THINK

AND

BELIEVE

THINK

AND

BELIEVE

Frederick W. Marks

EMMAUS
ROAD
PUBLISHING

Steubenville, Ohio
A Division of Catholics United for the Faith
www.emmausroad.org

Emmaus Road Publishing
A Division of Catholics United for the Faith
827 North Fourth Street
Steubenville, Ohio 43952

© 2012 Frederick W. Marks
All rights reserved. Published 2012
Printed in the United States of America
14   2 3 4 5 6

Library of Congress Control Number: 2012941071
ISBN: 978-1-937155-37-7

Unless otherwise marked, Scripture quotations are from Revised Standard Version of the Bible—Second Catholic Edition (Ignatius Edition) Copyright © 2006 National Council of the Churches of Christ in the United States of America. Used by permission. All rights reserved. Those drawn from the Confraternity Edition or New American Bible are marked CE and NAB respectively.

Excerpts from the English translation of the *Catechism of the Catholic Church* for the United States of America copyright © 1994, United States Catholic Conference, Inc.—Libreria Editrice Vaticana. English translation of the *Catechism of the Catholic Church: Modifications from the Editio Typica* copyright © 1997, United States Catholic Conference, Inc.—Libreria Editrice Vaticana. Noted as "CCC" in the text.

Cover design and layout by Julie Davis, General Glyphics, Inc., Dallas, Texas (www.glyphnet.com)

Nihil Obstat: Rev. John Cush. *Censor Librorum*
Imprimatur: Most Reverend Nicholas DiMarzio, Ph.D., D.D., Bishop of Brooklyn and Queens, NY
October 20, 2010

The *Nihil Obstat* and *Imprimatur* are official declarations that a book or pamphlet is free of doctrinal or moral error. No implication is contained therein that those who have granted the Nihil Obstat and Imprimatur agree with the contents, opinions, or statements expressed.

DEDICATION

To Mary

ACKNOWLEDGMENTS

I take complete responsibility for any errors of detail or interpretation in the following essay. But I should like to thank fellow members of the Catholic Evidence Guild of New York for challenging me to refine my approach to apologetics. I also owe a great deal to those who read early drafts of *Think and Believe*, and especially those who were kind enough to offer helpful suggestions, among them: Rev. Ray Ryland, Warren and Anne Carroll, James Drummey, Ronda Chervin, Piroska Haywood, Rev. Les Fairfield, Bruce Johnson, James Torrens, S.J., Louis Hellerman, Fr. Alkuin Schachenmayr, O. Cist., Fr. C. John McCloskey III, and Mike Sullivan. There is no way I can adequately thank Shannon Minch-Hughes and Chris Erickson of Emmaus Road Publishing for their patience and careful work on the editorial end; and last, but not least, comes family. My daughter, Mary Anne, lent me her computer expertise, along with her eye for detail and razor-sharp mind, while my wife, Sylvia, kept the sun shining through innumerable readings. Whatever rapport I may have achieved with the reader is due, in large part, to the patience of a loving spouse who has been on my case for close to fifty years.

TABLE OF CONTENTS

INTRODUCTION

Truth has such a face and such a mien
as to be loved needs only to be seen.
John Dryden

Religion seldom comes up in casual conversation. "Good taste" dictates that we stick to sports and the weather. Still, there are myriad intimations of the supernatural. Something said at a funeral may give us pause. The birth of a baby may cause us to wonder where the child came from originally and where it is headed after death. Loss of a job or a period of prolonged suffering may raise the question of destiny—in particular, how much of it we control. Occasionally, there will be a charity walk for suicide prevention. If we live in the city, we may see an ad on a bus or subway train for the free treatment of depression. What, we wonder, is the secret of happiness?

Ultimately, it is intangibles that shape one's outlook on life. How we react to illness and adversity, how we handle success, whether we are cheerful or morose, kind or cruel—it all depends on an immaterial "larger picture." Many of life's most basic priorities, including our choice of friends, are determined by an underlying value system, and oftentimes, this is determined by the circumstances of birth. From childhood on, whether we are believers or skeptics, we drink in a whole host of assumptions and prejudices, along with the air we breathe.

Think and Believe challenges the reader to set aside long-held assumptions and prejudices. Two thousand years ago, there lived a man who declared that "before Abraham came to be, I am"[1] (CE). Proclaiming himself to be "the Way, the Truth, and the Life," he guaranteed the salvation of all who believed in him.[2] He

1

called for repentance and not only forgave men their sins but ordained disciples to do the same.[3] No other human being ever spoke with such authority or made such demands, nor is there anything remotely comparable to the way he sacrificed himself on a cross to atone for the sins of mankind and open heaven to all who seek the truth with a sincere heart.

Five hundred years before the birth of Christ, a character in Plato's *Republic* is quoted as having said that if a truly righteous man were ever to come along, he would be such a thorn in the side of society that he would be subjected to every form of humiliation and eventually crucified.[4] Jesus, I submit, was such a man, and the extent of his suffering is but one of many ways in which he is unique. Among religious founders, he is the only one whose coming was foretold. He is the only one who proclaimed himself sinless.[5] He alone predicted the manner of his death, and his miracles, culminating in the Resurrection, are without parallel.[6] Above all, he is the only one who ever claimed to be God. His followers converted an entire empire without resort to violence, and after winning Rome they not only gave the world its calendar but transformed pagan culture beyond recognition.

These are hard, cold facts. My reader may question the reliability of the New Testament Gospels on which some of them are based. If so, there is an answer, and in chapter 2, I will give it. First, though, a few thoughts about the reasonableness of belief in general.*

---

* N.B. Throughout the text in chapter 1, as well as elsewhere, there are copious notes for easy identification of persons, events, or doctrines that may be unfamiliar. The reader will also find a detailed index, along with useful appendices, at the end.

Chapter 1

THE CASE FOR GOD

Consider, to begin with, the sheer usefulness of belief. Clinical studies show that rates of heart disease, stroke, and psychological depression are markedly lower among regular churchgoers.[1] There is also less incidence of AIDS and sexually transmitted disease. Drug addiction, alcoholism, and sexual promiscuity, all of which lead to destitution and higher taxes, are much reduced. The medical profession attests to a better rate of recovery for patients who pray or have prayers offered for them, and alcoholics who recover do so, almost without exception, by turning to a higher power.[2]

Beyond this, divorce and illegitimacy are radically lower among those who are devout. Conversely, reconciliation rates for separated couples are highest among those who are religiously observant, and if one combines regular church going with Bible reading, one is almost certain to have a stable family. Since children from single parent homes are likely to be troubled—and statistics show that out-of-wedlock births cost America dearly—society would appear to have a financial stake in promoting religious devotion.[3] Gallup polls indicate that churchgoers give four times as much to charity as non-churchgoers. They also volunteer twice as much time on an individual basis and are much less likely to cheat on their income tax.[4]

None of this proves the existence of God. But it does suggest a connection between religion and happiness while raising the question of purpose. We know from the physical world that the value of an object depends on knowing the intent of its maker. One cannot use a pencil as a can opener and expect good results. Complicated machinery comes with a manual of rules for maintenance, and if we want the manufacturer to honor his warranty, we must follow the book. So, too, with man. If he has a maker—and we will argue that he does—then he stands to benefit from reading the owners' manual, commonly known as the Bible.

Some regard belief as a crutch for weaklings unable to stand on their own two feet. As with all alluring falsehoods, this one contains an element of truth. We are all handicapped in one way or another and belief helps us stand erect by affirming the value of life regardless of circumstance. Material loss, loneliness, illness and death may be borne with equanimity and even joy in the knowledge that God is in control, that he will not ask more of us than we can give, and that there is a redemptive side to suffering. When crimes go unpunished or a man who has worked hard all his life dies poor, one senses, deep down, the need for an equalizer. Without a final court of justice where the world's valleys are raised up and its mountains laid low, life may seem unfair. Man's yearning for beauty and truth, like his yearning for goodness, cannot be satisfied this side of paradise. Was he born to be denied?

What critics fail to realize is that God's "crutch," which compensates for weakness, builds on strength and is, in turn, strengthening. It has been shown, for example, that those who were religiously motivated had the best chance, by far, of surviving Nazi concentration camps during World War II. They were strong in spirit because it is not easy to keep the Ten Commandments and carry out one's social responsibilities. Churchgoers are enjoined to correct their erring brethren and shun heretics, along with public sinners, and this requires spine.[5] Was Thomas More, Bolt's "man for all seasons," weak when Henry VIII forced him to choose between apostasy and death? Jesus had a mother who stood by him on Calvary, and the apostles, who continued to frequent a temple administered by men responsible for their Savior's execution, had to be psychologically robust.[6]

Many who put their faith in science regard religion as something of a "leap." In reality, though, is it not the men in the white coats who do most of the leaping? Scientific hypotheses are in constant flux. The medical theory of Hippocrates is full of errors by today's standards, as is the astronomy of Ptolemy. Aristotle's law of gravity, the received wisdom for two thousand years, has been superseded. For hundreds of years, scientists believed the heart's arteries pumped air, not blood. Bleeding as a medical treatment has been abandoned except in rare cases. The "laws" of energy and conservation have changed dramatically. As late as the 1990s, children were taught that nothing travels faster than the speed of light. No longer.[7] Science texts are continually being revised.

STANDARD PROOFS

Proof #1 for the existence of God hinges on the observation that nothing happens without a cause. We come from parents who came from other parents in a long line of procreation. How did the process get started? Physicists speculate about a "Big Bang" at the beginning. What caused the bang? Some may have heard the joke about the chemist who told God he had found a way to manufacture life. "Is that so?" replied the Lord. "How do you do it?" "Well," said the chemist, "I take this handful of dirt ..." "Stop right there," interjected the Almighty, "that dirt belongs to me!" Just so.

There is much talk of evolution. But if evolution actually occurred—and the theory is far from unassailable—what set it in motion? How can an inanimate object become a man? Flower A may evolve into flower B; animal A may evolve into animal B; but experience tells us that lower forms of life do not produce higher forms. A stone does not produce a flower; a flower does not produce an animal; animals do not produce human beings. There are no intermediate forms between stones and flowers, flowers and animals, or animals and people. The fossil record suggests that even between species there are no intermediate forms.

Believers argue, secondly, that God's hand is apparent in all that we see. How likely is it that random circumstance produced the complexity of the human eye? How can one gaze at the beauty of a rose or the glory of a sunset without feeling that they were fashioned by an intelligent being to gladden the soul? Is it pure happenstance that the moon, four hundred and ten times smaller in circumference than the earth, is also four hundred and ten times closer to the earth than it is to the sun, making possible the vision of a perfect eclipse? Trees and flowers grow in gratifying symmetry, and again, why is this so unless they were made for man? Belief in intelligent design cannot explain everything, but it certainly accounts for a great deal more than disbelief. Is it coincidental that the earth, which revolves 366 times in one orbit of the sun, is 366% larger than the moon, or that the moon, which takes 27.32 days to orbit the earth, is 27.32% of the earth's size? Consider, too, that the earth is 109.3 times smaller than the sun, while the circumference of the moon, when measured in kilometers, is 10,930 km!

THE ARGUMENT FROM CULTURE

A third proof for the existence of God, and one I will develop at length, is the argument from culture. If the Lord of the Universe is the source of all that is beautiful, good, and true, as he is supposed to be, then all that is most beautiful, most good, and most true should be God-made or, if not God-made, then made by godly men. And is this not what one finds? Nothing fashioned by human hands can match the grandeur of an alpine landscape. When it comes to goodness, no doctor can compete with Mother Nature. When it comes to healing, no pharmaceutical drug can soothe the psyche the way holy living does. No earthly teacher seeking to enlist students on the side of right can compete with the voice of conscience. And in the area of wisdom, Sacred Scripture surpasses the work of the greatest sages, men of the caliber of Plato, Dante, and Shakespeare. The Ten Commandments are still binding; the voice of the Psalmist is still vibrant; Sirach, Proverbs, Wisdom, and Ecclesiastes are a better guide to life than all of the works of secular literature put together.

GOD'S BOOK

Taking a closer look at the Book of Books, it contains something on the order of a thousand prophecies, none of which have ever been known to fail, while an estimated 688 have been fulfilled. God told Abraham that his descendants would be as numerous as the stars in the sky, and so they are if one counts Christians and Muslims. There was a time when observers, pointing to the 1,022 stars visible to the human eye, faulted Genesis for likening the multiplicity of stars to grains of sand along the seashore. Then along came the telescope in the seventeenth century, and skeptics wedded to the notion of conflict between science and religion fell into embarrassed silence.[8]

Jeremiah and Ezra foretold the return of the Hebrew people from Babylon, and Jeremiah, in conjunction with Isaiah, forecast the fate of Babylon itself.[9] If they had said about Nineveh what they said about Babylon, they would have been dead wrong, and the accuracy of their prophecy was not confirmed until long after their deaths.

With Ezekiel and Zephaniah, it is much the same. Had Ezekiel forecast for Thebes what he forecast for rival Memphis—namely, that God would put an end to its monuments—or for Sidon what he foretold for rival Tyre—that diverse peoples would demolish its walls, scrape down its rubble to bare rock, and turn it into a place to spread fishnets "out in the sea," never to be rebuilt—he, too, would have

About Fr. McCloskey   Featured Articles   Audio/Video   Book Reviews   All Articles   Cardinal Newman

A Catholic Lifetime Reading Plan

by Father John McCloskey

- Catechism of the Catholic Church – Catholicism Explained/Theology
- Adams – The Spirit of Catholicism – Catholicism Explained/Theology
- Augustine – City of God – Spiritual Classics
- Augustine – Confessions of St. Augustine – Spiritual Classics
- Aumann – Spiritual Theology – Spiritual Reading
- Baur – Frequent Confession – Spiritual Reading
- Baur – In Silence with God – Spiritual Reading
- Belloc – The Great Heresies – History and Culture
- Belloc – How The Reformation Happened – History and Culture
- Belloc – Survivals and New Arrivals – History and Culture
- Benedict XVI – Opera Omnia – Misc
- Benedict XVI – Day by Day with the Pope – Misc
- Bennet – The Temperament God Gave You – Misc
- Bennet – The Emotions God Gave You – Misc
- Benson – Lord of the World – Literary Classics
- Bernanos – The Diary of a Country Priest – Literary Classics
- Bouyer – Spirit and Forms of Protestantism – Catholicism Explained/Theology
- Boylan – Difficulties in Mental Prayer – Spiritual Reading
- Boylan – Tremendous Lover – Spiritual Reading

Dialogues") – Spiritual Classics

- Cervantes – Don Quixote – Literary Classics
- Chautard – Soul of Apostolate – Spiritual Reading
- Chesterton – Everlasting Man – Spiritual Classics
- Chesterton – Orthodoxy – Spiritual Classics
- Chesterton – St. Thomas Aquinas
- Chesterton – St. Francis of Assisi – Holy Men and Women
- Chevrot – Simon Peter
- Cizek – He Leadeth Me – Spiritual Reading
- Crocker – Triumph – History and Culture
- Caussaude – Abandonment to Divine Providence – Spiritual Reading
- Dante – Divine Comedy – Literary Classics
- Dawson – Christianity and European Culture – History and Culture
- Day – Long Loneliness – Holy Men and Women
- de la Palma – The Sacred Passion – Spiritual Reading
- de Sales – Introduction to Devout Life – Spiritual Reading
- de Sales – Treatise on the Love of God – Spiritual Reading
- d'Elbee – I Believe in Love – Spiritual Reading
- Eliot – Christianity and Culture – Literary Classics
- Endo – Silence – Literary Classics
- Enzler – My Other Self – Misc
- Escriva – Christ is Passing By – Spiritual Reading
- Escriva – Way, Furrow, Forge – Spiritual Reading
- Escriva – Way of the Cross – Spiritual Reading

been mistaken. Interpolation is again out of the question because the fate of these cities was not settled until the time of Alexander the Great (in the case of Tyre) and the rise of Islam (in the case of Memphis). Memphis and Thebes were once Egyptian capitals, and both had vast numbers of statues, pyramids, sphinxes, and obelisks. When the Muslims established a military camp fourteen miles away from Memphis, they used it as a stone quarry. Its statuary was recycled, and today it is merely a suburb of Cairo.[10] All of its grandeur is gone. As for Zephaniah, he correctly forecast different fates for Ekron and Askelon, two flourishing Philistine cities, and in this instance, the outcome was not known until the time of the Crusades.[11]

The best way to appreciate the accuracy of biblical prophecy is to set it alongside worldly prognostication. Parson Malthus warned in the early 1800s that the growth of the world's population would outstrip the ability of farmers to feed it, while Thomas Jefferson, around the same time, predicted that most Americans would soon be Unitarians.[12] Both men were mistaken. Malthus failed to anticipate the Green Revolution, and Jefferson underestimated the staying power of Trinitarianism.

CREATIVE GENIUS

But back to the idea that God is the source of all beauty, goodness, and truth. We can do more than recognize the superiority of his handiwork. We can compare the work of mortals who are divinely inspired with those who aren't. "Enthusiasm," one of the prime requisites of creative genius, is a word derived from the Greek *en theos* meaning "in God," and what we know about the spiritual commitment of the world's greatest artists bears this out. Those whose output has stood the test of time have been exceptionally close to God—even when one takes into account the age in which they lived, which was more religiously oriented than our own. Similarly, the cynical post-Christian West has fared less well artistically than the age of belief, and we know from history that whenever governments make a concerted effort to stamp out religion, the result is always the same: art, architecture, music, and literature languish.

ARCHITECTURE, SCULPTURE, AND PAINTING

The medieval cathedrals, in a class by themselves, were built, in large part, to honor the Virgin Mary, and before the cathedrals came Constantinople's Santa Sophia (Hagia Sophia today), the most admired and imitated edifice of its time. The product of five years of intensive labor on the part of a hundred thousand workers and a prototype for Islamic as well as Christian architecture, Santa Sophia was erected by

Justinian, a ruler who fasted and prayed regularly. Or take the Taj Mahal. Anyone who has ever gazed at its haunting beauty knows that its walls are covered with verses from the Koran and that the man who built it as a mausoleum for his deceased wife was exceptionally chaste, pious, and God-fearing. Additional examples can be found among the ruins of Central America. Nothing is more beautiful than the ancient temple pyramid at Chichén Itzá built by a Toltec leader devoted to the defense of life. He waged a one-man war against human sacrifice and, for a time, succeeded. In Paris, one will hear the story of King Louis IX, a canonized saint beloved by the French, who commissioned the windows of Sainte Chapelle, the most exquisite example of stained glass anywhere in the world.

In the field of sculpture, Phidias, who stands at the head of a long line of Greek geniuses, was highly devout. Two thousand years later, Michelangelo, who has been described as "pious," sculpted his *Pietà* and painted the ceiling of the Sistine Chapel relatively early in his career. Already, he was on fire spiritually. In comparison with other artists, he devoted much of his time to spiritual themes, including an unforgettably powerful sculpture of Moses, and his sonnets are evocative of the Psalms and Book of Job.

Painting is close to sculpture, and Rembrandt, whose name is synonymous with excellence, was the only Dutch master of his century to favor biblical themes. Never more in his element than when limning such masterpieces as *The Prophetess Anna Reading the Bible, Susanna, Simeon in the Temple,* and *Christ at Emmaus,* he painted only one seascape, *The Storm on the Sea of Galilee.* Rubens, another titan of the art world who stands out for the number of biblical themes he executed, was a daily communicant. Closer to our own time, Corot, the founder of the French Impressionist School, was devoutly Catholic, and in America, the distinguished Hudson River School of painting whose canvases grace the world's finest art galleries had one overarching goal: to reveal God in nature.[13]

MUSIC AND LITERATURE

For those whose passion is music, Ludwig van Beethoven, born and buried in the Church, covered the periphery of his writing desk with sayings about God. Johann Sebastian Bach and Johannes Brahms were pious Protestants, with Bach marking all his manuscripts "for the greater glory of God." Joseph Haydn, father of both the symphony and the string quartet, was a Rosary-praying Catholic, as was Wolfgang Amadeus Mozart, the most popular classical composer of all time.

The Mostly Mozart Festival, a New York institution for over forty years, features the music of a man whose middle name means "lover of God" and whose life was dedicated to Mary.[14]

The most frequently performed of all operas, *The Magic Flute*, is also the most spiritual of Mozart's dramatic masterpieces, while the most beloved of all oratorios, Handel's *Messiah*, was struck off by a man said to have exclaimed at the end of his labors, "I did think I did see all heaven before me, and the great God Himself." *Messiah* happens to be the only sacred oratorio Handel ever wrote, as well as the only one of his works performed in a consecrated place during his lifetime.

Shifting to the field of literature, Aesop was religious, as was Dante, the world's greatest poet. Milton, who rivals Dante, drew his inspiration from the Bible. Then there is Shakespeare, whose work resonates with Judeo-Christian values.[15] Drama *itself*, as we know it, is religious in origin. In ancient Greece, a performance of the *Oresteia* was a blend of entertainment and worship, and Sophocles, the premier Greek tragedian, was a priest.[16]

In modern times, Goethe may have been a pantheist, but his most illustrious work, *Faust*, is Christian to the core in the way it addresses suffering, conversion, and redemption. Among other acknowledged greats, Victor Hugo, Tolstoy, Dostoevsky, and Dickens were all well versed in the Bible. The author of *David Copperfield* and *Oliver Twist* wrote more than any other well-known contemporary writer about Christmas, and unbeknownst to most of his readers, he penned a life of Jesus that came out posthumously in 1934. Hugo devoted the first eighty-five pages of his greatest novel, *Les Miserables*, to a detailed description of an ideal priest who is not only witty, learned, and profoundly philosophical, but also humble, prayerful, courageous, kind, and true to his priestly duties. Leo Tolstoy, along with Henrik Ibsen and a number of other luminaries, sowed their wild oats as youths. But it was not until they settled down morally that they were able to harness their magnificent talent.

SCIENCE

Looking beyond literary masterpieces to scientific achievement, Sir Isaac Newton is known by many as the chief architect of modern physics. Inventor of calculus, father of the laws of gravitation, Newton explained tides and taught us to speak of inertia and momentum. Trained to be an Anglican clergyman, he remained intensely interested in religion to the day of his death. His library overflowed with works on theology, indeed he wound up writing more about religion than science.[17] Louis

Pasteur, the man behind pasteurization and winner of the battle against anthrax, cholera, and rabies, prayed the Rosary. Sir Charles Simpson, the mastermind of anesthesiology, asked to name his greatest discovery, is said to have replied, "When I discovered that Jesus Christ is my savior."

History offers any number of examples. Robert Boyle, the father of modern chemistry (along with Lavoisier), wrote books on religion and established a foundation for the promotion of evangelization. Albert Einstein, whose views on religion were more complicated than many might think, held that there must be a supernatural intelligence behind the physical world. How many atheists or agnostics can one put up alongside Boyle and Einstein?[18]

SOCIAL SERVICE

When it comes to humanitarianism, one would expect something special from the professed servants of a God who is the source of all goodness; and again, the paradigm holds. No two people in history have done more to improve the lot of the poor, the elderly, and the ill than Vincent de Paul and Mother Teresa of Calcutta, both of whom were bound by religious vows. Francis of Assisi embraced a leper. Damien de Veuster succumbed to leprosy in order to bring comfort to victims of the dread disease on the island of Molokai. Another priest, Maximilian Kolbe, who was incarcerated at Auschwitz during World War II, gave his life for a fellow inmate. Camp rules dictated that when a prisoner escaped, ten others chosen at random were automatically put to death. In this instance, a family man with wife and children was chosen for execution, and Fr. Kolbe, overcome with pity, volunteered to take his place in the starvation bunker.[19]

Where, one wonders, are the Damiens and Kolbes in the annals of non-belief? Skeptics such as Jean Jacques Rousseau, Karl Marx, Bertrand Russell, Jean-Paul Sartre, Margaret Mead, Sigmund Freud, Pablo Picasso, and Alfred Charles Kinsey were notably cold. Margaret Sanger, the founder of Planned Parenthood, was a racist. Historians Paul Johnson and E. Michael Jones, in chronicling the private lives of leftist paragons, have shown how cruel they were in relation to kith and kin, and how unhappy.[20] Nietzsche, who pronounced God dead, died in an insane asylum. Virginia Woolf, who saw "something obscene" in a "person sitting by the fire believing in God," committed suicide, as did Hitler and a great many others who turned their back on religion.

STATESMANSHIP

In politics, those who have brought the greatest measure of peace, justice, and happiness to their people have again been exceptionally spiritual.[21] For example, Justinian, Charlemagne, Otto I of Germany, Stephen of Hungary, Louis IX of France (already mentioned), Jadwiga of Poland, Isabel of Spain, Maria Theresa of Austria, George Washington, Abraham Lincoln, Queen Victoria, and Ronald Reagan.[22] Rome entered its era of greatest peace, prosperity, and culture under the leadership of Caesar Augustus, an emperor who founded a new order of priests, erected many temples, contributed to the building of synagogues, outlawed adultery, encouraged large families, and was married for fifty-two years to the virtuous Livia.

Contrast that with those guilty of mass murder and genocide. Hitler hated the Catholicism of his youth and massacred ten million people. Stalin left the Orthodox Church and did away with many more. Mao, another anti-religious zealot, dispatched an estimated seventy million, while Pol Pot, his opposite number in Cambodia, slaughtered a fifth of his people.[23]

Such savagery cuts two ways, of course. It underscores the consequences of skepticism, but it also raises the question of how an all good and all powerful God can create a world in which there is genocide, murder, and rape. How can he permit a tsunami to sweep away thousands? Why does a girl of seven, the soul of sweetness, die of leukemia before the eyes of parents down on their knees in prayer?

THE PROBLEM OF EVIL

There is no totally satisfying answer to the problem of why good men suffer, but if God is as great as he is supposed to be, earthlings can no more fathom his grand design than a month-old baby can see the need to save for college. "My thoughts are not your thoughts," says the Lord, "neither are your ways my ways."[24] At the same time, believers are not entirely mystified. They see rape, murder, and genocide as coming not from God but from man, who has the gift of free will. Cancer and natural disasters, which did not exist in the Garden of Eden, are viewed as God's response to the sin of Adam and Eve, along with our own sin. Perhaps the Lord knew that without the fear of suffering and death, man would be intolerably proud. The kindest and dearest souls tend to be those who have suffered the most without succumbing to cynicism. Conversely, those for whom life has gone relatively smoothly are apt to be vain and selfish. A good parent will put children to the test on occasion and assign them unpleasant chores—all in a spirit of love—and God is, of course, the best of all parents.

Believers may not be able to make perfect sense of life's greatest enigma, but they have two great advantages. First, they are confident that when suffering is borne cheerfully and offered up (to God as a sacrifice), it can be a source of much good. More on this shortly. Secondly, they are animated by the same hope that sustains parents of infants. We all know that babies suffer. Their problem may be gastrointestinal, or it may be teething. Whatever the case, parents are not terribly upset because they know the trail of tears will end, their child will grow up, and the future will be bright. Believers feel the same about themselves. With their sights fixed on heaven and viewing pain as temporary, they are not unduly alarmed.

But enough. Since we will have a second look at suffering in chapter 5, we can proceed apace to one last charge commonly leveled by the critics of organized religion: namely, the idea that religion causes war.

RELIGION AND WAR

The notion is not so much wrong as misleading. Religion can indeed lead to war. Judas Maccabeus fought for Judaism. During the 1920s and 1930s Mexico's Cristeros entered the lists for Catholicism. Many have died in defense of religious freedom. But men fight for a host of things, including national honor and decency. Are we to discard patriotism and virtue because they can bring on hostilities? What is one to make of the fact that the most irreligious of all centuries, the twentieth, has produced more in the way of war, devastation, and cruelty than any other?

By nature, men are aggressive, and history indicates that they fight more viciously and more frequently without religion than with it. The lion's share of conscientious objectors—for example the Quakers and Jehovah's Witnesses—have been religious. Then, too, Christ's counsel to those bent on driving the Romans out of Palestine was: "Render therefore to Caesar the things that are Caesar's." Had Jewish leaders heeded such advice, millions of lives would have been spared, as there would never have been war between Rome and Jerusalem. The temple would still be standing.

It is true that God ordered Joshua to exterminate neighboring tribesmen engaged in cult prostitution (along with child sacrifice, cannibalism, and sexual deviance). But before he did so, he sent swarms of bees as a warning. The Canaanites clung to their evil ways. From a religious standpoint, God controls the gates of life and death; he can use whatever means he chooses, including an avenging army, to call men home for judgment; and he can do so whenever he pleases.[25]

Most of the time it is acquisitiveness that leads to war. Although religion was a major cause of the Thirty Years War (1618–48), dynastic, territorial, and economic issues were also important. Protestant princes helped themselves to the Church's extensive landholdings, and by the time the conflict ended it was simply another round in the age-old struggle between Catholic France and the Catholic Hapsburgs. The pope himself was accused of favoring the Protestant side.[26] Much the same may be said with respect to medieval pogroms on Good Friday, North/South Irish strife, and Taliban violence. Oftentimes religion is used as an excuse or apology for war with secular considerations lurking just beneath the surface, and those who are truly devout are rarely the ones to blame when the tinder box explodes.

The Bible commands us to love our enemies and turn the other cheek. We are to take no revenge, cherish no grudges, and forgive seventy times over.[27] Hardly a formula for strife. Armed robbery, homicide, and rape are far more likely to result from too little religion than too much—ask any policeman—and the same holds true on the world stage where the most aggressive figures have been anti-religious.

Why is it that religious communities such as the Franciscans, Benedictines, and Dominicans have been more successful at preserving harmony than secular utopias like Brook Farm and Fruitlands? During the Middle Ages, when religion wielded immense power, warriors adhered to a code that set strict limits on the time, place, and target of hostilities. As we shall see in chapter 8, the Crusades were primarily defensive, and it was not until religious enthusiasm waned during the Renaissance that Europe imploded—in the name of religion.

Closer to our own time, conflict in the Middle East is primarily territorial. Scripture has been cited as a justification for the Jewish state, but Zionism was not a religious movement, and Israel, with its small minority of orthodox believers, is not a religious nation. As for the United States, it has fought ten wars in a little over two centuries, not counting its War for Independence and the Civil War, but religion was not a motive for any of them. Although America's abolitionist movement was driven by the churches, the Civil War had a lot to do with issues such as the tariff and territorial expansion. Theodore Roosevelt, who won the Nobel Prize for mediating between Japan and Russia, did not fire a single shot at a foreign foe during his presidency of seven years, and this was a man who taught Sunday school at Harvard and, later in life, urged his fellow Americans to go to church.[28]

In sum, religion has given the world a fair measure of security in addition to great art, great music, great literature, and monumental works of charity. The argument from culture that I have chosen to highlight does not appear in standard apologetics texts, but it should appeal to those conscious of history. The other line of thought that may be unfamiliar to certain readers and one we have only pursued tangentially thus far hinges on the reliability of God's Book, the Bible. In discussing truth as a divine attribute, I touched briefly on the accuracy of Old Testament prophecy; but the case for biblical integrity extends far beyond prophecy, and since Scripture is crucial to all that follows, I will present additional evidence in chapter 2.

Lastly, I would advise anyone who remains wedded to agnosticism to consider Pascal's Wager, along with a special prayer. Blaise Pascal, a brilliant seventeenth century French mathematician, reasoned as follows: If God does not exist, one has little to lose by living the life of a believer. But if he does exist and one refuses to acknowledge him as Lord, life in the next world could be gravely disappointing. As for the prayer, it is very simple: "If you exist, Almighty God, give me the grace to recognize the truth, whatever it may be, and to embrace it, whatever the cost."

Chapter 2

THE CASE FOR
GOD'S WORD

Allegations of biblical error are always popular, for without continual reassurance in the media that traditional morality is ill founded, the guilt of a great many would be well nigh unbearable. Not that all skeptics are scapegraces. But to the degree that they are, their mindset frees them from responsibility. If the received texts are shot through with error, why should one keep the Commandments? One need not fast, attend weekly assembly, or give to charity.[1] In the case of the Gospels, Christ claimed to be God, proved it by the miracles he worked, and established an organization to teach in his name. But again, if the text is faulty, the reader may do whatever he pleases. He needn't hang on Jesus' every word if the words themselves are in doubt.

Attacks on Sacred Scripture are nothing new. Tatian, a student of Justin Martyr, felt impelled to write a defense of biblical inerrancy in AD 170. Two centuries later, Augustine devoted an entire volume to the subject, refuting hundreds of allegations. In every age the debate has raged, but beginning with the second half of the eighteenth century, disbelief mounted rapidly, especially in the West. Thomas

Jefferson put out an edition of the Gospels devoid of all reference to miracles, and by the end of the nineteenth century liberal exegetes were firing off multiple broadsides. Old Testament authors were dismissed as fanciful storytellers; Moses' awesome feats were called into question; Matthew, Mark, Luke, and John were portrayed as men with an agenda.

We will address each of these challenges in turn. But before doing so, we would do well to ponder the prophetic nature of God's Word. The accuracy of forecasts involving the fate of specific cities, as seen in chapter 1, is but a small sampling of what can be adduced. Jesus, for example, foretold that the poor would always be with us, and so they are in spite of all that has been done on their behalf.[2]

IMPLIED PROPHECY

There is also what one might call "implied prophecy." Our Lord remarked that "the wind blows where it wills . . . you do not know whence it comes or whither it goes" (Jn. 3:8). Such words can be taken to mean that man will *never* know, in which case they are prophetic *by implication*. Enormous progress in the field of meteorology notwithstanding, tornadoes still take us by surprise and forecasts are often wrong. When Hurricane Ivan unleashed its deadly fury in 2004, one weatherman admitted freely that "you can't know exactly where those storms will go."

Breathtaking discoveries over the past century in the field of medicine have done nothing to render obsolete a statement made over two thousand years ago by the author of the Book of Sirach: "The number of a man's days is great if he reaches a hundred years."[3] In like vein, Scripture lists grinding toil and pain in childbirth as consequences of original sin. Modern labor-saving devices have not eliminated the daily grind, and in spite of enormous strides in the field of anesthesia—visits to the dentist are no longer dreaded—women continue to suffer pain in childbirth.

One can go further. Jesus told his listeners they could not add a single cubit (eighteen inches) to their height or prevent their hair from turning white.[4] If the pharmaceutical industry were ever to hit upon a formula for doing either of these things, it would be worth a fortune. But it has not happened. Again, Christ is quoted in the thirteenth chapter of Matthew as referring to agricultural yields of thirty-fold, sixty-fold, and a hundred-fold. Every year, the United States Department of Agriculture spends a tidy sum on research and development, but today's farmer, using the best seed available, finds it virtually impossible to obtain an increase of a hundred-fold. Thirty-fold is average and sixty-fold outstanding—just as it was in Jesus' time.

THE ENDURING WORD

Ninety-nine out of a hundred species have disappeared over the years; yet all that are mentioned in the Bible have survived—one more sign of the singularity of God's Word. The sparrow, the eagle, the swallow, the dove, and even the hyena can be seen today. Mustard trees, fig trees, and olive plants have survived. In spite of breathtaking advances in chemistry, iron is still subject to corrosion, moths still leave holes, and weeds grow up with the grass—just as they do in Christ's parables. We are still sewing patches; we are still sowing seed; leaven is still used to make bread rise.[5]

Not that the Bible would be discredited if science eliminated toil or OBGYNs found a way to scotch pain in childbirth—the account of original sin in Genesis is inconclusive with regard to the duration of the penalties. For that matter, neither would the disappearance of this or that biblical species undercut God's Word. If chemists were to get the better of moths and rust, it would simply mean that biblical language, like all language, is vulnerable to the march of time. But given the historical record of three or four millennia, Scripture seems timeless in a way that is nothing short of marvelous.

HISTORY AND THE BIBLE

Shifting to what history, archaeology, and science tell us about the accuracy of the Bible, let us begin with history. Was there really a prolonged drought at the time of Elijah? The Tyrian historian Menander confirms it. Were 185,000 Assyrians suddenly struck down at the time of Hezekiah? Herodotus, master chronicler of Greece, not only alludes to it but offers an explanation.[6] Flavius Josephus (c. AD 37–100), priest, general, and by far the greatest Jewish historian of ancient times, tells us much about the early Church. We learn things about Jesus and Pilate, John the Baptist, and James the first bishop of Jerusalem, that one would never know from the New Testament. All of it is complementary, and at the same time perfectly compatible with Christian teaching. Josephus says nothing that contradicts anything found in the Gospels or Acts of the Apostles.[7]

When problems relating to the historicity of the Bible arise, as they will from time to time, the solutions are not always apparent. But answers to the toughest questions have a way of surfacing, and when they don't—when Scripture and the secular record remain unreconciled—one must bear in mind that record keepers are fallible.

Those who stay abreast of archaeological research know that discoveries by the hundreds vouch for the accuracy of the Word while not a single dig has ever proven it conclusively wrong. For years, scholars regarded Belshazzar's Feast as fictional because Nabonidus was the last recorded king of Babylon. Then came Sir Henry Rawlinson's "pick and shovel" discovery that Nabonidus had a son named Balsarussur, who ruled in his own right. Could Goliath have stood six and a half feet tall, as recorded in 1 Sam. 17? To many, the notion appeared suspect because Middle Easterners tend to be short. No matter that Joshua and his fellow scouts reported finding giants when they reconnoitered the Promised Land. Doubt lingered in the mind of academicians until skeletons were found confirming that men as tall as Goliath existed thousands of years ago.

THE TESTIMONY OF SCIENCE

Science, too, is on the side of Scripture. There is a 1,750-foot tunnel that channels water from the Spring of the Virgin beyond Jerusalem's walls into the Pool of Siloam. Did Hezekiah really build it, as the Bible says? Scholars thought it beyond the capability of Hezekiah's engineers until carbon 14 testing proved otherwise.[8] Were Sodom and Gomorrah really destroyed by fire and brimstone? Geologists found an area of burned out oil and asphalt at the southern end of the Dead Sea. A stratum of rock salt lies beneath Mount Sodom on the west shore of the sea, and the salt is overlaid with a stratum of marl that, in turn, is overlaid with free sulfur (brimstone) in a very pure state. When the gases given off by oil and asphalt catch fire, an explosion occurs that can send red hot salt and sulfur high into the air.[9]

No longer do scholars doubt the existence of Abraham; no longer do they deny that Moses was able to write. Archaeology supports the biblical account of the complete destruction of Canaanite cities, and Old Testament details relating to Jewish exile in Egypt have been accepted as accurate down to the price of a slave at the time of Moses (twenty shekels).[10] The existence of the Hittite tribe to which David's victim Uriah belonged is acknowledged; the Queen of Sheba is no longer regarded as fictional.[11]

Turning to the Christian era, the Gospel of Luke tells us that Joseph and Mary journeyed to Bethlehem because Roman regulations stipulated that men register in their own town, and Joseph was of the House of David. Skeptics knew of no such regulations, but archeologists active in Egypt unearthed a Roman edict containing just such a regulation. Similarly, when scholars doubted the story about Jesus sleeping "inside" the stern of a boat during the storm on the Sea of Galilee, no one had ever heard of a Galilean fishing boat with a covered compartment. But such a boat was eventually found.[12] Exegetes doubted Jesus' cure of a paralytic at the Pool of Bethesda because the pool is described as having five porticoes, and they knew of nothing pentagonal in Jewish architecture at the time of Jesus. Eventually, though, they discovered such a structure—exactly on the site where the Pool of Bethesda was supposed to have stood.[13]

Finally, it is becoming increasingly clear that the Shroud of Turin, which confirms the reliability of contemporary accounts of Jesus' Passion and death, is the authentic burial cloth of Our Lord.[14] Measuring approximately fourteen by three and a half feet, with blood stains at all the points one would expect, it registers no less than one hundred sixty wounds caused by the blows of a Roman whip. There are marks indicating penetration of the temple by a crown of thorns; there are stains caused by laceration of the face; there are knee abrasions that testify to repeated falling under heavy weight. There is further evidence of nails driven through wrists and feet, and one can make out telltale signs of an opening in the victim's side. Researchers using a microdensometer, a VP-8 image analyzer, and a spectroscope, have even discovered that the Shroud bears marks of a brief scorching flash (cellulose oxidation) at a level of energy approaching the thermonuclear.[15]

EYEWITNESS TESTIMONY

Approaching the subject from a slightly different angle, Aristotle used three criteria to determine historical reliability. The first of these is eyewitness testimony, and we have it in abundance because two of the four Gospel writers, Matthew and John, were apostles. We know this because Bishop Polycarp of Smyrna (c. AD 69–156) who studied under John, and Bishop Irenaeus of Lyons (c. AD 125–203) who studied under Polycarp, both affirm it. Bishop Papias of Hierapolis, a third witness quoted by the historian Eusebius (c. AD 263–339), maintained midway through the second century that the first Gospel was written by Matthew. Hermas, a brother of Pope Pius I (d. circa AD 155), identified Luke and John as the authors of the third and fourth Gospels.[16] And a century later, Tertullian, one of the theological greats of the early Church, distinguished between Matthew and John, whom he describes as "apostles," and Mark and Luke, whom he calls "apostolic men." Even the earliest heretics agreed that the first three Gospels came from the pen of Matthew, Mark, and Luke, and at dates that coincide with Christian tradition. One thinks of Cerinthus in the first century, for example, along with Valentinus (c. AD 136–c. 165), Marcion (c. 110–165), Basilides (early second century), and Tatian (late second century).

Since these scholars had access to information that has long since disappeared, their testimony is invaluable.[17] Few today know the name Hegesippus, father of the successor to James, Bishop of Jerusalem, because his history of the early Church has been lost. But the Church fathers, who were far closer in time and culture to the Gospels than we are today, may well have consulted Hegesippus, along with Papias, whose work, once again, is no longer extant.

Still another indication that the Gospels of Matthew and John are eyewitness accounts is the fact that what we know about their authors squares with what they wrote. Matthew is reputed to have been a tax collector, and his Gospel is uniquely concerned with money.[18] It alone recalls Jesus' paying the temple tax with a coin drawn from the mouth of a fish (Mt. 17:27), and instead of relating, as Mark and Luke do, that Judas received "money" for betraying Jesus, it specifies kind and amount: "thirty pieces of silver" (27:3).

The apostle John, who claims in his Gospel to have been an eyewitness and whose claim went unchallenged, is said to have been from a priestly family, and again, this is borne out by his writing.[19] He alone gives two accounts of the driving of money changers from the temple just as he alone tells of Jesus being interrogated by Annas before being brought to Caiaphas. John gives the fullest account of what Jesus said and did in Jerusalem on religious feasts, even as he demonstrates special knowledge of Siloam and Bethesda. Also, because we know from Scripture and Tradition that John took Mary into his home, we would expect the Johannine text to reflect a special relationship with the Blessed Mother, and it does. It alone tells of Mary's inauguration of Jesus' public ministry at Cana, just as it alone informs us of what Jesus said to John from the Cross: "Behold, your mother!" (Jn. 19:27).

Mark and Luke were not eyewitnesses. But what we know about them is again borne out by what they wrote. Mark, Peter's secretary in Rome, gives us an extra verse on Peter's mother-in-law, and he is the only evangelist to describe Jesus as indignant, angry-looking, and incredulous. If anyone is likely to have recalled sternness and shock on the part of Jesus, it would have been Peter, who knew Christ's indignation firsthand, and, as the leader of the apostolic band, would have had sensitive political antennae.[20]

As for Luke, who traveled with Paul, he is known to have been a doctor, and his Gospel stands out for its singular use of medical terms. For the word "needle" he uses a term signifying a surgical instrument, as compared with the kind used for sewing, and he alone records Jesus' words, "Physician, heal yourself."[21]

OUTSIDE SOURCES

Aristotle's second criterion for historical reliability, corroboration of eyewitness testimony by disinterested sources, is as easily met as his first. We have already mentioned the testimony of Josephus, but we also have Celsus, one of the best-known critics of Christianity during the late 100s, who affirmed the virgin birth, the visit of the Magi, the flight into Egypt, the slaughter of the Innocents, Jesus' miracles culminating in the Resurrection, and the descent of the Holy Spirit on Pentecost.[22] If one consults early editions of the Talmud, the second holiest book of Judaism, one finds corroboration that Jesus went to Egypt, worked miracles, and was crucified on the eve of Passover. Mention is even made of the amnesty granted to Barabbas.[23]

Towering above all else, though, in the matter of outside sources is something historians call negative evidence. No Jew, Gentile, heretic or apostate during the early years of Christianity ever denied the overall reliability of the Gospels. The Jews, in particular, had every reason to do so since they were in the driver's seat politically on the aftermath of the crucifixion. Yet the only thing they ever denied was the Resurrection. Apologists from Justin Martyr to St. Augustine challenged Jewish leaders to give the lie to anything else found in the Gospels, and the answer was silence.[24]

MANUSCRIPT EVIDENCE

Aristotle's third criterion for reliability is the age and number of surviving manuscripts, and once again, the Gospels are impressive. Although we do not have the originals, we do have copies in Greek dating as far back as the fourth century, and portions of Luke and John are thought to be even older. There is also a manuscript dated about AD 135 that contains some verses of John. Considering that the average interval between the initial appearance of ancient works and the date of the oldest surviving copy is roughly seven hundred years, this is extraordinary. As far as numbers are concerned, surviving copies of secular works of antiquity are remarkably few by comparison with what we have for the Gospels—one copy each, for instance, of Homer's *Odyssey* and the first six books of Tacitus' *Annals*, as compared with thousands of manuscript (hand-written) copies of the Gospels.[25]

All of which makes the New Testament the best attested Greek or Latin work in all of the ancient world. In addition to thousands of copies in Greek, we have manuscript copies in other languages that number in the scores of thousands, not to mention over a million quotations from the pens of patristic writers. The documentation is so overwhelming, in fact, and the discrepancies so few that one can be certain of 99 percent of the text.[26]

Reliability is further confirmed because relatively little time elapsed between the year Christ ascended into heaven (AD 30 most likely) and the date the Gospels first appeared in writing. One hundred fifty years intervened between the death of Mohammed and the first written accounts of his life, and if one examines the origin of Buddhism, the documentation is even shakier. Compare that with the Gospels, which, according to the vast majority of scholars, appeared within seventy years of the Resurrection at a time when eyewitnesses could challenge any and all instances of inaccuracy. Many academicians believe that the synoptic Gospels (Matthew, Mark, and Luke) were written no later than twenty to forty years after the Resurrection.[27] Using state-of-the-art power microscopes, experts have put a date of AD 50 on three postage-stamp-sized fragments of Matthew on deposit at Magdalene College, Oxford, and some of the latest philological research places all four Gospels between the early AD 30s and 60.[28]

According to some scholars, portions of Mark's Gospel (6:52–53), along with a verse from 1 Timothy (4:1b), are decipherable in what is known as the Dead Sea Scrolls, and we know the scrolls predate AD 68, the year the caves in which they were found were permanently closed due to war between the Romans and Jews.[29] Indicative, too, is the fact that Luke, in his Acts of the Apostles, speaks of having written a "former book" which relates "all that Jesus began to do and teach" (Acts 1:1). Both volumes are dedicated to Theophilus and both have key words, phrases, and grammatical constructions in common. Equally important, because Acts ends abruptly with Paul's house arrest in Rome, we may assume that it was written by AD 62, the year of his release, and the third Gospel could hardly have come later. Luke refers to other accounts, most likely the Gospels of Matthew and Mark, and some of St. Paul's letters written no later than twenty-five to thirty years after the Resurrection, which replicate Gospel teaching on divorce and celibacy, along with the mystery of the Eucharist and the reality of Christ's Resurrection.[30]

All circumstantial evidence points one way. Chemists, paleographers, and papyrologists can identify the time frame within which a given type of paper, parchment, ink, or shape of writing was used, and they, too, are on the side of early dating.

Similarly in the case of philologists and linguists, who rely, like Professor Henry Higgins of *My Fair Lady* fame, on style and manner of expression. Historians, for their part, come at it from still another slant (if, for example, they find reference to a steam locomotive in a particular manuscript they know it must be late nineteenth or early twentieth century).In the case of the Gospels, there are hundreds of details relating to people, places, and events that would have been unfamiliar to authors of a later period.

MEMORY POWER

Still another factor underscoring reliability is the memory power of Christ's followers, which must have been awesome. At a time when few could afford books, pens, or paper, the rabbis used to say that a good student was like a cistern that never leaked.[31] There were scribes who knew all of the Old Testament by heart, and for centuries, the Babylonian Talmud, which ran to sixty volumes, was routinely recited by memory.[32] We must take care not to view the ancient world through twenty-first century lenses. To regurgitate all twenty-two thousand lines of the *Iliad* and *Odyssey*, as Greek story tellers did, would be out of the question for most of us today, even in the world of entertainment. Roman school children were expected to memorize the entire legal code of the decemvirs, and in AD 632, the year Mohammed died, there were so many Muslims who knew the Koran by heart that it was only when eyewitnesses began dying that the text was committed to writing.

In Christian circles, St. John Chrysostom had the New Testament memorized and St. Paula could recite all four Gospels in Greek. Anyone who aspired to enter one of the monasteries of St. Pachomius in Egypt had to commit the New Testament and Psalms to memory, and it was no different in medieval times. St. Anthony of Padua carried most of the Bible in his head.[33] As late as the nineteenth century, there were American Sunday school teachers who expected their students to memorize several chapters of the Bible every week, and during the twentieth century, Africans who relied on memory because they lacked typewriters, tape recorders, computers, and copy machines were highly regarded.[34] The communication of the nomadic people of Somalia was exclusively oral and if a storyteller made a single slip, his listeners would beat the ground with their sticks until he got it right. A missionary reportedly gave a copy of the Gospel of Luke to a Ugandan convert only to have the man return a few days later, saying, "I know it now."[35]

It is easy to forget that Matthew and John sat for years at the feet of the greatest teacher the world has ever known, and Jesus, for his part, must have used every conceivable device to stamp his teaching indelibly on their minds. Beyond that, he promised to refresh their recollection by sending "the Counselor, the Holy Spirit" to recall to them all that he had said (Jn. 14:26).

SPECIOUS CHARGES OF FAKING

Deliberate faking on the part of the evangelists has been alleged. But since when do men lay down their lives for what they know to be a lie? According to Tacitus, the dean of Roman historians, "an immense multitude" of Christian witnesses to the Gospel endured the cruelest torture imaginable at a time when there were thousands still alive who had known Jesus personally.[36] Secondly, the Gospels ring true. What charlatan or spin artist would burden readers with something as inconsequential as the fact that one of Jesus' followers ran away naked from the Garden of Gethsemane (Mk. 14:52)? There are also passages in which the disciples are portrayed negatively as, for instance, when they argue about who is greatest.[37] Why would editors include such material if they were self-seeking? Why would men upholding the doctrine of Christ's divinity quote the Lord as saying, "The Son [of God] can do nothing of his own accord"; "What I say . . . I say as the Father has bidden me"; and again, "the Father is greater than I"?[38] Jesus is portrayed as having told his apostles that places of honor in the kingdom of heaven were not his to give, just as he is shown praying for God's help.[39]

Thirdly, faking would have been profoundly disrespectful, reflecting on the master as much as it did on the student. Great teachers choose their words with care. They expect to be quoted accurately, and for any student to do otherwise would not only have been deceitful but fatuous. Such fraud would surely have come to the attention of fellow students, in this case one of the apostles.

THE HONOR AND INTEGRITY
OF THE EARLY CHRISTIANS

Charges of duplicity would have rung particularly hollow in the ears of a first-century Roman, owing to the reputation for honesty enjoyed by contemporary Jews and Christians. Lying and misrepresentation are common today. Journalists and directors of motion pictures think nothing of palming off fiction as truth. Over the years Communist functionaries have been perfectly shameless in this regard. Lenin is famous for having said that "promises are like pie crusts, made to be broken," a throwback to the Lombard invaders of ancient Rome who kept their word only when convenient.[40] This, however, was not the Judeo-Christian standard.

Sarah's duplicity in denying laughter at the thought of pregnancy in old age became the basis for the Jewish prohibition against female testimony in court. The price Jacob paid for his trickery made a lasting impression, as did the leprosy contracted by Elisha's deceitful servant Gehazi. Isaiah condemns duplicity in the harshest of terms, as does Sirach, and we know that the tradition was very much alive in Jesus' time. A contemporary rabbi went so far as to forbid "white lies."[41] According to Shammai, one could not even tell a homely bride on the day of her wedding that she looked beautiful.[42] Jesus' description of Nathaniel as a "true Israelite without guile" says as much about the Jews as it does about Nathaniel, and lest any doubt remain, Tacitus described the Jews, whom he disdained, as "inflexibly honest."[43]

Moses' command, "Thou shalt not bear false witness" was taken especially seriously when it came to Holy Writ. To add or subtract from the Pentateuch was a heinous offense in the eyes of the Pharisees and strictly forbidden by Scripture.[44] One reads in the Book of Proverbs: "Every word of God proves true . . . Do not add to his words."[45] Woe, therefore, to any priest who falsified or embroidered. He could be deposed.[46] The Ark of the Covenant containing the Ten Commandments could not even to be *touched* by unauthorized human hands, and when it was the guilty party was struck dead.[47] Even today Torah scrolls may not be trashed or burned. If worn or damaged to the point of being illegible, they must be buried as one would bury an honored member of the family. Small wonder that when Josephus combed through a mountain of documentation to write his definitive history of the Jews—tapping Egyptian, Greek, Chaldean (Babylonian), and Tyrian (Lebanese), as well as Jewish sources, many of which have been lost—he concluded that Hebrew Scripture was every bit as trustworthy as the rabbis contended.

Rooted in this ancient tradition, Christianity raised the bar still higher. In the New Testament, lying is associated with murder and idolatry (Rev. 22:15), and Satan is known as "the father of lies" (Jn. 8:44). Ananias and Sapphira are struck dead for misinforming Peter about their contribution to the common purse.[48] The earliest Christian conduct book outside of the Bible, the *Didaché*, goes so far as to forbid equivocation, and early in the second century, Aristedes, alluding to the apostles' emphasis on truth telling, puts honesty on a par with compassion as a Christian virtue.[49]

It was customary for ancient historians to put words into the mouths of the figures they chronicled. Josephus, for instance, does it for Herod. But Eusebius (c. 260–339), the first Christian historian of prominence, refused to follow suit. How likely is it that Christians who shrank from literary license in portraying secular figures, would use it in the case of the God-Man? Skeptics point out that Plato took liberties in his literary sketch of Socrates, but Plato was neither Jewish nor Christian, and he certainly did not regard his subject as God.

Christian insistence on truth telling runs like a leitmotif through the New Testament. Peter condemns deceit repeatedly, and Paul tells us to gird our loins with the truth.[50] According to James, truth is what gave us birth, and John, whose writing might be called "the Gospel of Truth," recalls that Jesus prayed twice in rapid succession so that his followers would be "sanctified" in the truth.[51] The word "truth" appears over and over again in John, several times within a few lines on one occasion (Jn. 17:17–19). He begins his Gospel by picturing the Lord as "full of truth" (1:14) and ends it by affirming the truth of his own testimony (19:35; 21:24). Then, in the Book of Revelation, he fires a warning at those who would add to his words or subtract. To the man who adds, "God will add to him the plagues," he thunders, and to the one who subtracts, God will "take away his share in the tree of life."[52] It is John who quotes Jesus as saying that the truth will make us free, John again who recalls Christ's description of himself as "the Way, and the Truth, and the Life."[53] In John's view, Jesus' very *raison d'être* was "to bear witness to the truth," and those who are "of the truth" will hearken to him.[54]

A self-proclaimed Christian by the name of Cerinthus denied Jesus' Resurrection and divinity, and John, on encountering him at the baths, exclaimed, "Let us fly [from here] lest even the bathhouse fall down because Cerinthus, the enemy of truth, is within."[55] Polycarp was John's student through and through. When he met with Marcion, who rejected the Old Testament, Marcion asked him if he knew who he [Marcion] was, and Polycarp shot back: "You are the first born of Satan!"[56]

One of Polycarp's contemporaries, Pliny the Younger (62?–113), observes in his letters to Emperor Trajan that Christians are bound by oath never to falsify their word or deny a pledge. Eleven hundred years later, Thomas Aquinas, true to tradition, will insist on absolute integrity of speech. Add another six hundred years and Victor Hugo will present the lovable Sister Simplice of *Les Miserables* as a woman who never lies. Forced to do so in order to conceal the whereabouts of a kindly master hounded by a cruel enemy, she thinks she will faint. Today, the Catechism of the

Catholic Church goes so far as to condemn adulation in the sense of hollow flattery even when one's goal is to avoid evil.[57]

This is not to say that every version of the Bible is flawless. Translators make mistakes, and there have always been typographical errors—"copyist" errors, as they were called in the days when scribes, bending over a manuscript by candlelight, were prone to fatigue. Nor is it to say that the New Testament Gospels are any more inerrant than the rest of Scripture. It is just that, in the case of the Gospels, the word "reliability" seems to be written on every page. While they may differ on occasion, they are never contradictory.

EXAMPLES OF ALLEGED CONTRADICTION

There are two versions of the Lord's Prayer, one of them abbreviated, but the discrepancy is easily explained. Jesus must have taught children, as well as adults, how to pray.[58] The Sermon on the Mount recorded by Matthew is longer and slightly different from the sermon on the plain found in Luke.[59] But again, this is not a problem. Our Lord must have delivered the same basic speech hundreds of times, varying it to suit his audience and the time at his disposal. Undoubtedly, there were short, long, and medium versions. Was it late in the day? Was there a thunderstorm brewing?

That we have different words in different Gospels for the consecration of bread and wine at the Last Supper is equally understandable. Bread was distributed more than once at a seder. Jesus could have served his apostles individually, and there was more than one raising of the cup. Typically four cups of wine were blessed and consumed at four different times, two of them during the latter part of the meal, and a gifted teacher knows how to say the same thing in a variety of ways.[60]

Allegations of contradiction such as those just mentioned have been rampant for decades, but there are affordable encyclopedias of Bible difficulties that deal handily with each and every one.[61] Genesis 1 may be squared with Genesis 2.[62] Matthew's account of the death of Judas is reconcilable with that found in Acts.[63] Then, too, the "God of the Old Testament" does not differ from the "God of the New." Mercy figures prominently in the Old Testament while there is no lack of condemnation in the New.[64] As often as the Israelites abandoned the Lord, he never abandoned them, and Jesus castigated whole classes of people along with entire towns and cities.[65]

In point of fact, it is the *absence* of contradiction that is striking. If one Gospel named Bethlehem as Jesus' birthplace and another Nazareth, or if one referred to Joseph and Mary instead of Zachary and Elizabeth as the parents of John the Baptist, there would be cause for concern. If the lists of apostles differed in length or Peter's name appeared on only one of them, lights would again flash red.[66] But this is not the case; and Jesus himself is always the same. His tender regard for children coupled with a steady insistence on worldly detachment are constants. First, last, and always, he stresses the need for repentance.

TAMPERING RULED OUT

Certain non-believers, Muslims in particular, will argue that however accurate the Gospels may have been to begin with, they were corrupted—i.e. tampered with. Tampering, however, is as improbable as faking, and for many of the same reasons. One can point to the extraordinary uniformity of thousands of manuscripts found in many different parts of the world. How could falsifiers have corrupted all four Gospels while their authors were alive? The originals were undoubtedly copied and disseminated at a steady rate during the lifetime of the evangelists, and even more rapidly after their death. How could chicanery artists have corrupted all of them? There is no trace of any other story. Hand-copied Gospels were precious and, as such, would have been well guarded. Surely there would have been too many reliable copies in one or another place for the work of a falsifier to escape detection, and once detected it would have aroused the anger of a faith community that imposed severe penalties for such conduct.[67]

In the Muslim tradition some have held it permissible to twist or distort the truth in order to instill virtue or foster submission to the law.[68] But, as pointed out, this was never an option for Christians. We know from St. Augustine that the slightest deviation from the authorized text on the part of a lector was loudly protested.[69]

MODERN BIBLICAL CRITICISM

Surprisingly, it is not Islam that offers the greatest challenge to the integrity of the Gospels, but rather intellectuals sailing under Christian colors. As a case in point, Rudolf Bultmann (1884–1976), professor of biblical studies at the University of Marburg in Germany and the father of modern "demythologization," declared it "impossible to use electric light . . . and at the same time to believe in the New Testament world of spirits and miracles."[70] On a tour of the United States in 1958, he delivered an influential series of lectures entitled "Jesus Christ and Mythology," and from then on, it has been open season on the Bible in America. Many of the most prominent theologians, even in Catholic circles, have seconded Bultmann's preposterous claim that we can know practically nothing about Jesus' life and personality.

We will revisit biblical criticism in chapter 5. Suffice it to say at this point that Bultmann's thesis piles assumption on top of assumption while treating speculation as fact. At once unscholarly and unhistorical, it is not even scientific. Scholars in the Bultmann mold have stated categorically that "Mark came first" (before Matthew in chronological order), which is again unprofessional because it is only theory dressed up as fact, and not very well grounded theory at that. As apologist Karl Keating has pointed out, the "Q" source theory often used to prop up the idea that Mark preceded Matthew is overwhelmed by countervailing data. But "Q" marches merrily on.[71]

Bultmann-like skeptics, many of them distinguished enough to be classed as "experts," occupied influential positions in biblical scholarship during the second half of the 1900s. But this is changing, and we know from history that so-called "experts" can be wrong. Christ's response to the scribes and Pharisees, the most highly respected Scripture scholars of his time, was nothing if not scorching: "Woe to you, lawyers! for you have taken away the key of knowledge; you did not enter yourselves, and you hindered those who were entering" (Lk. 11:52). Tertullian (c. AD 150–c. 220), the author of thirty-three books and the foremost Christian theologian of his age, wound up apostatizing because he could not abide the practice of absolving persons guilty of grave sexual sin. In the fourth century most of the Church's theologians questioned the divinity of Christ, and centuries later a preponderance of brains held that a Church council could override the pope. Both of these theories, Arianism and Conciliarism, were badges of academic respectability in their day, and both have been scrapped.

THE DEUTEROCANONICAL BOOKS

One last word. Many books were read aloud by early Christian lectors, among them the *Shepherd of Hermas* and the *Epistle of Barnabas*. As time passed, the Church had to decide which of these volumes belonged in the Bible and which didn't on the basis of reliability, and it made this decision in the late 300s (Hermas and Barnabas were, in fact, excluded). For over a thousand years, Rome's decision went unchallenged. But at the time of the Reformation, questions arose over the canonicity of some of the books included by the Fathers. These books, the deuterocanonicals ("apocrypha" in the Protestant lexicon), are: Sirach, 1 and 2 Maccabees, Judith, Tobit, Wisdom, Baruch, and parts of Daniel and Esther.[72]

The original King James Bible retained the deuterocanonicals in an appendix, but later Protestant editions omitted them altogether, and this is unfortunate. Sirach was the conduct book of the early Christian Church—also known as *Liber Ecclesiasticus* or "Book of the Church"—and, in many respects, it is superior to Proverbs. Maccabees commemorates the courage of the ninety-year-old Eleazar, who preferred to undergo torture and die rather than appear disloyal to his faith, along with a brave mother who urged her seven sons to do the same. Judith is another story of feminine courage. Tobit and Wisdom are absolutely marvelous, as are the portions of Daniel and Esther that fell beneath Luther's axe.

Protestant reformers may or may not have known that the Septuagint, the Greek translation of the classical Hebrew Bible updated to contain the deuterocanonicals, was the edition favored by Jesus and his disciples, along with the vast majority of the world's Jews at the time of Christ, most of whom lived outside Palestine. It is still read by Ethiopian Jews. Of approximately three hundred fifty quotations drawn by the New Testament from the Old, roughly three hundred come from the Septuagint, and the writings of the Church fathers are positively peppered with allusions to it.[73]

One thing Luther did know: the deuterocanonicals contradicted his theology. The doctrine "once saved, always saved" is countered by Sirach's "call no one happy before his death" (11:28). Sirach also prophesied that the Aaronic priesthood would never pass away (45:13), and, as we know, most Protestant denominations are priestless. The second book of Maccabees supports two other things denied or condemned by Luther: namely, the existence of purgatory and prayer for the dead.[74] Calvin taught predestination while Luther was enamored of the idea that one is saved by faith alone: "be a sinner and sin stoutly" [i.e. without doubting your salvation].[75] But Sirach testifies to the existence of free will, and hence to the necessity of works: "Say not: 'It was God's doing that I fell away' . . . If you choose, you can keep the Commandments . . . If you have sinned, sin no more"[76] (CE). In like vein, Sirach depicts God as judging men according to their "deeds," and this is, of course, echoed by the *Letter of James* (another book Luther wished to do away with).[77]

In discarding the deuterocanonicals, the Reformers pointed out that this is what Jewish leaders did when they met at Jamnia in northern Palestine toward the end of the first century. But the question is, why? The Book of Wisdom rebukes those who condemn the "son of God" (described as one "who boasts that God is his Father") to a "shameful death" (2:16–20) and makes clear reference to an afterlife (3:1–9), which would have been objectionable to the Sadducees. Secondly, Sirach, the volume chosen by the earliest Christians as their conduct book, refers to the priesthood as perpetual, and this would have been as disturbing to the Jews of AD 90 or 100 as it was to Reformation Protestants. Thirdly, the seventy-two rabbis who translated the Hebrew Scriptures into Greek (for the deuterocanonical-inclusive Septuagint version) were unanimous in holding that the Hebrew word 'almâ, used in reference to the mother of the Messiah, meant "virgin" (Is. 7:14). 'Almâ can mean young woman *or* virgin, depending on the context, but in the Greek Septuagint there is no such ambiguity, and this bolsters the case for Christianity.

Needless to say, these were not the reasons given by the men who met at Jamnia. Instead, they objected because some of the books in question were not sufficiently ancient (divine inspiration was thought to have ceased after the time of Ezra and Nehemiah c. 400 BC). They were also partial to books that were written in Hebrew, or at least available in Hebrew. Judith, along with Tobit, Baruch, Wisdom, and 2 Maccabees, were available only in Greek, and there was nothing to indicate that the latter two had even been written in Hebrew.

It should be clear that none of the above arguments favoring the Hebrew version of the Bible over the up-dated Septuagint version are relevant from a Christian point of view. The Gospels and their companion volumes were all written after the so-called "age of inspiration," just as the oldest surviving copies of the New Testament are all in Greek. In sum, the Church has done well to keep the deuterocanonicals. The Old Testament accepted by Rome is the one most often cited by Jesus and the fledgling Church, and even if this were not so, it is hard to imagine how Christians under the continual guidance of the Holy Spirit promised them by Jesus could have erred on such an important matter for over a thousand years.[78]

Chapter 3

THE CASE FOR CHRIST

The Library of Congress catalogue contains something on the order of seventeen thousand entries under the name "Jesus," twice the number for any other figure—Shakespeare runs a distant second. The Galilean carpenter, who lived for thirty years in total obscurity before rising to a position of greater influence than anyone else in history, is radically unlike any other man born of woman. Terms like "fascinating" and "intriguing" are woefully inadequate when it comes to describing a man who allowed the apostle Thomas to call him "my Lord and my God," who said that "all authority in heaven and on earth" had been given him, who claimed he could raise himself from the dead, who promised eternal life to all who believed in him, and who said that one day he would come with his angels to judge the living and the dead.[1]

This individual applied the Jewish name for God, "I am" (Yahweh), to himself. When Moses asked the Lord what he should tell his people if they asked who commissioned him to deliver them from bondage, the Almighty replied, "Say this to the sons of Israel, *I Am* has sent me to you." Jesus used the same words when he said, "Before Abraham was, *I am*."[2]

God alone is sinless and capable of forgiving sin. Yet, as mentioned earlier, the man from Nazareth not only pronounced himself sinless but presumed to forgive others their sins and conferred this power on his apostles.[3] Instead of claiming to *have* the truth, he declared himself to *be* the truth.[4] He called himself "lord" of the Sabbath and "the Son of God," insisting that "he who has seen me has seen the Father," for "I and the Father are one."[5] Peter and Paul reminded their listeners that they were human like anyone else; but Jesus, who called himself meek and humble of heart, said that he was wiser than Solomon, greater than Jonah, greater even than God's temple.[6]

The divine makeup of the God-man is especially evident in his claims to pre-existence. "Father," he prayed, "glorify thou me . . . with the glory which I had with thee before the world was made." Then again, "I saw Satan fall like lightning from heaven."[7] Those who heard these words wanted to put him to death because "he not only broke the Sabbath but also called God his Father, making himself equal with God." At one point, picking up rocks to stone him, they charged him outright: "You being a man make yourself God."[8] When the high priest asked him if he was "the Son of God," he answered, "You have said so" (meaning "yes"). At which point the priest tore his robes, declaring, "He has uttered blasphemy" while others, unable to contain themselves, spat in his face.[9]

Such claims, incredible as they may sound, were no more incredible than the way they were validated. Elijah and Elisha raised a man from the dead, but Jesus raised at least four, himself included. He alone cured at a distance, changed water to wine, calmed the wind, walked on water, and restored a severed ear to its owner.[10] John tells us that "the world itself could not contain the books that would [have to] be written" if all the miracles he worked had been recorded (21:25). In an instant, those suffering from paralysis, leprosy, and mental illness were made whole. Peter's mother-in-law shook off a fever at his touch.[11] He drove out unclean spirits, healed a chronic hemorrhage, gave sight to a man *born* blind (something altogether unprecedented), and when he restored a demoniac to health, the crowd, aware of the uniqueness of the moment, exclaimed: "Never was anything like this seen in Israel."[12]

One marvels at the sheer variety of it all—from the healing of a man with a withered hand to the feeding of five thousand persons with two fishes and five loaves. When Peter needed money to pay the temple tax, Jesus told him to cast his net into the sea, and on doing so he caught a fish with a coin of exactly the right denomination in its mouth.[13] At the sound of Christ's curse, a barren fig tree withered; at the touch of his hand, a deaf mute spoke and heard. He passed unseen through a hostile crowd; he filled Peter's fishing net to capacity after the apostle had labored all night in vain; he straightened the spine of a woman badly bent for eighteen years. Restoring the health of a man who had lain helpless for thirty-eight years and curing a victim of dropsy—all of this was routine.[14]

Any one of these miracles is impressive in and of itself, but together they are astounding, and since God is the essence of truth and cannot endorse falsehood, there is only one conclusion. Jewish leaders, denying none of the signs save one, attributed them to a form of black magic. But magic cannot calm the wind or raise the dead, and the one sign called into question, the Resurrection, is the exception that proves the rule, as we shall see.[15]

THE MESSIANIC PROPHECIES

Forecasts of the coming of the God-Man even before his birth single him out among religious founders, and the accuracy with which those forecasts predict the most minute details of his suffering is incredible. Hundreds of years before Mary gave birth to the Messiah, Old Testament prophets spoke of a servant who would be scourged, mocked, spat upon, pierced in the hands and feet, and thrust through; a servant, moreover, who would suffer for the sins of mankind and be counted among the wicked. His executioners would cast lots for his clothing. Not one of his bones would be broken because he was the Passover Lamb; neither would his body undergo corruption.[16]

There was also the expectation that his mother would be a virgin (Is. 7:14); that he would be born in Bethlehem (Mic. 5:2) of the tribe of Judah in the line of David, and that he would rule by the "rod of his mouth," eschewing violence. Isaiah predicted that he would be called "God" and that his name would be "God with us." Finally, it was foretold that he would be a light to the Gentiles, that his betrayer would receive thirty pieces of silver, and that he would inaugurate a universal priesthood of the laity that, by inference, would give ordinary folk privileged access to the Holy of Holies.[17]

Scholars have indentified hundreds of messianic prophecies.[18] The odds against any one person fulfilling all of them, as Christ did, are roughly 8,400,00 0,000,000,000,000,000,000 to 1. Jewish rabbis have their own view of the prophecies, but even they will admit, in many cases, that their interpretation is open to question.

While we are dealing with prophecy, Jesus himself foretold everything from a catch of fish to a chance encounter with a man carrying water (something highly unlikely since women did most of the carrying). Judas' betrayal, along with Peter's denial, were on the Master's lips before they occurred, and his apostles heard him say that he would be mocked, spat upon, scourged, crucified, and raised up.[19] He likewise anticipated the destruction of Capernaum, Corozain, Bethsaida, and Jerusalem—Capernaum was ransacked by the Persians in AD 614 and never rebuilt; Corozain and Bethsaida no longer exist; and Jerusalem was demolished in AD 70.[20] This man assured his followers that they, too, would one day be privy to "things that are to come," and they were. Peter anticipated the death of Sapphira, and Paul predicted not only that the magician Bar Jesus would go blind but also that God would strike down Ananias, the Jewish high priest—Bar Jesus lost his sight for three days and Ananias was murdered in AD 66 by a band of Sicarii.[21]

If Jesus' signs and prophetic utterances were all one had to go on, they would be stunningly indicative. But there is more. He established a covenant between himself and mankind and worked miracles without invoking the name of God.[22] When Moses confronted Pharaoh, he began with the words, "Thus says the LORD," (Ex. 11:4). Peter likewise commanded a crippled beggar to rise and walk "in the name of Jesus Christ of Nazareth" (Acts 3:6). Christ, on the other hand, spoke three words to a man four days in the tomb: "Lazarus, come out" (Jn. 11:43). In comparison with Jeremiah, who prefaced his teaching with "thus says the LORD" and Moses, who called upon God to show him the way, Jesus proclaimed himself to *be* the way![23] One can only wonder what his followers must have thought when he insisted that they love him as much as they loved their own parents.[24]

JESUS' HUMANITY

None of this is meant to obscure Our Lord's pain and disappointment, thirst and anxiety. He wept with Mary over the death of Lazarus. And even as he told the scribes, "I . . . came forth from God . . . He sent me," he implored the Father's help in time of need.[25] For this reason the Church has always viewed Jesus as fully human, *as well as* fully divine, with two distinct wills and two separate intellects. And the distinction is one that matters. A mere mortal can no more atone for Original Sin, which is an offense by man against God, than a dog can compensate his master for ripping his pants. Man is man; God is God. But Christ, being God, as well as man, was uniquely equipped to reconcile beings of different orders.[26]

Needless to say, the apostles never allowed the human side of Christ to prejudice them against his divinity. Peter, in one of his letters, spoke of him as "the Author of life," while for Paul he was the "fullness of deity." Jude has him chaining the fallen angels and John uses the first and last letters of the Greek alphabet (alpha and omega) to describe him "who is and who was and who is to come."[27] Pliny, a Roman administrator, remarked in the year AD 112 that the Christians "sang hymns to Christ as God."[28] In short, the evangelists who demanded so much in the way of faith were certain of what they were asking.

The Old Testament sage who prophesied that the Messiah would be "God with us" could not have been more prescient.[29] Beauty, truth, and goodness, the essence of the Godhead, are reflected in the singular beauty of Jesus' words, the unmatched profundity of his wisdom, and the unparalleled sublimity of his love. Scripture tells us that God is mercy and justice alike (Sir. 5:7; 16:12), and again, we see both qualities brilliantly displayed in the Son.

JESUS' MERCY

In his mercy, Jesus intervenes to save the life of an adulteress.[30] He weeps over the impending doom of an unbelieving Jerusalem and he pardons his executioners.[31] Compassion such as one finds in the parable of the Prodigal Son is nowhere to be found in the Brahmanas and Upanishads of Oriental religion. The caste system of Hinduism with its notion of untouchability is a far cry from Jesus' "blessed are you poor" (Lk. 6:20), and while Buddhism values compassion more highly than Hinduism, it is not on a par with Jesus' willingness to use the word "friend" in reference to a man whom he knew to be both a thief and a traitor.[32]

The founders of major religions have much to recommend them, but there is nothing in their history comparable to the way Jesus valued children. Where, outside the New Testament, does one find an infant leaping for joy in his mother's womb at the approach of another unborn infant? God himself becomes a child. He embraces youngsters, blesses them, holds them up as models of humility, and instructs parents to let them come to him.[33] The Lord of Creation, after recalling Jairus' daughter to life, asks that she be given something to eat.[34]

By entering the world and leaving it the way he did, Jesus embraced the marginalized, and by extending the Jewish scope of neighborly concern to include Samaritans, he brought all mankind under the umbrella of brotherly love.[35] Preaching that many who are last in the world will one day be first, he gave his followers a taste of what was to come by raising a reformed prostitute to immortal fame and canonizing a contrite thief on the cross.[36] Just as he invited Matthew, a hated tax collector, to join his band, so, too, did he dine at the table of another outcast, Zacchaeus.[37] So radical was his call to charity that the early Church held all goods in common.[38] Finally, while his cures are legendary, he showed still greater kindness by forgiving men their sins and dying for his enemies.[39]

That his death was voluntary is clear not only from his mission statement: "The Son of Man [has come] . . . to give his life as a ransom for many" (Mk. 10:45), but also from what he told the Pharisees: "No one takes it [my life] from me, but I lay it down of my own accord" (Jn. 10:18). In preparing his followers for the crucifixion, he explained that, "as Moses lifted up the serpent in the wilderness, so must the Son of man be lifted up [on Calvary], that whoever believes in him may have eternal life" (Jn. 3:14–15). And he made the same point at the Last Supper when he raised a cup of wine and said: "This is my blood of the new covenant, which is poured out for many for the forgiveness of sins" (Mt. 26:28).

JESUS' JUSTICE

In comparison with mercy, justice is a somewhat harder quality to discern in Jesus' public ministry, but the Old Testament describes it as a band around the waist of the Messiah, and if one looks for it in the life of Christ, one will find it.[40] The first word of his public ministry was "repent," and when he forgave the woman caught in adultery, he instructed her to "sin no more."[41] In describing Judgment Day, he included, among the various deeds to be weighed in the balance, sins of omission, along with "every idle word." Those who had failed to acknowledge him before men would be met with a reciprocal failure on his part; he would not plead their case before the Father.[42] Then, on the last day, mankind would be divided into two groups, the "sheep" and the "goats," with the former going to heaven and the latter to hell.[43]

Isaiah expected a Messiah who would "slay the wicked" with the "breath of his lips," and Jesus did not disappoint, denouncing lawyers as a class, along with scribes, Pharisees, and chief priests—practically the entire Jewish establishment.[44] Judas, at the moment of betrayal, was dubbed the "son of perdition."[45] Peter, in a moment of weakness, was called "Satan."[46] Where the Old Testament speaks elliptically of hell, referring to it simply as "death," Jesus is more graphic.[47] It is "everlasting fire" accompanied by "weeping" and "gnashing of teeth."[48] Those, he warned, who did not respond to the signs of his ministry would die in their sins, and Jerusalem, along with the temple, would perish utterly because its inhabitants had not recognized the time of their visitation.[49] As for Capernaum, his headquarters in Galilee, it would go down to "hell."[50]

Except when he fashioned a whip of cords and used it to drive money changers from the temple, the fury of the Messiah was not physical.[51] Still, there is nothing in the history of religion to compare with his choice of epithets: "fools," "sons of hell," "hypocrites," "blind," "liars," "serpents," "vipers," and "whited sepulchers" (pure on the outside and putrid within).[52] At times he referred to pagans as "dogs" and "swine."[53] Jeremiah and Ezekiel were known for their invective, but in comparison with what came from the tongue of Jesus, their words sound almost lyrical.

A man unlike any other, he condemned hypocrites out of hand, equated lustful looks with adultery, and outlawed remarriage after divorce, raising the bar generally and showing himself to be Justice as well as Mercy incarnate.[54] Yes, he embraced children and wept at the death of his friend, Lazarus. But he could be uncompromisingly stern, as in his refusal to allow a candidate for discipleship to return home to bid his family farewell.[55] Even at his most compassionate, he was all business.[56]

JESUS' DIVINITY

Which raises the question of identity. As C. S. Lewis put it, Jesus was either a lunatic (i.e. a madman), or he was what he said he was, namely God incarnate. If he was not the Word made flesh, the splendor of the Father, he was the greatest liar and braggart the world has ever known. Clearly, though, he was not a liar. Liars do not foretell the future—not, at least, with unfailing accuracy. Neither was he a braggart or megalomaniac. Such people are showy; they seek to overawe. The man from Nazareth would have none of this. He bathed his apostles' feet and served them breakfast.[57] When he raised people from the dead, he did so before relatively small groups, and there were times when he even forbade his followers to spread the news.[58]

Some have suggested that he was mentally unbalanced, but again, where is the evidence? In response to barbed questions, he was steady, lucid, and self-assured. Parables as great as those of the Good Samaritan and the Prodigal Son, with their unique blend of subtlety and simplicity, do not roll off the lips of a lunatic. His words, intelligible to a child yet inexhaustibly deep, are perennially fresh. With every new reading, imagery and symbols once blurred come into focus; lessons and applications once obscure are all of a sudden clear.[59]

So powerful were Jesus' words that they should have sufficed, in and of themselves, to establish his identity. But the miracles really push skepticism to the wall.[60] Nicodemus, who came to Our Lord at night seeking instruction, had it right when he said that "no one can do these signs that you do unless God is with him." So, too, in the case of the man born blind who asked: "How can a man who is a sinner do such signs?"[61]

Jesus expected the same kind of logic from Jewish leaders, telling them: "If the mighty works done in you had been done in Sodom, it would have remained until this day. But I tell you that it shall be more tolerable on the day of judgment for the land of Sodom than for you" (Mt. 11:23–24). Just as Moses assumed that the stream of marvels worked in Egypt would sustain his leadership in the desert, so too did Jesus expect the Jews of his generation to recognize him as divine on the basis of his miracles even though they were looking for a different kind of Messiah. In both cases the penalty for disbelief was severe: forty years in the desert for Moses' people, and destruction of the Jewish state and priesthood following a forty-year trial period (AD 30–70) for those who spurned the Gospel.[62]

Because Christ's expectations apply to men and women of every era, they raise the question of whether modern man is disadvantaged in comparison with the early Christians who saw the God-man with their own eyes and had access to first-hand testimony. The answer is no.[63] The Bible tells us again and again that God is impartial, and this is but one of many ways in which we can glimpse his refusal to play favorites.[64] That the ancients knew the Lord personally is a given. They also lived at a time when faith in the supernatural was stronger than it is today, a time when a king as worldly as Herod Antipas could suppose that Jesus might be John the Baptist reincarnated.[65] If Paul and Barnabas were to return to Lystra today, they would not be greeted as gods.[66] Nevertheless, there are distinct advantages to being a twenty-first century Christian, among them the knowledge on hindsight that Christianity converted the Roman Empire. Never in their wildest dreams could Jesus' contemporaries have imagined their successors enriching Roman culture, performing spectacular feats of charity and, in the end, causing the world's calendar to turn on the fulcrum of the Lord's birth. Modern man also has the benefit of Scripture in its final form. For many years, Christians had to rely on oral tradition for defense of the Faith, as written copies of the Gospels were costly and rare, and it was not until late in the fourth century that they had the privilege of reading the

New Testament as we know it today because it took that long for the canon to be established.

THE RESURRECTION

Returning to Christ's miracles, we come finally to the Resurrection, which is the most striking and the most fiercely contested of all the proofs for his divinity. Skeptics suggest that those who saw the Risen Lord may have been victims of hallucination or hypnosis. But let us look at the record. Jesus upbraided his apostles for their *lack* of faith and hardness of heart.[67] Although he prepared them for the Resurrection, telling them plainly what would take place, it took the sight of an empty tomb to convince a badly shaken John.[68] They refused to believe the good news even when they heard it from two different sources: women returning from the grave and men who had broken bread with the Risen Lord at Emmaus (Mk. 16:11–13). Hard-bitten Thomas would not listen until Christ appeared to him personally, inviting him to put his hand into his side (Jn. 20:28). Why, if the apostles were credulous, did Jesus feel the need to assure them that "a spirit [i.e. ghost] has not flesh and bones as I have" (Lk. 24:39).

The Risen Lord appeared not once, but many times, first to Mary Magdalene, then to Peter, then to his disciples bound for Emmaus, and finally to the Eleven. On one occasion five hundred saw him at once. He also showed himself to Paul. Altogether, he appeared at least twelve different times over a forty-day period, and in each instance he was seen and heard. Twice he was touched by human hands. Twice he displayed his wounds. Four times he took food.[69] Hallucinations and hypnosis do not occur under such circumstances, do not last for hours, and do not account for the empty tomb.

Some are puzzled because Christ was not instantly recognized by Mary Magdalene. His disciples on the road to Emmaus and those who saw him on the shore of the Sea of Galilee experienced similar difficulty. But the reason is plain. His resurrected body was "glorified," that is to say "perfected," and this must have affected his *voice*, as well as his visage. When a man is seriously ill or lying in repose, he may be hard to recognize even though he is the same person with the same DNA and genes. With Jesus, it was the reverse. Instead of going from good to poor physically, he went from good to glorious, and the fact that men preaching the Resurrection admitted difficulty recognizing him is simply another sign of their integrity.

It has been suggested that Jesus may never have died, but this again makes little sense. Even his harshest critics on the Sanhedrin never went this far. He suffered the worst scourging allowable under Roman law. A crown of thorns pierced his temple so that he bled from the head, as well as from the wrists and feet. Soldiers, acting on orders to dispatch their victims so they could be buried before the Sabbath, broke the legs of the criminals on either side of Jesus, and so it is safe to assume that Our Lord had stopped breathing by the time they reached him since they left his legs alone. One of them, wishing to be certain of his death, drove a lance into his chest, whereupon blood and water poured out, a sure sign of death.[70] After this, they wrapped his body in a burial shroud and laid it in a heavily guarded tomb. Even if he had reached the sepulcher alive and remained conscious for two nights and a day without food or water, he would have been in no condition to exit a burial chamber sealed by a stone too large for three women to move. Mark tells us that it was huge (Mk. 16:3–4; also Mt. 27:66).

THE EMPTY TOMB

Could the body have been stolen? In an effort to explain away the empty tomb, the chief priests made this very claim:

> They gave a sum of money to the soldiers and said, "Tell people, 'His disciples came by night and stole him away while we were asleep.' And if this comes to the governor's ears, we will satisfy him and keep you out of trouble." So they they took the money and did as they were directed; and this story has been spread among the Jews to this day. (Mt. 28:12–15)

Those assigned to guard duty were normally posted in groups of four and changed every few hours. For the story to be true, therefore, several soldiers had to be asleep at the same time, something highly unlikely because the penalty for dereliction of duty was death. Following Peter's prison break, his guards were executed.[71] Paul's guard in Phillipi contemplated suicide when he thought his charge had escaped, and during Paul's shipwreck, the soldiers aboard his vessel were prepared to kill every last prisoner rather than risk the escape of one.[72]

But even if one can imagine soldiers on active duty sleeping side by side, why would the disciples have risked their lives to steal a corpse? Where would they have put it and how could they have concealed its whereabouts? Why, too, would they take the time to unwrap it and roll up its head cloth? John tells us that he and Peter found burial clothes in the empty tomb, along with a head cloth that had been folded or rolled up.[73] Why, finally, would men risk martyrdom to preach a lie? Christian proselytizing was a capital offense in the eyes of the Jews. So dejected were the apostles on the aftermath of the crucifixion that some returned to their former trade as fishermen. All of a sudden, gloom turned to joy and a band of ordinary men despised by the establishment was set to win the world for Christ.

Not all were ordinary, of course. Absent the Resurrection, how does one explain the conversion of Paul, a high-powered Jewish intellectual with sterling academic credentials who had been accustomed to arresting believers and overseeing their execution?[74] Suddenly the man from Tarsus claims that Jesus appeared to him personally and we see him embracing Christianity mind, heart, and soul, speaking of the Resurrection as if it were an established fact.[75]

The Roman procurator who asked, "What is truth?" was not ordinary either. Pontius Pilate appears to have been a convert, along with his wife.[76] Admired by Tertullian and canonized by the Ethiopian Copts (his wife, a canonized saint of the Greek Orthodox Church, has her own feast day), there is a mountain named after him in Switzerland (Mount Pilatus), as well as a memorial in Vienne, France where he is said to be buried.[77] Why would he have converted, again with nothing to gain and everything to lose, if Jesus had not risen?[78] According to the non-canonical *Acts of Peter and Paul* mentioned by Justin Martyr, as well as by Tertullian and Eusebius, Pilate sent a report to Rome that described Jesus' Resurrection as a fact. This would make sense because Eusebius tells us that it had "long been customary for provincial governors to report to the holder of the imperial office any change in the local situation, so that he might be aware of all that was going on."[79] It also squares with Tertullian's contention, confirmed by Eusebius, that Jesus was nominated by Emperor Tiberius for inclusion in the Roman pantheon of gods.[80]

THE TESTIMONY OF GOOD FRIDAY

Still another approach to the Resurrection is to extrapolate from a series of events that occurred on Good Friday. Reports of the crucifixion tell of the temple veil splitting from top to bottom, along with earthquake activity and a solar blackout lasting three hours.[81] The earthquake, undoubtedly the cause of the veil splitting, had to be a sign of divine intervention given its timing; and the blackout, as we shall see, must have been miraculous because it could not have been caused by an eclipse. Once one accepts the existence of a miracle on Friday, along with highly suggestive auxiliary signs, it is not hard to believe that something similar occurred two days later.

For evidence of the splitting of the temple veil, we do not have to rely on Matthew, who furnishes circumstantial evidence (i.e. his report of earthquake activity), because we have it on the authority of Josephus, along with the author of the apocryphal *Gospel of the Hebrews* cited by St. Jerome.[82] Circumstantial evidence comes from Tacitus, Josephus, Celsus, and the authors of the Talmud, all of whom tell of a mysterious opening of the gigantic bronze gate of the temple, which separated the Court of the Women from the Court of the Israelites and normally required twenty men to move.[83] The opening occurred in AD 30, one of two likely dates for the crucifixion, and short of a miracle, earthquake activity is the only thing that could account for it. Seismic disturbance is further confirmed by the work of the celebrated thirteenth-century Dominican scholar, Jacobus de Voragine, who cites Eusebius along with the Roman historian Orosius.[84]

The most remarkable of all the signs that occurred on Friday is the blackout. It could not have been caused by an eclipse of the sun because such eclipses do not occur when the moon is full or close to full. We know that Jesus was crucified the day before Passover (Jn. 19:14), and Passover is always celebrated around the time of the full moon. Furthermore, astronomical records show that there could not have been any solar eclipses during the period AD 30-33, and even if such an eclipse had occurred so as to obscure the sun totally, it would not have lasted for hours. Evidence of coincident darkness in Bithynia, Rome, and Egypt was noted by Voragine, who cites Eusebius and Orosius, along with Dionysius, the first bishop of Athens. Dionysius had been in Heliopolis, Egypt, when he experienced the unearthly phenomenon, and though he knew at the time that it could not be an eclipse, it was not until he heard Paul recount the events of Good Friday that he grasped its real significance.[85] Further confirmation comes from Phlegon, a freedman of Emperor Hadrian, as well as from the Palestinian historian Thallus, who was cited by Julius Africanus in AD 221.[86]

Celsus, an anti-Christian pagan mentioned earlier, affirmed the historicity of the Resurrection in the late 100s; Josephus observed that many believed Jesus to be a god after his crucifixion; and one of the most unlikely of all sources affords a final piece of evidence.[87] The Jewish Talmud is the last place one would normally go to find support for Christianity, but it tells us that once a year, after the high priest entered the Holy of Holies on Yom Kippur to offer sacrifice for the sins of the people, a scarlet thread that hung on the temple door was expected to turn white. When it did, people took it as a sign that God had accepted the priest's offering. But beginning with the year AD 30, the scarlet thread never again turned white.[88] To be sure, this is not direct proof of the Resurrection. But it confirms the Christian theory of substitutional atonement found in the Letter to the Hebrews: "Every [Jewish] priest stands daily . . . offering . . . sacrifices, which can never take away sins" (Heb. 10:11). Something happened in AD 30 that defies worldly explanation. The cessation of the miracle of the scarlet thread, the seismic disturbance, and the three-hour blackout are all of a piece.

A PROFILE OF SKEPTICISM

Only one question remains. If there is so much evidence for the Resurrection, why does it not settle, once and for all, the issue of Christ's divinity? Sadly, there are many reasons. Clarity of thought does not come easily for those involved in substance abuse, gambling, or pornography. There are numerous roadblocks along the way to belief even for those who are sane and sober. Many are loathe to admit that they have been wrong and led others astray. Intellectual pride, endemic to the human condition, is especially deadly when it stands in the way of accepting anything miraculous.

Some would-be converts, aware of how quick the world is to punish signs of religiosity, may lack the requisite courage. With the proverbial sword of Damocles hanging over their heads, they are justifiably afraid of being cut off from family and friends. They could be disinherited. They could lose their jobs. They might have to sever valuable cultural ties. No serious follower of Jesus will be wanting in enemies—powerful ones—and the average man simply wants to be popular around the water cooler. Lastly, without courage and a modicum of self-discipline, it is well-nigh impossible to accept Christian teaching on sexual morality.

This is not to deny that there is such a thing as sincere doubt. It is only natural to wonder why an all-powerful Creator would suffer excruciating pain when he could have saved mankind by a split-second act of his sovereign will. He may have acted as he did in order to underscore the redemptive value of suffering. But one cannot be sure. There is a built-in futility about trying to probe the mind of the Infinite. At the same time, there is no reason why the believer has to shelve his intellect. Take, for example, the question of how a perfect God can take on an imperfect human nature. It seems impossible on the face of it. Yet if a perfect Being can create beings who are imperfect, then such a Being can take on imperfection. At times the faith of a Christian may transcend reason, but it never contradicts it.

Scandalous behavior on the part of believers is still another obstacle in the way of the sincere seeker even though such incongruity is not uniquely Christian. If one examines the history of the Jews, the litany of woe that poured from the mouths of such prophets as Elijah, Jeremiah, and Ezekiel is as good an indication as any of the depravity of God's chosen people for hundreds of years. Out of dozens of Jewish kings only a handful were upright, and among the priestly class few stand out for their virtue. The high priest Alexander Janneus kept concubines. Another murdered his brother in the temple.[89] Even before the time of Janneus, bribery figured in the appointment of Jewish spiritual leaders, and beginning in 63 BC when Pompey brought Judea under the Roman yoke, the office of high priest was controlled by Rome. Annas and Caiaphus, who are familiar from the Gospels, were little more than puppets of the imperial authorities.[90]

My point should be clear: whether Abraham's descendants were moral or immoral—and it was mostly the latter for many years—they were still the Chosen People and, as such, bearers of the truth. Judah was the stage upon which God worked his greatest miracles. From Judaism came the Messiah. However tempted a believer might have been in 800 or 900 BC to apostatize, desertion was not the answer. In every age there have been exemplary Jews, and religion must be judged by the conduct of those who take it seriously—every religion.

Some deny the existence of truth, but this makes little, if any, sense, for by denying truth, they deny the existence of absolutes, which is itself an absolute. Just as puzzling is the stubborn denial of divine intervention when such intervention is as apparent as the noonday sun. After witnessing a dramatic cure at Lourdes, French novelist Émile Zola refused to examine the evidence, and in his novel, *Lourdes*, he cooked the facts. Later, on finding that one of the victims of his fabrication was alive after having pronounced her dead, he offered the woman hush money to avoid exposure as a fraud.[91]

The best example of how impervious the world can be to signs of the supernatural is the way it reacted to what happened in the Portuguese village of Fatima on October 13, 1917. Scores of thousands witnessed the most thoroughly authenticated miracle in the annals of history. Yet few took it to heart, fewer still know of it today, and among those who know, many choose to look the other way, refusing to credit anything that smacks of "popular religion."

FATIMA

The story of Fatima is easily told. On the basis of an apparition of the Virgin Mary, three children claimed to know that a great miracle would occur in three months' time. When the appointed day arrived, seventy thousand had gathered, including atheists, agnostics, hard-bitten journalists, and anti-clerical officials, all awaiting what they confidently expected would be a non-event. It rained long and hard the previous night and many were soaked, but around noon, the sky brightened, the clouds parted, the spectators found themselves dry as a bone, and the sun, after spinning rapidly and throwing off a variety of colors, appeared to zigzag and hurtle at tremendous speed toward the earth. Many fell terrified to the ground. A full account appeared in the anti-clerical Lisbon newspaper, *O Seculo*, along with various other newspapers. Hundreds were interviewed, some of whom witnessed the miracle from as far away as six or eight miles, and their testimony is substantially in agreement.[92]

Authenticity is further confirmed by two things reported by the children well before October 13. First, they quoted the Virgin as having said that without prayer and mortification, Russia would fall into error and spread lies around the world (within a matter of days of the miracle of the sun, Communists seized power in Russia). Secondly, they mentioned a promise from the Virgin that, in answer to their request, two out of the three seers would soon join her in heaven. This, too, came to pass. A flu epidemic at the end of the decade took the life of Jacinta and Francisco, but Lucia, the oldest child, lived to be almost a hundred.

History students can pore over their texts in search of an event that is as telling as it is curious, and few will find it because Fatima is off the radar screen for most academicians. A Marian apparition four centuries earlier at Guadalupe, Mexico resulted in the rapid conversion of millions of native Indians, and this, too, is off the screen. Clearly, Fatima's obscurity is not due to any lack of measurable impact.

How right Jeremiah was when he warned that "the heart is deceitful above all things, and desperately corrupt; who can understand it?"[93] People of intelligence have denied the very *existence* of Jesus, including a fair number of Jews living in New York during the first quarter of the twentieth century. So adamant were they in their denial that Rabbi Stephen Wise, speaking at New York's Carnegie Hall in 1925, was compelled to admit: "For years I have been led to believe, like thousands of other Jews, that Jesus never existed. I say this was not so."[94] If one can doubt Jesus' existence, it is possible to doubt that he was God.

When we survey the history of the Church that Christ founded, we shall find that it furnishes still another argument for his divinity. But before examining Church history we need to pause for a moment and reflect on what the God-Man intended by way of ecclesiastical organization.

Chapter 4

THE CASE
FOR CHRIST'S CHURCH

Forty days after Jesus rose from the dead, he bid farewell to his followers and ascended to heaven. What kind of an organization did he leave behind? How did it function? Who was in charge? To what extent was it based on Jewish tradition? What, in short, were Christ's blueprints? It is easy to exaggerate the novelty of Christianity and, in so doing, overlook its derivative character. But the Faith of the Fathers was, and remains, a continuation of the essential teaching and practice of Judaism.[1]

God, the author of both the Old and the New Testament, cannot change any more than human nature, created in his image and likeness, can change. We know that Jesus valued tradition, along with Scripture, because he told his followers to observe and do all that the scribes and Pharisees taught without following their example. He had not come to "abolish" the Law but rather to "fulfill" it, and "not an iota, not a dot" would pass away, he insisted, until all had been accomplished.[2]

CONTINUITY

Although he introduced much that was new, Our Lord was not a revolutionary.[3] Nothing he said or did ran counter to the Ten Commandments or the moral law articulated by the prophets. Although he tightened the rules on divorce and remarriage—more on this in a moment—he was squarely in line with the Book of Malachi, which teaches that God "hates" divorce, and his aim was to restore marriage to what it had been "from the beginning."[4] Was he liberal or conservative? A progressive or a reactionary? The God-Man is hard to label.

Celibacy, a privilege hitherto reserved for scribes "married" to their work, was now open to all and recommended to the apostles.[5] But even here there were precedents. As Roy Varghese points out, once the Jewish prophets received their call, they seem to have lived as if they were celibate. Priests of the old dispensation abstained from marital relations while on temple duty, and, as we know, priests of the New Covenant are expected to officiate every day of their lives.[6]

It is true that Jesus broke with convention when he stopped to speak with a woman he did not know. He also cured on the Sabbath, dispensed with ritual ablution, and downgraded the importance of dietary regulations. Nonetheless, he never dispensed with anything essential. From the day Mary presented him in the temple to the day he submitted to judgment before the high priest, virtually everything we know about the life of Christ is strictly in accord with tradition. On Saturdays he attended services at the local synagogue, and every year he accompanied his family to Jerusalem to celebrate the Feast of Passover, even though this was only required of those living in close proximity to the Holy City (Lk. 2:41; 4:16). In like manner, he went up for other feasts such as Tabernacles and Succoth (the Dedication of the Temple) much the way medieval pilgrims would make their way to Rome, Canterbury, and Santiago de Compostella.[7] Although he is the only prophet known to have driven money changers from the temple, his behavior was anything but radical, since his aim was to restore God's sanctuary to its proper function as a "house of prayer."[8]

Baptism replaced circumcision as a sign of salvific initiation, but again, this was hardly new. David Goldstein, a twentieth century convert from Judaism, observes in his *Letters to Mr. Isaacs*:

> Baptism by immersion preceded the ceremony of circumcision of converts (proselytes of righteousness), who, when they stepped out of the water, were each considered by the Rabbis to be "as if he were a little

50

child just born." Mikwa is the name of the ritual of purification, baptism by immersion in running water, to which high priests, women at childbirth or after menstruation, etc. were obliged to submit (p. 178).

Far from objecting to the Jewish ecclesiastical establishment, Jesus sent his followers to the priests for the certification of cures and told them to "practice and observe" everything told them by the authorities, even when it came to minute regulations.[9] He likewise retained the male priesthood though he could have adopted the pagan custom of ordaining priestesses.[10] The chief image used to describe his mission, that of the good shepherd, was borrowed from Jewish Scripture, as were most of the Beatitudes and a fair portion of the Our Father and Magnificat.[11] Even the notion of loving one's enemy was familiar from the Old Testament: "You shall not take vengeance or bear any grudge."[12] According to Exodus and Leviticus, if one's enemy is hungry, one must give him food, and if his ox or ass goes astray, one must return it to him.[13]

Following the Ascension the apostles were continually in the temple, and when traveling abroad they preached at the local synagogue and celebrated Jewish feasts.[14] Paul continued to support the Jewish nation financially long after his conversion. He registered his Nazirite vow with the temple authorities after he completed his missionary journeys, and when describing "all Scripture" as "inspired by God and profitable for teaching, for reproof, for correction, and for training in righteousness," his reference was to the Hebrew Bible.[15] So slow were the early Christians to chart an independent course that it took them twenty years to decide whether or not to waive circumcision as a requirement for Gentile conversion. Then, too, out of deference to the Jewish establishment, they called their priests "elders."

A major change occurred in AD 70. The temple went up in flames, and among the many priceless objects lost in the fire were the official genealogical records. Priests of the Old Covenant were required to demonstrate maternal descent from Aaron. Since they could no longer do so, the Jewish priesthood came to an end, and those who were curious must have wondered. Sirach had prophesied that the priesthood of Aaron would last "perpetually" (45:7, 13, 17, 24–25) and Moses had referred to the showbread kept in the Holy of Holies as Aaron's by "perpetual" right (Lev. 24:9).

With the fall of the temple, Christ's ecclesiastical establishment came into its own much the way David had come into his own on the death of Saul. David was king *de jure* for many years, but it was not until Saul died that his successor's kingship went uncontested. Many priests of the old dispensation joined the Church (Acts 6:7) encouraged, no doubt, by the apostolic commitment to traditionalism. When Jesus entrusted Peter with the keys of the kingdom, the Lord ensured that the role of the high priest with power to teach, judge, and prescribe ritual would survive the destruction of Jerusalem; and when he instituted the "pure offering" prophesied by Malachi (1:11) at the Last Supper, Christian priests were equipped to carry out their ministry. Following the Ascension, Jesus himself was offered in unbloody manner at every Mass as the Lamb of God.[16]

The theme of continuity has many variations. Catholic churches are open daily just as the temple was, and there is daily sacrifice.[17] The costliness of appointments, the splendor of priestly vestments, the grandeur of architectural design—all of this ordained by God—has been maintained, especially in the larger churches, basilicas, and cathedrals.[18] The vigil lamp illuminating Catholic tabernacles serves the same purpose as the lamp that burned in the temple, and since the tabernacles themselves are sacred repositories of Jesus' flesh and blood under the appearance of bread and wine, they fulfill God's promise made through Ezekiel that his sanctuary would last "for evermore."[19]

So extensive is the linkage between old and new that one hardly knows where to begin. The Church's use of holy water and the washing of the priest's hands is based on the Jewish practice of ablution (Ex. 40:32). The ringing of bells at the consecration of the Mass to signal the coming of the Lord echoes the bells that sounded when the high priest made his entrance—bells sewn into his garments.[20] The miter ordained by Leviticus for the high priest (Lev. 8:9) is worn by the bishop, Moses' weekly assembly rule is enforced, and the use of incense at Benediction and high Mass recalls not only the gift of the magi but also the practice of Moses, Judith, and Jewish priests.[21] Gabriel came to Zachary in a cloud of incense.[22]

Catholics engage daily in still another Jewish practice. One reads in the Book of Isaiah, "To me every knee shall bow" (45:23), and again in Psalms 95, "Let us kneel before the Lord" (v. 6). Solomon knelt when he dedicated the temple, and Daniel fell to his knees three times daily. Jesus also knelt in prayer, as did Peter, Paul, and the other apostles.[23] James, the first bishop of Jerusalem, spent so much time on his knees that they were said to be as calloused as his feet, and several hundred years later, Eusebius would call kneeling the "normal attitude" of the Church.[24]

MARIAN DEVOTION

The reverence accorded the Jewish queen mother finds a counterpart in the veneration of Mary. Bathsheba had privileged access to her son Solomon and sat on a throne next to his, as was true of all the mothers of Jewish sovereigns. Genealogies normally traced a man's lineage through the father, but when a king is introduced in the Old Testament or in Josephus, it is generally the mother who is named.[25]

A wealth of information points to Mary's veneration as queen mother from the earliest days of Christianity. Having given us her Son at Bethlehem, she is depicted as giving him a second time at Cana when she launches him on his mission (Jn. 2:5). Conversely, the son gives us his mother when he says to John at Calvary under the eye of Salome, John's biological mother: "Behold your mother," referring to Mary (Mt. 27:56; Jn. 19:27). The Book of Revelation presents Mary as a queen with a crown of twelve stars and the moon beneath her feet. She is likewise "clothed with the sun" (Rev. 12:1), an image hitherto reserved for God himself (Psalms 104:2).

Mary is important if for no other reason than the fact that she is the spouse of the Holy Spirit, the Third Person of the Blessed Trinity! One can likewise assume from the words addressed to her by the Angel Gabriel (Lk. 1:28) that she was set apart from all other mortals prior to the Incarnation because God "favored" her (perfect passive participle) and also was "with" her—in some special way, presumably. When Elizabeth calls her "blessed among women" (Lk. 1:42), we can assume further that "blessed" in this context means "most blessed among all women" since Hebrew and Aramaic do not have superlative forms.[26]

Christians of the first generation would certainly have known that, out of hundreds of prophecies contained in the Bible, Mary is the subject of the first and most important. Any doubt as to the identity of "the woman" of Genesis 3:15 is obviated by Jesus' use of the term "woman" in reference to his own mother, and surely, it is more than a coincidence that she "bookends" Sacred Scripture.[27] Genesis, the first volume of the Bible, proclaims her enmity with Satan (3:15) while Revelation, the last book of the New Testament, depicts her in regal attire (Rev. 12:1).

Finally, apart from the fact that mothers are by nature close to their sons, especially if they are widowed with an only child, apart, too, from the fact that the miracles of Guadalupe, Lourdes, and Fatima suggest that Our Lord chose Mary to act as mediatrix (more on this in chapter 9), no one else in Scripture is the object of such impressive salutations, ranging from Gabriel's "*kecharitomene*" to Elizabeth's "blessed . . . among women." Elizabeth could have asked, "Why is this granted me that my Lord should come to me?" Instead, she exclaims, "Why is this granted me that *the mother of my Lord* should come to me?" At which point Mary prophesies that "all generations will call me blessed" (Lk. 1:48).

Many who believe that Catholic devotion to Mary detracts from the worship of her Son are unaware that Mary is merely venerated. At Marian shrines, Eucharistic devotion is at the heart of all pilgrimage activity, and while Mary's statues grace Catholic churches, they traditionally yield pride of place to the tabernacle that contains Christ's body. In most churches there is also a crucifix front and center recalling Moses' elevation of the serpent and Jesus' prophecy, "I, when I am lifted up from the earth, will draw all men to myself."[28] For more on Mary, see Appendix F.

THE NOTION OF HIERARCHY

Returning to the linkage between Old and New Testament practices and noting, in particular, a marked consistency in the ecclesiastical line of command, it is important to recall the position of the high priest, whose word on faith and morals, as well as on liturgical and disciplinary matters, was final.[29] Aaron and his successor, Eleazar, may not have been known as "high priests," but they filled the office.[30] Next in line to the high priest and under his aegis came the seventy-member Sanhedrin, exercising legislative and judicial power, with the figure seventy derived from the number of elders chosen by Moses. According to some sources there was also a ten-member executive committee.[31]

The Christian hierarchy looked much the same. Peter came first, followed by the Twelve as a whole, and the Twelve stood over seventy-two (Lk. 10:1). The kind of Church that Jesus intended to found was therefore pyramidal in structure, with functionaries appointed from above. The presbyters (priests or elders) charged with administration in such towns as Lystra, Iconium, and Pisidian Antioch were designated by Paul and Barnabas.[32] Titus, after being delegated by Paul, appointed presbyters for Crete.[33] Paul and Barnabas did not embark upon their missionary journeys nor did Timothy take up his apostolate until after the leaders of the church of Antioch had *laid hands* on them.[34] In the same way, the Sacrament of Confirmation, along with ordination to the deaconate, was conferred by an official laying on of hands.[35] Peter and John confirmed the Samaritans, Paul confirmed the Ephesians, and even the seven deacons were confirmed by the laying on of hands.[36]

If Church policy had been decided at the local level, Paul would not have gone all the way to Jerusalem for an apostolic ruling on the question of exempting

Gentile converts from circumcision, nor would he have told the faithful at Antioch in reporting the Council's decision that he was acting under the authority of "the Church's apostles and the elders."[37]

That the early Church functioned hierarchically is indisputable. Very early, one finds reference not only to deacons and elders (or priests), but also to bishops. Paul instructs Titus, bishop-to-be of Crete, to "appoint" elders in every town (Tit. 1:5), just as he tells Timothy, bishop-to-be of Ephesus, how to deal with erring or sinful elders. Timothy is not to credit any accusation against them unless it is supported by the evidence of two or three witnesses. Only if the elders are found guilty and persist in sin after all the evidence is weighed is he to "rebuke them in the presence of all" (1 Tim. 5:19–20).

Five of seven letters by Ignatius, Bishop of Antioch, on his way to martyrdom (c. AD 110), refer to the office of bishop (*episkopos* in Greek). He insists on obedience to the bishop as if he were "the Lord himself," mentioning the office of bishop first whenever he speaks of it in connection with the deaconate or "presbytery." To the Smyrneans, he writes, "Follow the bishop as Jesus Christ follows the Father, and the presbytery as you would the apostles." In his letter to the Magnesians, he describes their deacon as "subject" to the presbytery as to "the law of Jesus Christ" but subject to the young bishop "as to the grace of God." Then again, in his missive to the Trallians: "Be subject also to the presbytery," but "do nothing without the bishop," who is "a type of the Father," for while presbyters preside "in place of the Council of the Apostles," the bishop presides "in place of God."[38]

None of the Church fathers can be understood in any other way. *The Shepherd of Hermas* speaks not only of deacons and teachers (priests or presbyters), but also of bishops. Origen (c. 185–254) alludes to a "continual succession" of bishops, while Irenaeus (identified earlier as one of the most distinguished of the early apologists, as well as a student of Polycarp, who was himself a student of John the Evangelist), claims he can name all the bishops of all the Church's sees.[39]

THE PAPACY

Above the bishops came a single individual, the Christian equivalent of the Jewish high priest, who stood in for Jesus after the Ascension and whose power was derived from the Lord's words to Simon: "You are Peter" (meaning Rock) "and on this rock I will build my church, and the powers of death shall not prevail against it. I will give you the keys of the kingdom of heaven, and whatever you bind on earth shall be bound in heaven, and whatever you loose on earth shall be loosed in heaven."[40] Peter alone received the keys, and this is especially telling because in Isaiah 22, power is conferred on Hezekiah's steward, Eliakim, when he is given his keys, the ultimate symbol of authority. Jesus, in commissioning Peter, uses language practically identical to that used in the commissioning of Eliakim; and Eliakim, like Peter, was called to be a "father" to his people.[41]

Peter was unique among the Twelve in receiving a new name, and again this is telling because name changes occur only on momentous occasions in salvation history as, for example, when God changed Abram's name ("exalted father") to Abraham ("father of many peoples"). Peter was also firmly in charge of the apostolic band.[42] When questions were directed to Jesus by the apostles, they almost always came from Peter; likewise, when queries traveled in the other direction, the Fisherman generally acted as spokesman. Our Lord told him, and him alone, to feed his sheep.[43] His name comes first on every list of apostles.[44] At the same time, he is the only disciple bidden to strengthen his brethren, as well as the only one Christ is known to have prayed for individually.[45]

Peter is further distinguished by being the first to enter the empty tomb (Jn. 20:6). He alone among the apostles has his tax paid by Jesus (Mt. 17:27), just as he alone furnishes the boat from which Christ teaches (Lk. 5:3), and hence the phrase "bark (or barque) of Peter." Finally, he alone sheds tears of remorse after having identified himself as a sinner (Lk. 5:8). With Judas there is bitter regret, but no tears.

Peter's prominence becomes even clearer after the Resurrection. He recognizes the need to replace Judas and decides on the method.[46] He is the first to address the rulers of the Jews, the first to preach on behalf of the Church, the first to work a miracle, the first to cure, the first to take Christianity to the Gentiles (Cornelius and his family), and the only one of the Twelve to raise a person from the dead.[47] Luke tells us that Peter's power over illness was such that the sick waited patiently just to have his shadow fall upon them.[48] He is also the only one of the Twelve in whose presence a man and woman are struck dead (for lying to him).[49] When Paul goes up to Jerusalem after spending time in Arabia and Damascus, it is Peter who hosts him (for fifteen days).[50] At the Council of Jerusalem, when the question of requirements for Gentile conversion sparks heated discussion, it is Peter who restores calm by telling the council what must be done based on the revelation he has received.[51] Judging from the Acts of the Apostles, no decision of any importance was taken without Peter's approval.[52] He may have been rebuked by Paul for not following through consistently on an agreement to waive circumcision for Gentile conversion (Gal. 2:11).

But this was unexceptional. The current Holy Father listens every day to disgruntled cardinals, and he may well take their advice; yet he remains in charge.

Compare Peter's position to that of the man from Tarsus. As we have seen, Paul takes the issue of requirements for Gentile conversion "to the apostles and the elders" at Jerusalem (Acts 15:2). He delivers their decision to the people of Asia Minor (Acts 16:4) and, in one passage, he clearly distinguishes between himself and men of authority (Gal. 2:6). Not so in the case of the first pope, who spoke with an unmatched air of command. He is the only author of Sacred Scripture to pronounce judgment on a fellow author, warning that Paul's writing is liable to be misunderstood by those who are either uneducated or weak in their faith.[53] Ruling that no prophecy of Scripture is made "by one's own interpretation," he exempts himself and uses the magisterial "we" ("We have the prophetic word . . . you will do well to pay attention").[54] He also pens the New Testament's most extensive analysis of the anatomy of evil.[55]

To be sure, the visibility of the head apostle diminishes almost to the vanishing point halfway through Acts. But by then the administrative pattern had been set, and Peter had established himself at Rome, the imperial capital and hub of Christian operations.[56] The apostles traveled far and wide—Thomas to India, Andrew, it is thought, to Ukraine, and James, the son of Zebedee, reputedly to Spain. But all roads led to Rome. The second half of Acts is really Paul's story, due, in large part, to the fact that Luke was Paul's biographer and constant companion.

PETRINE SUCCESSION

The next question concerns the transfer of papal power, which is a sticking point among Protestants owing to the dearth of evidence that succeeding bishops of Rome exercised Peter's authority. Recall in this connection that Christianity was outlawed for several hundred years, and so it is unlikely the popes would have left much in the way of an administrative paper trail. One thing, however, is clear. When dissention broke out in the church of Corinth in AD 95, Pope Clement, the fourth bishop of Rome, sent a letter to the Corinthians that is highly magisterial in tone:

> We have been somewhat tardy in giving heed to the matters of dispute that have arisen among you . . . . Dearly beloved, we write, not only as admonishing you . . . [Our Apostles knew] there would be strife over the name of the bishop's office . . . *They appointed* [persons], *and afterwards they provided a continuance* . . . . It is shameful,

dearly beloved, yes, utterly shameful and unworthy of your conduct in Christ, that it should be reported that the very steadfast and ancient Church of the Corinthians, for the sake of one or two persons, maketh sedition against its presbyters . . . Let us therefore root this out quickly . . . submit yourselves unto the presbyters and receive the chastisement unto repentance . . . But if certain persons should be disobedient unto the words *spoken by Him* [i.e. the Holy Spirit] *through us,* let them understand that they will entangle themselves in no slight transgression and danger . . . . [italics added for emphasis].

Whether or not Clements's opinion was requested, it was heeded and read aloud by Corinthian lectors for centuries, and it is doubly suggestive of papal primacy since John the Evangelist was far closer to the Corinthians than Clement. If anyone was well situated morally, as well as geographically, to act as arbiter, it was Christ's "beloved disciple." Yet it is Clement who intervenes. Worth noting, too, is that, half way through the second century, Bishop Polycarp of Smyrna in Asia Minor traveled to Rome to obtain a ruling on the date of Easter.[57]

All the testimony of the early Church fathers points in the same direction. Ignatius of Antioch, who died around AD 107, showed deference to one and only one see, Rome, which, as he put it, held "the presidency."[58] Irenaeus, who was martyred about a hundred years later, insisted in like vein that "with this Church [at Rome] . . . all churches must agree . . . because in it the Apostolic tradition has always been preserved." According to the bishop of Lyons, it was through Rome, and Rome alone, that the tradition of the apostles and the preaching of the truth had "come down."[59] Just as Josephus, in his *Contra Apionem* (Bk. 1), said he could name every high priest going back two thousand years, so, too, did Irenaeus claim to have the names, not only of all the Church's bishops but also of all her popes in chronological order.[60] Speaking of the church "founded and organized at Rome by the two most glorious apostles, Peter and Paul," he repeats himself: "With this church, because of its superior origin, all churches must agree, that is, all the faithful in the whole world; and it is in her that the faithful everywhere have maintained the Apostolic tradition."[61]

Unity, which is the *raison d'être* of the papacy, was important to Christ. He stressed it time and again—no less than four times in three verses of the Gospel of John (17:21–23). He doubtless foresaw the rise of innumerable heresies, and since history indicates only one institution is capable of holding the Church together, it is hard to see why he would want his organizational model discarded. In the Old Testament, when Eliakim replaced Shebna as Hezekiah's steward, it was assumed he would have a successor, and, as mentioned above, Jesus went out of his way to recall Eliakim's installation when he commissioned Peter.[62] Those familiar with Jewish history would also have recalled what happened when Solomon appointed a second high priest. Each priest backed a different claimant to the throne with results that were nothing less than disastrous.[63]

PAPAL PRIMACY

Initially, pontiffs may not have appointed all of the world's bishops or even *approved* their appointment, but as the Church grew there was a corresponding growth in the exercise of papal prerogative.[64] By the mid 200s we find Novatian, an antipope, installing new bishops in all of the Church's sees. Novatian's legitimacy was in doubt, but not, it would seem, the right of a pope to depose bishops and appoint successors. Cyprian, a contemporary bishop of Antioch, held that "there is . . . one church and one chair founded by the voice of the Lord upon Peter . . . [the] principal chair in which sacerdotal unity has its source."[65] During the fourth century, when warring theologians sought the support of the bishop of Rome, Ambrose held that "where Peter is, there is the Church," and his student Augustine agreed. "The acts of two councils were sent to the Apostolic See," wrote the bishop of Hippo; "Rome has spoken, the case is closed."[66]

Church records show that the Council of Constantinople (381) adopted a canon ranking the bishop of Rome above the patriarch of Constantinople.[67] Furthermore, although the Fourth Ecumenical Council (451) at Chalcedon recognized the see of Constantinople as having "equal privileges" with the see of Rome, it stated that "the primacy before all others and the chief dignity should belong to the archbishop of Rome." Likewise, when members of the Council wanted a formal sentence of excommunication pronounced on Dioscorus, the Monophysite patriarch of Alexandria, it was to the pope's representatives that they applied.[68]

Pope Siricius (384–99), who referred to the bishops of Rome as "heirs" to Peter, issued the first known papal directives or "decretals" to churches from Greece to Spain, and the move seems to have met with little, if any, opposition. Interestingly, not until the fifth century did any of the popes feel impelled to cite Scripture as a confirmation of the apostolic origin of their authority.[69] As late as the sixth century, when Theodora, the wife of Emperor Justinian, exiled Pope Silverius to an island off the coast of Asia Minor, the local bishop of Patara, aware of Silverius' plight, entreated Emperor Justinian as follows: "In the world, there are many kings, but there is none like the Pope who is over the Church of the whole world, but is now expelled from his see." At about the same time, when Pope Agapitus deposed an eastern bishop for heresy against the wishes of the imperial authorities, no one, including the emperor and empress (Theodora), questioned his right to do so.[70]

As Warren Carroll points out in his magisterial history of Christendom, papal primacy was invoked in appeal after appeal, even in the Eastern Church, "right down to the time of Photius" (c. 820–892).[71] The patriarch of Constantinople recognized it in 861, and in western regions it went absolutely unopposed.[72] Charlemagne declared at an assembly of archbishops, bishops, abbots, priests, and lay noblemen that, "We dare not judge the apostolic see, which is the head of all the churches of God . . . [and] is judged by none."[73]

THE INDISSOLUBILITY OF MARRIAGE

This concludes our discussion of church hierarchy, but not our review of ecclesiastical blueprints. There is virtually nothing in Catholic teaching that does not find support in the Bible and early Christian tradition, and since nothing is more characteristic of Catholicism, apart from the papacy, than its defense of conjugal indissolubility, naturalness in sexual relations, and the Real Presence of Jesus in Holy Communion, is to these three doctrines that we now turn.

Looking first at indissolubility, there are five separate prohibitions against remarriage after divorce in the New Testament: Mt. 5:32; 19:3–9; Mk. 10:7–12; Lk. 16:18; and 1 Cor. 7:11.[74] We also know that the practice was prohibited by the Fathers and unknown among early Christians, whose commitment to marital indissolubility appealed to the best in Rome's past.[75] According to William Lecky's *History of European Morals* and William Barclay's Bible commentary, divorce was virtually unheard of in republican Rome for a period of five hundred years, and even in the days of the empire, it was a liability for anyone with political ambitions.[76]

In spite of this, many of our Protestant brethren view the ninth verse of the nineteenth chapter of Matthew as an escape clause. Jesus is quoted as allowing a man to put away his mate in cases of *"porneia,"* a Greek word meaning "fornication," and the passage is taken to be an exception to the general rule. The question, though, is *what kind* of exception? If it is the one claimed, it is obviously important and one has to wonder why it goes unreported by Mark, Luke, and Paul. As mentioned earlier,

Papias and Hermas hold that the Gospel of Matthew predates those of Mark and Luke, and since there is nothing in early Christian literature to indicate otherwise, it seems safe to assume that any ambiguity on the part of Matthew was scotched by his fellow synoptics. By the time John published his Gospel, the whole question of remarriage after divorce would appear to have been a non-issue since John fails even to mention it.

Approaching the subject from a somewhat different angle, we have already mentioned that the Greek word *porneia*, in its most literal sense, means "fornication."[77] Traditionally, in many Catholic editions, as well as in the King James Bible, that is how it is translated, and such a rendering makes sense.[78] Nevertheless, certain translations render *porneia* as "unchastity" or "immorality," and this poses a problem because these are umbrella terms.[79]

For many years, the Anglicans, who allowed divorce and remarriage if adultery could be proven and an act of Parliament obtained, found themselves on a slippery slope. Today, they permit divorce (and remarriage) on virtually any ground while accepting the remarriage of spouses who have been "put away" in clear violation of Scripture (Mt. 19:9).

Another problem with taking *porneia* to mean adultery is that even if Jesus' contemporaries had understood it this way, it would not have precluded a ban on remarriage after divorce because the penalty for adultery under the Mosaic law was death by stoning (Lev. 20:10; Deut. 22:24). Anyone whose spouse has been stoned to death is obviously free to remarry!

Again, if Jesus had meant to admit adultery as an exception to the rule of indissolubility, why did he insist that "from the beginning" man and woman were meant to be "one" in marriage and that what "God has joined together, let no man put asunder" (Mt. 19)? Why, in addition, did he speak unequivocally in his initial response to the Pharisees (Mt. 19:1–6)? Only when questioned did he refer to cases of "*porneia*," and later, returning to the subject in private conversation with the Twelve, his language was again unequivocal: "Whoever divorces his wife and marries another, commits adultery against her; and if she divorces her husband and marries another, she commits adultery" (Mk. 10:10–12).

Taking the argument a step further, the Jews and Greeks had a word for adultery. Why didn't Jesus use it if he intended to admit adultery as an exception to the rule of indissolubility? Several times in the New Testament *porneia* appears alongside the Greek word for adultery, indicating that the words were regarded as separate and distinct.[80] Finally, a well known rabbi by the name of Shammai was already teaching that one could divorce one's wife on grounds of adultery. If Jesus was merely following Shammai, why were the apostles so astonished at what Jesus had to say—to the point of questioning the viability of marriage itself ("if such is the case . . . it is not expedient to marry")?[81]

Needless to say, Catholicism recognizes civil divorce on a *de facto* basis for legal and financial purposes. It also allows separation of spouses in cases of extreme difficulty. Much has been made of the granting of marital annulments, with critics going so far as to suggest that annulment is merely divorce Catholic style. But this is not so. An annulment is simply a formal declaration that a couple has never been validly married. For a marital contract to be valid, both parties must understand the meaning of marriage, they must be free to make a reasoned choice, and there are various other requirements, some of them involving age and distance of kinship. To be sure, there appear to have been cases of tribunal abuse, especially in the United States where 5 percent of the Catholic population worldwide has received 80 percent of the world's annulments. But for anyone, even in America, to have more than one annulment is virtually unheard of. The Church has fought long and hard to preserve the integrity of the marriage bond for those whom God has truly "joined together."

CONTRACEPTION

All of which leads to a consideration of something else God has joined together, namely the unitive and procreative function of the marital act. Here again, the Catholic position is not only Bible-based but squarely in line with early Church practice and teaching. Among the Fathers of the Church, all who refer to contraception, abortion, or sterilization condemn them, and the list is long. It includes Clement of Alexandria, Lactantius, Chrysostom, Jerome ("Some go so far as to take potions that they may insure barrenness and thus murder human beings almost before their conception") and Augustine ("Cruel lust resorts to such extravagant methods as to use poisonous drugs to secure barrenness; or else if unsuccessful in this, to destroy the conceived seed").[82]

In Scripture, the biblical admonition to "be fruitful and multiply" is repeated four times: once to Adam, twice to Noah, then again to Jacob.[83] That human life and the act that produces it are sacred in the eyes of the Lord was also clear from the time that God struck Onan dead for wasting his seed in an act of birth control.[84] Onan may have been selfish in refusing to raise up issue to the wife of his deceased brother (as commanded by Moses at a later date). But judging from the swiftness and severity of the punishment, it was due to the *way* in which he shirked his duty. The Mosaic sanction for refusal to raise up issue was exceedingly light by comparison with what happened to Onan.[85]

In the New Testament, Jesus restores marriage to the way it was "in the beginning," and there was no contraception in the Garden of Eden. The term "one flesh" used by Our Lord to describe husband and wife (translated literally) is likewise inapplicable to couples using contraception. There can be no artificial barrier between oneself and oneself.[86] Paul, for his part, stresses the importance of "natural relations" between husband and wife (Rom. 1:26–27), and clearly, contraception is unnatural.

Still another line of argument worth considering is based on the idea that contraception, widespread even at the time of Jesus, was euphemistically referred to as "using magic" or "using drugs," and Paul and John both prohibit the use of *pharmakeia* (literally "drugs" or "potions" but variously translated as "secret potions," "magic," and "witchcraft").[87] Notice in this connection the wording of the *Didaché* (AD 60–100), mentioned earlier as the first extra-biblical Christian conduct book: "You shall not use magic. You shall not use drugs. You shall not procure abortion. You shall not destroy a new-born child."[88]

Less telling, but noteworthy nevertheless, is that one of the thorns in Peter's side on his visit to Samaria was Simon Magus, a practitioner of "magic" and the only person Peter is known to have denounced as hell-bound (Acts 8:20–23). The closest one comes to Simon Magus is Bar-Jesus (also called Elymas, a name meaning "magician"), who was struck blind by Paul. Interestingly enough, Elymas practiced his arts on Cyprus, an island known for its harlot priestesses and worship of Venus.[89]

In sum, naturalness in sexual relations makes eminently good sense in light of Scripture and the writings of the Fathers (for more on the subject, see Appendix E). This does not mean, however, that Catholic teaching will ever be popular. Hormones are powerful and human pride reacts viscerally to any kind of sensual constraint. The only reason the Church continues to emphasize the importance of unity in both marriage and church organization is because its mission is to proclaim the truth.

THE EUCHARIST

Eucharistic devotion is a third area in which the principle of unity is central to Church teaching. On the spiritual plane, the man who receives Holy Communion experiences oneness with God comparable to the physical intimacy experienced in marriage, and the facts concerning the institution of the Eucharist may be simply stated. In the sixth chapter of John, soon after the multiplication of loaves, Jesus tells his followers that they must "eat" his flesh and "drink" his blood if they are to have eternal life. They recoil, calling it a "hard" saying. But he refuses to retract a single word, repeating the phrase "eat my flesh" six times and insisting that "my flesh is food indeed, and my blood is drink indeed." They continue to object. He continues to insist.

That he allowed "many" of his followers to part company with him on the matter of the Eucharist (Jn. 6:67) and indeed was willing to let the Twelve go as well highlights, better than anything else, his insistence on being taken at his word. Would the many who bolted have done so had they thought he was speaking symbolically? Would the world's greatest teacher have allowed them to go on the basis of misunderstanding? We know from Mark that he "explained everything" to his disciples (Mk. 4:34), and we see it in the way he followed up on questions such as those pertaining to his parables (e.g., Mt. 13) and the need for rebirth in the Spirit (Jn. 3). In reference to Lazarus' "sleep" and the "leaven" of the Pharisees, he elaborated without even being asked, and when his apostles were incredulous at the thought of marital indissolubility—so much so that they asked, in effect, "Who, then, should marry?"—he made himself clear by recommending celibacy. When he said that it is harder for a rich man to enter the kingdom of heaven than for a camel to pass through the eye of a needle, and they asked in wonderment, "Then who can be saved?" he brought home to them the unyielding nature of his position with the observation that all things are possible with God.[90]

Careful reading of John 6 furnishes us with several additional clues. By linking the Eucharist with the Ascension, Jesus implies, first of all, that it is a miracle: "'Do you take offense at this [the Eucharist]? Then what if you were to see the Son of man ascending where he was before?'" (Jn. 6:61–62).

Secondly, the discourse on the Eucharist comes on the aftermath of a mystery involving multiplication. If Jesus could feed five thousand with five loaves and two fish—Elisha's feeding of a mere hundred with twenty loaves was regarded as miraculous (2 Kings 4)—he could do more, and in this case, he did, as a loaf of consecrated bread, broken into fragments, will feed thousands.

Thirdly, Christ describes his apostles as "taking offense" at what he told them (Jn. 6:61).[91] Nowhere else in the Gospel narrative are they so described, but the reader will recall that this is the way Mark characterizes the Nazarenes who sought to throw Jesus over a precipice (Mk. 6:3), and there is another occasion on which Our Lord, anticipating an obstacle to belief yet to be revealed, used the word "blessed" to describe those who would not "take offense" (Mt. 11:6).

Fourthly, the word "believe" occurs nine times in the space of forty verses. That those repelled by Jesus' words *understand*, but do not *believe*, is clear from what the Master himself says: "there are some of you that do not believe." Peter, too, when queried by Christ, frames the issue in terms of faith, not reason. He could have said, "we have understood." But instead, he answers, "we have believed" (Jn. 6:64, 69). If Our Lord had wanted his words taken metaphorically, John would not have added that "Jesus knew from the first who those were that did not believe, and who it was who should betray him" (6:64). Judas faced a spiritual crisis at this juncture, and his failure to measure up caused Christ to call him a "devil" (6:70). We know, too, that on the night of the Last Supper, Jesus no sooner presents the Eucharist as his "body" than this same Judas falls a second time, allowing Satan to "enter in" to him (Jn. 13:27).

Who can deny that Jesus' teaching on the Bread of Life was and remains a challenge? In the case of the apostles, they did not abandon Jesus, as the others did, but they must have wondered how they were ever going to partake of the body of the Lord. Then, at the Last Supper, Jesus took bread in his hands and said, "Take, eat; *this* is my body," and, raising the cup, he said, "Drink of it, all of you, for *this* is my blood" (italics added for emphasis).[92] Note that he did not say, "This is a *symbol* of my body" or "This *represents* my body," but rather, "This *is* my body." Even so, it is extremely unlikely that the apostles grasped the sacrificial significance of the first Eucharist since the crucifixion had yet to occur. But once Jesus died, once he rose from the dead, and once he was recognized in the breaking of the Bread (at Emmaus), things changed.

That transubstantiation was the understanding of the early Church is clear from Paul's warning that those who receive the Eucharist "in an unworthy manner" without "discerning the body" are guilty "of profaning the body and blood of the Lord" and drinking "judgment" unto themselves.[93] St. Ignatius of Antioch, a contemporary of John the Evangelist on his way to Rome to be martyred in AD 107, described the Host as "the Flesh of our Savior," observing that skeptics "abstain from the Eucharist and from prayer because they do not confess that the Eucharist is the Flesh of our Savior Jesus Christ." Justin Martyr, midway through the second century (c. 150), provides additional evidence:

We call this food Eucharist, and no one . . . is permitted to partake
of it except one who believes our teaching. . . . Not as common bread
nor common drink do we receive . . . food which has been made into
the Eucharist by the Eucharistic prayer set down by Him . . . The
change of which our blood and flesh is nurtured is both the flesh and
the blood of that incarnated Jesus.[94]

One can also cite Origen and Chrysostom, along with Cyril of Jerusalem
and Augustine.[95]

That Jesus should give himself continually under the appearance of bread
and wine is consistent not only with the Gospels and patrologia, but also with his
birthplace in Bethlehem, a town whose name means "House of Bread." As an infant,
he was laid in a trough for the feeding of cattle (the manger), and as an adult, he
styled himself the "bridegroom" and his Church the "bride."[96]

Bride and groom become "one flesh" on the physical level, and it is through
the Eucharist that we are made "one flesh" with God. Occasionally, someone will say
in jest, "I'd like to eat you up!" Incredible as it may be, such is what the Lord invites
us to do every time we come to his dinner party. This tremendous lover who touched
the tongue of a deaf-mute with his saliva, who put his fingers into the ears of a man
hard of hearing, and who made a solution of mud paste with his spittle and applied
it to the eyes of a man born blind, this Giver of Givers calls each and every one of us
to a union that is unimaginably close.[97]

Yes, the doctrine of the Real Presence can be difficult—Lord, I believe; help
my unbelief! But illogical it is not. If one were to eliminate every tenet of Christian
dogma that transcends human understanding, the Eucharist would be only one of
many to go. There would be no Virgin Birth, no Incarnation, and no Resurrection.
It hardly seems likely, besides, that the patristic understanding of the Last Supper,
which informed all of Christendom for fifteen hundred years and still informs most
of it, could be false in light of Jesus' promise that the Holy Spirit would teach his
followers "all the truth" and dwell with them "for ever."[98]

Chapter 5

MORE BLUEPRINTS

We will now apply the blueprint test to a broad range of ecclesiastical teaching and practice, asking at each step along the way what it means to be truly Christian. Rome's attitude toward Jewish fugitives during World War II will come under scrutiny, as will the Church's rejection of the doctrine of "once saved, always saved" and its preference for clerical celibacy. First, though, a follow up on a line of thought introduced but not fully fleshed out in chapter 2.

DEFENSE OF SCRIPTURE

Confidence in the Bible has waxed and waned over the years depending on the setting, but the Church has always held it to be inerrant. Paul regarded the sacred texts as "inspired by God," as well as useful, without exception, for "teaching . . . and for training in righteousness," and this is the Catholic view in a nutshell.[1] St. Augustine, one of the earliest to refute charges of contradiction and error, laid down a hallowed rule of interpretation when he wrote that one should never "depart from the literal and obvious sense [of Scripture] except . . . where reason makes it untenable or necessity requires." Many centuries later in 1893, when scriptural skepticism appeared to be carrying the day in Protestant circles, Pope Leo XIII not only upheld Augustine's rule but labeled any interpretation "foolish or false" that "makes the sacred writers disagree one with another." All books of the Bible, wrote Leo, "are written wholly and entirely, with all their parts, at the dictation of the Holy Spirit" and "it is impossible that God Himself, the Supreme Truth, can utter what is false."[2]

At the Second Vatican Council (1962–65), Cardinal König took issue with the principle of inerrancy, alleging error in three specific cases. But all three of his charges were found wanting by the Council fathers, and Pope Paul VI made certain that the language of the Council's *Dogmatic Constitution on Divine Revelation* (*Dei Verbum*) didn't so much as *give the impression* of admitting error in any area, including history and science.[3]

Vatican II's teaching on Scripture, as set forth in *Dei Verbum*, speaks of Scripture as "truth" (seven times), as "the word of God" (nine times), and as written "under the inspiration of the Holy Spirit" (seven times). One is assured that the evangelists "consigned to writing what he [God] wanted and no more"; that they did it "truthfully and without error"; that after the Ascension, they "handed on to their hearers what he had *said* and done" (italics added); that they then handed on, in writing, "the same message they had preached." Matthew, Mark, Luke, and John are named as authors of Gospels that tell us "the honest truth about Jesus." Finally, the Bible is described as "unalterable," a book that "stands forever." It is hard to imagine a sixteen-page document going any further by way of reassurance.

A number of Catholic scholars influential during the 1960s and 1970s denied the inerrancy of Holy Writ. One of them, Raymond Brown, became head of the Pontifical Biblical Commission (PBC). The papacy, however, was not moved by what Brown and his fellow skeptics were saying. In 1971, Pope Paul VI fired a warning shot across the bow of the PBC, placing it under the aegis of the Congregation for the Doctrine of the Faith, and in 1995 Pope John Paul II had stern words for its members: "Your ecclesiastical task," he told them, " should be to treat the sacred writings inspired by God with the utmost veneration and to distinguish accurately the text of Sacred Scripture from learned conjectures, both yours and others' . . . A certain confusion can be noted inasmuch as there are some who have more faith in views which are conjecture than in words that are divine."[4]

For Catholic theologians to find fault with Scripture is almost a contradiction in terms, for, in so doing, they contradict what their Church has been teaching for two thousand years and continues to teach with the utmost confidence. They set themselves at odds not only with Sacred Tradition and common sense, but also with the Catechism, the doctors of the Church, a long line of pontiffs, and the infallible pronouncements of ecumenical Church councils.

It is greatly to the Church's credit that no pope or ecumenical council has ever distorted Scripture to advance a political agenda as did Henry VIII, founder of the Church of England, when he cited Leviticus 18:16 and 20:21 to justify the annulment of his eighteen-year marriage to Catherine of Aragon, his brother's widow. Although the verses prohibit a man from having intercourse with his brother's wife or marrying her, they say nothing about a man's marrying his brother's widow. By disregarding a passage in Deuteronomy *requiring* such a union when the widow is childless (as was the case with Catherine), Henry violated one of the cardinal rules of scriptural interpretation—he made the sacred writers disagree with one another.[5] By using a carrot and stick approach to the universities, he was able to enlist the support of a significant portion of the intellectual world. But this did not make him any less wrong.

WHY FAITH ALONE?

Luther's approach was equally dubious. In trying to justify his doctrine of salvation by faith alone, he inserted the word "alone" in the text of Paul's letter to the Romans.[6] Such tampering exposes the entire corpus of Scripture to arbitrary embellishment, and, like Henry, the man who triggered the Reformation was guilty of making the Bible contradict itself. His phrase "faith alone" is diametrically opposed to what one finds the Epistle of James: "a man is justified by works and not by faith alone."[7] In addition to James (who also says that "even the demons believe—and shudder . . . faith apart from works is barren"), we have Paul's testimony. In his letter to the Romans, he states that God will repay "every man according to his works," and in addressing the Corinthians, he warns that "Neither the immoral, nor idolaters, nor adulterers, nor homosexuals, nor thieves, nor the greedy, nor drunkards, nor revilers, nor robbers will inherit the kingdom of God."[8] Peter teaches that God judges each "according to his deeds," and Jesus himself states that God "will repay every man for what he has *done*" (italics added).[9]

The Church avoided still another error when it rejected the notion that all who accept Jesus as their personal savior are automatically saved—"once saved, always saved." Popular in non-Catholic circles, the idea is inconsistent not only with Jesus' parable of the sower (in which good seed is eventually choked by thorns) but also with Paul's warning that one must work out one's salvation "with fear and trembling" and Peter's exhortation, "Brethren, strive even more by good works to make your calling and election sure . . . [and] be on your guard lest, carried away by the error of the foolish, you fall away from your own steadfastness"[10] (CE). In the Old Testament, Ezekiel speaks of a man who is upright all his life losing his soul if he spurns God on his deathbed. In the New, Jesus tells us we must "persevere" to the end, and Paul, after confessing to the Philippians that he himself has not "already obtained" his reward, says that he "presses on" and "strains forward" to arrive at his goal. To the people of Corinth he writes, "I am afraid that as the serpent deceived Eve by his cunning, your thoughts will be led astray from a sincere and pure devotion" to Christ.[11]

WHY SCRIPTURE ALONE?

Here, as elsewhere, Catholic teaching is fully in accord with Scripture. Nevertheless, the Church does not rely on the Word alone. Tradition has a legitimate part to play as well, and this raises still another question. Many of our separated brethren subscribe to the idea that Scripture is the sole source of truth (*sola scriptura*) even though it was not the Bible that gave us the Church, but rather the reverse.

For well over three hundred years, there was no "New Testament" as we know it, and the vast majority received the Faith by word of mouth. Even when one searches the Bible itself one finds no justification whatever for *sola scriptura*. On the contrary, Paul tells his followers to "hold to the traditions which you were taught by us, either by word of mouth or by letter" (2 Thess. 2:15). If Jesus had wanted his followers to adhere to the doctrine of *sola scriptura*, he would not have told them to obey all the teachings of the scribes and Pharisees, many of which were based on tradition.[12]

Sola scriptura is not simply wrong; it is *dangerously* wrong because it leads to private interpretation that, in turn, leads to disunity, and disunity is inconsistent with the spirit of the early Church, which prided itself with being "of one heart and soul."[13] Choose ten people at random, put them in ten different rooms, tell them to make sense of Jesus' teaching on the Eucharist, and you will have ten different interpretations. Without a clearly designated arbiter specially equipped to speak authoritatively because he is guided by the Holy Spirit, the unity that Jesus prayed for and that the apostles insisted upon is simply unattainable. The apostles exhorted their followers again and again to avoid schism and sects. Nevertheless, our separated brethren have split into scores of thousands of denominations, giving those outside the Christian fold a frequently cited reason for staying where they are. Once again, the Church of Rome and the Bible are as one.

RELICS, THE TITLE "FATHER," AND GRAVEN IMAGES

Some regard Catholic veneration of relics as superstitious because they do not find it in Scripture, but they have not looked far enough. A corpse was restored to life after touching the bones of Elisha, and contact with Jesus' cloak was all it took for people of faith to be cured. Articles of Paul's clothing had the same property: when applied to believers, they wrought miraculous changes.[14]

Others take Catholics to task for calling their priests "father," citing Christ's warning not to call anyone "father" but God. Again, this is based on a lack of familiarity with the divine Word because Christ also instructed his followers not to call anyone but God "good"—or "teacher" or "master."[15] Clearly, this is Hebraic hyperbole. If he had wanted to be taken literally, Peter and Paul would not have called their disciples "sons." Neither would Paul have referred to himself as a "teacher" or called Abraham his "father."[16] In the Old Testament, Elisha calls Elijah his "father," and Isaiah tells Eliakim that he is to be a "father" to his people.[17]

Those who view the biblical prohibition against graven images (Ex. 20:4) as barring statues in churches are caught up in a similar kind of literalism. God, who cannot contradict himself, commanded the Israelites to fashion images of cherubim, and when they were bitten by poisonous snakes he instructed them to gaze at a bronze serpent.[18] What is forbidden is not the images themselves but rather the act of worshipping and bowing down to them (Ex. 20:5). Otherwise, it would be sinful to take a picture of one's wife or husband.

JESUS' "BROTHERS"

One last example of how easy it is for the private interpreter to lose sight of overall context is the widespread impression that Jesus had blood brothers. Leaving aside that such a notion flies in the face of tradition—it took fifteen hundred years to surface—it is not borne out by Scripture. Mark refers to four so-called "brothers" of the Lord, along with an unspecified number of "sisters" (6:3). But he must be understood in light of Semitic culture. There was no word for "cousin" in Aramaic, the language spoken by Jesus; hence "brothers" and "sisters" covered a wide range of relations.[19] That Mark's "brothers" and "sisters" are not what they appear to be is clear from Paul's Letter to the Galatians that identifies James as "the Lord's brother." Only two apostles had the name James, and neither was the son of Mary and Joseph.[20] We also have Matthew, who refers in one passage to James and Joseph as Jesus' "brothers" but identifies them elsewhere as sons of another Mary.[21]

Matthew, the Gospel of record, tells us that Joseph did not "know" Mary "until" she brought forth her "first-born" son. But again, appearances are deceptive. The expression "first-born," in the popular idiom, did not imply the existence of other children. It was simply the title given to the male that opened the womb.[22] Jewish usage of the word "until" did not imply future action. The childless Michal, daughter of Saul, was said to have had no children "until the day of her death." In like manner, the Book of Deuteronomy tells us that the location of Moses' grave was not known "to this day" (literally "until this day") when, in point of fact, it was never known.[23]

The "sibling" thesis leaves too many questions unanswered. Why did Mary respond to Gabriel's prophecy of future conception by asking: "How can this be?" unless she had taken a vow of virginity? It would have been only natural for a woman in her position to have had high hopes for a child. Why, in addition, did she abstain from marital intercourse during pregnancy?[24] It is hard to imagine a woman espoused to the Holy Spirit, the third person of the Blessed Trinity, having carnal relations with a man. One must ask, too, why Jesus entrusted Mary to John at Calvary if, by the Protestant reading of Mark, she was the mother of at least four sons and two daughters. Under Jewish law, the oldest surviving son was bound to provide for a widowed mother.[25]

THE CASE FOR CELIBACY

One of the reasons Mary's commitment to virginity is so fiercely contested is that it ties in with another controversial practice, that of clerical celibacy, which must again be put to the test. Where does it stand in relation to Scripture and the standard of the early Church? "There are eunuchs," Jesus said, "who have been so from birth, and there are eunuchs who have been made eunuchs by men, and there are eunuchs who have made themselves eunuchs for the sake of the kingdom of heaven. He who is able to receive this, let him receive it" (Mt. 19:12). On another occasion, when Peter told him, "We have given up our possessions to follow you," the Master replied: "Truly, I say to you, there is no man who has left house or wife or brothers or parents or children for the sake of the kingdom of God who will not receive [back] manifold more in this time, and in the age to come eternal life" (Lk. 18:29–30). One finds more of the same in Paul's first letter to the Corinthians (ch. 7).

Christ did more than recommend the single life; he and his closest associates lived it. Martha and Mary, along with John the Baptist and the apostle Paul, were celibate, and going by the Gospel, it would appear that every one of the Twelve made a conscious decision to renounce family life. We know that Peter was married, but he was probably a widower or separated when called to the priesthood because his wife remains nameless, and when he hosts Jesus, the meal is served by his mother-in-law (Mk. 1:31). Anna, the prophetess at Jesus' presentation was a widow who never remarried and, like today's cloistered nuns, she worshiped "night and day" with "fasting and prayer" (Lk. 2:37).

Those who question clerical celibacy point to the fact that Eastern Rite priests in communion with Rome may marry provided they do so before ordination. Many are aware, too, that priests in the early Church were married.

All of the Eastern Rites followed the Catholic practice of clerical celibacy for priests, as well as bishops, until the Council of Trullo (692), and even now all of their bishops are single in deference to Christ's clearly stated preference for celibate ecclesiastical leadership.

With regard to priests of the early Church, many, if not most, were indeed married; but there was a reason for it. The life they lived was not normal. In antiquity, one had to be older in order to command respect, and since virtually all "elders" were married, Paul and his fellow missionaries had to be flexible in their choice of pastors for newly founded Christian communities. But this said, a married clergy in the early days of Christianity did not mean what it means today. State-of-the-art research has shown that priests were expected to live as brother and sister with their spouse, and if the wife conceived, her husband could be expelled from the presbyterate. A bishops' conference in Carthage in AD 390 decided that "what the apostles taught [in this regard] and what antiquity itself observed, let us also continue."

In sum, clerical celibacy was imposed early on; it was reemphasized in the 1100s; and there have been cases of Eastern Rite Catholic communities returning to the celibate priesthood after experimenting with a married clergy (e.g., the Syro-Malabar rite). For more on celibacy, see Appendix D.[26]

THE CASE FOR POVERTY

Catholicism has a long record of men and women, many of them from noble families, giving up a good deal more than marriage in response to Jesus' charge to the rich young man, "If you would be perfect, go, sell what you possess and give to the poor" (Mt. 19:21). The evangelical counsels of poverty and celibacy go together, and working in harness they can be spectacularly empowering. After St. Anthony of the Desert (c. 250–355) took Jesus at his word and gave away all that he possessed, people in search of spiritual advice flocked to his hermitage. Anthony was relatively well off before he left the world. But men and women of far greater affluence have been known to bid farewell to their possessions. Charlemagne's brother, Carloman, along with Emperor Charles V of Spain, sacrificed entire kingdoms to live as monks. Elizabeth of Hungary (d. 1231), widowed at the age of twenty-two, declined a royal offer of marriage in order to lead a life of humble service to the poor. Likewise in the case of her contemporary, Margaret of Hungary (d. 1270). Elizabeth refused an emperor, Margaret a king.

CHRISTIAN CHEERFULNESS

Thus far, we have dealt mainly with Catholic *teachings* and *practices*, but there are hallmarks of Christ's Church as found in the Gospel that relate more to personal character, three of which are worth considering before closing out the chapter. They are: cheerfulness amid hardship and mortification, suffering in the face of persecution, and magnanimity toward the enemy.

As regards cheerfulness, Scripture has it that Jesus' disciples were not only unmoved by the loss of property. They were downright delighted at being flogged for preaching the Good News, for, as they put it, they had been "counted worthy to suffer dishonor for the name." When Paul was thrown into prison, he positively rejoiced, urging his followers to do the same: "Rejoice in the Lord always; again I say rejoice!"[27]

Clearly, cheerfulness amid adversity is characteristically Christian, and if one examines the historical record, one finds that the most outstanding exemplars of such virtue were Catholic. In imitation of Peter and Paul a millennium and a half later, a group of Carthusian monks on their way to torture and execution under Henry VIII appeared to be as happy as "bridegrooms" going to their marriage.[28] Farther down the road, an English weaver by the name of Wreno was being hanged for his Catholic faith when the rope accidentally broke, causing him to fall unharmed to the ground. Protestant ministers rushed forward to remind him that he could still save his life if he agreed to take the oath acknowledging England's king as head of the Church, but Wreno, hurrying back up the scaffold, declared to his amazed captors, "If you had seen that which I have just now seen, you would be as much in haste to die as I now am."[29]

Among those who suffered for the Faith under Henry and his daughter, Elizabeth, were a number of Oxford and Cambridge graduates, one of whom, on seeing his heart torn out and the executioner fingering it, is said to have exclaimed, "O happy day!"[30] Thomas More, chancellor of England under Henry and second only to the king, flagellated himself and wore a hair shirt that bloodied him. Yet, in spite of it—or perhaps on account of it—he was the soul of wit. No one could have been better company or a dearer friend, nor could anyone have been jollier *in extremis*. Ascending the scaffold to meet his executioner, he joked with his guards: "See me up safe, I pray you. At my coming down, let me shift for myself." Minutes later, as the axe was about to fall, he managed to get off one last quip. Removing his beard from the chopping block, he was heard to murmur, "This, at least, has done no treason."[31]

More's combination of mortification and cheerfulness, quintessentially Catholic, may again be seen as something patterned directly on the life of the early Church. One thinks of Paul, who abstained from food and drink for three days following his conversion and strove unceasingly thereafter to bring his body into subjection. As he told the Corinthians, "I pommel my body and subdue it, lest after preaching to others I myself should be disqualified" (Acts 9:9; 1 Cor. 9:27).

Two centuries before More laid down his life for the Faith, Catherine of Siena (1347–80) was the most joy-filled member of her family. She loved to sing and arrange flowers. Yet she ate almost nothing between the ages of six and twelve. Her parents, being of a worldlier disposition, objected when she took a vow of virginity and cut her hair. In desperation, they dismissed their servants and assigned all the menial work to Catherine—only to find that she loved it! Each of her tasks became a prayer. Brilliant like More, she used a whip to mortify herself and risked her life to relieve victims of the plague. Sleeping for a mere half hour each night and subsisting for fifty-five days on the Eucharist alone, she was not only contagiously merry but charismatic enough to exert more influence on princes and potentates than any other figure of her time, male or female.

Mother Teresa of Calcutta, a final example of a soul animated by an authentically Christian spirit, received periodic death threats from those who did not want her to build in their neighborhood, but she went right ahead. Suffering, she liked to say, is "a kiss of Jesus," and we should be happy "when he stoops down to kiss us. I hope we are close enough that he can do it." At the height of her fame, struggling against heart disease, she insisted on traveling third class and, when at home, she rose punctually at 4:40 a.m., refusing to sleep with a fan on even the hottest of nights.[32] Like Peter and Paul, she suffered much in the way of opposition. She also experienced a "dark night of the soul" in her later years. But whatever her battles, the gleam in her eye was such that one would have thought her the happiest person in the world, and she was forever urging her sisters to smile.

THE SOURCE

The source of such cheerfulness is the Gospel, pure and simple. Instead of teaching stoical submission in the face of the world's slings and arrows, the Church, in line with Scripture, holds that pain, as ordained by God and embraced by his Son, is something positive because Christ's death on a cross is what opened the gates of paradise, and when an individual offers up his pain in union with Christ, he gains a share in the Savior's sacrifice. Peter speaks of "partaking" in the Lord's redemptive suffering (1 Pet. 4:13) and Paul, in like vein, believes that what was "lacking in Christ's afflictions" he is "completing" in his flesh for the sake of the Church.[33] No one suffered more than Paul; yet he boasts of his "stripes" as if they were so many medals of honor.[34] "For the sake of Christ, then, I am content with weaknesses, insults, hardships, persecutions, and calamities," he tells us, "for when I am weak, then I am strong."[35] He is likewise convinced that by bearing in his body "the death of Jesus," he will make the Lord "manifest" to others.[36]

Jesus himself said his crucifixion would "draw all men" to himself (Jn. 12:32), and when asked if a man's blindness was due to his sins or those of his parents, he replied that the handicap had been given so that "the works of God" might be "made manifest" (Jn. 9:3). Who can pass a blind man on the street, especially one with a smile on his face, without marveling at the power of spirit over matter, without thanking God for the gift of sight, and without being ashamed of one's petty complaints?

When viewed through the prism of Catholic teaching, material deprivation and illness, even death itself, are heaven-sent *opportunities*. The Olympic gold medalist and the paraplegic are both destined for eternal happiness if they cooperate with God's grace, and both can be supremely happy in *this* world, as well as in the next. Believers, like anyone else, engage doctors and lawyers. But if their health or finances fail through no fault of their own, they are not prostrate. Just as Paul "gloried" in an unnamed infirmity—his so-called "thorn" in the flesh—confident that "God is faithful" and would not let him be tempted beyond his strength, so, too, does the

Church encourage its sons and daughters to lift up their hearts in the knowledge that they are at all times and in all circumstances the apple of the Lord's eye.[37] It has not lost sight of the Babe in the manger. While celebrating the Resurrection, it remembers the God-Man with no place to lay his head, and it strives to have ever before it an image of the King of Creation expiring on Calvary. Catholic crosses bear the corpus of the Lord, and a Catholic saint, Francis of Assisi, popularized the nativity scene.

This is not to say that Catholic theology is totally unique in the way it views suffering. Jewish rabbis have said that tears are to the soul what soap is to the body; during the 700s, Habib al-Ajami, a Sufi saint of Islam, taught that suffering was a precious prize; and Church of England apologist C.S. Lewis wrote that "in our pleasure God whispers to us; in our conscience God talks to us; in our suffering God shouts to us."[38] Catholics are not alone. Yet the literature they have turned out on the subject of suffering is unparalleled in breadth and depth. Thoroughly rooted in Scripture, it is also in complete harmony with the teaching of the Fathers. Notice, for example, how close Cardinal Newman (1801–90) comes to Paul and Ambrose. First Paul:

> We have this treasure in earthen vessels, to show that the transcendent power belongs to God and not to us. We are afflicted in every way, but not crushed; perplexed, but not driven to despair; persecuted, but not forsaken; struck down, but not destroyed . . . we are always being given up to death for Jesus' sake, so that the life of Jesus may be manifested . . .
>
> We commend ourselves . . . in honor and dishonor, in ill repute and good repute. We are treated as impostors, and yet are true; as unknown, and yet well known; as dying, and behold we live; as punished, and yet not killed; as sorrowful, yet *always rejoicing;* as poor, yet making many rich; as having nothing, and yet possessing everything (2 Cor. 4:7–9,11; 6:4, 8–10—italics added).

Here is Ambrose:

> How can a truly virtuous man fail in anything? In what situation will he not be powerful? In what poverty will he not be rich; in what obscurity will he not be brilliant; in what inaction will he not be industrious; in what weakness will he not be strong; in what solitude

will he not be accompanied? For he will have for company the hope of a happy eternity; for clothing he will have the grace of promises of a halo of glory!

Listen now to Newman:

I will trust Him—whatever, wherever I am. I can never be thrown away. If I am in sickness, my sickness may serve Him; if I am in sorrow, my sorrow may serve Him. He does nothing in vain. He knows what He is about. He may take away my friends. He may throw me among strangers. He may make me feel desolate, make my spirits sink, hide my future from me. Still, He knows what He is about.

THE WAY CATHOLICS SUFFER

Among the many things common to the life of Paul, Ambrose, and Newman was intense anguish and suffering on account of the Faith, and here we have a second sign of the true Christian that is at once Bible based and uniquely exhibited by members of the Church.

It goes without saying that the suffering endured by Jesus at the hands of his enemies was unique. But just as unique is that he promised *even greater* suffering for those who followed him: "'A servant is not greater than his master.' If they persecuted me, they will persecute you" and "if they do this when the wood is green, what will happen when it is dry?"[39] Intense suffering in the face of persecution is thus one of the specifications found in our Gospel blueprints and we need to review Catholic history with this in mind.

There is no question that the early Church suffered greatly, first at the hands of the Jews, then under the emperors—Nero, who beheaded Paul and crucified Peter, executed an enormous number of Church members, and if Edward Gibbon, author of *The Decline and Fall of the Roman Empire*, is correct, Domitian (AD 81–96) put thousands more to death.[40] But what is interesting is what came after Nero and Domitian (and Marcus Aurelius and Diocletian and Julian the Apostate).

Rome had its moments of glory, to be sure. One thinks of Pope Stephen II accepting the papal states from Pepin, then, too, of the way Germany's mighty Henry IV humbled himself before Gregory VIII. But such moments were as rare for the Church as they were for its Founder who rode in triumph on Palm Sunday. On the one hand, the papacy wielded immense power during the Middle Ages. On the other, there has never been a time when its missionaries have not borne a heavy cross. Neither has there ever been a century when Rome's bishops were not exposed to a steady stream of indignities.

Following the Reformation and up to the eighteenth century, the practice of Catholicism was a capital offense in such countries as England and Sweden. During the French Revolution, all priests were deported, and of those who managed to stay, a thousand were martyred along with four thousand laity. In Korea several generations later, two bishops, six missionaries, a priest, and eight thousand men, women, and children were martyred. Close by, in Vietnam, one hundred fifteen native priests, one hundred nuns, and more than five thousand faithful perished between 1857 and 1862. During Germany's *Kulturkampf* (1870–86), Bismarck imprisoned more priests than Hitler, and Catholics were excluded from the civil service.

In Mexico, from 1931 to 1936, four hundred eighty Catholic churches, schools, orphanages, and hospitals were closed and hundreds of priests put to death. The governor of Tabasco Province, who named his children Lenin, Lucifer, and Stalin, exiled all clerics who would not agree to marry, and few did. Spain, during the same period, turned into an inferno. Nuns were raped; clergymen disappeared. It took only six months for thirteen bishops and nearly seven thousand priests, seminarians, monks, and religious to be murdered.

Without wanting to dwell on the negative or suggest that Catholics are the only ones who have ever suffered, the story of what the Church has endured over the years deserves to be told because there is nothing quite like it this side of the Jewish Holocaust. During the Russian Revolution (1917–25), the Orthodox lost an estimated one hundred thousand priests, but those in union with Rome paid an even greater price. Some fifty-three hundred of their churches and chapels were destroyed, and two hundred thousand men, women, and children, along with their bishops, simply vanished.[41] In Communist Yugoslavia several decades later, six hundred priests were martyred while many more languished in prison. In Communist Lithuania during the decade 1945–55, four bishops, 185 priests, and 275,000 Catholic laity were kept under lock and key.[42] The faithful suffered terribly in Red China where they were subject to summary arrest, torture, and execution even after the civil war ended in 1949. Bishop James E. Walsh was held captive from 1958 to 1970, and recently, a Catholic bishop died after thirty-five years behind bars.

The Nazis were as ruthless as the Communists, closing convents and seminaries, suppressing cultural and charitable institutions run by the Church, banning Catholic journals, pressuring parents to boycott parochial schools, shutting them down altogether in 1939, and eventually killing hundreds of thousands. Across the border, in German-occupied Poland, a third of the priests were either shot or maltreated to the point of "natural death" while in nearby Bohemia and Moravia, hundreds of priests were deported, and seventy-three died in concentration camps.

The United States has been blessed with a relatively large measure of religious freedom, but even here, priests ministered at the risk of their lives during the colonial period. Maryland offered a haven for a brief interval, but after 1698 it was no safer than any other English colony. Following the War for Independence, in which Americans benefited from French and Spanish military operations, Catholics won a measure of toleration, but it was generations before they could vote or hold office, and, in the meantime, a number of convents and churches were burned to the ground. Provocateurs posing as disillusioned ex-nuns and ex-priests told salacious tales of alleged goings-on in the convent and rectory, and their stories were widely believed.[43] Nativist violence fell off after the Civil War, but not the hatred. In the words of Professor Philip Jenkins, anti-Catholicism remains deeply embedded as "the last acceptable prejudice."[44] Not long ago at New York's St. Patrick's Cathedral, homosexuals vented their spleen by chaining themselves to pews, flinging condoms into the air, and spitting the Holy Eucharist on the floor.[45]

Anti-Catholic caricature flourishes in the form of comic books disseminated by Chick Publications. On a slightly higher plane, Lorraine Boettner's *Roman Catholicism* remains in print even though it is egregiously off base factually, as well as interpretively, and on the university level, there are still professors at prestigious institutions who skewer the Faith by dwelling on errors, excesses, and scandals.

A MARVELOUS MAGNANIMITY

Summing up, the Christ who suffered disproportionately promised that his Church would suffer in like measure, and it has; and just as we have spoken of the joy displayed by the early Christians and their successors—joy amid great hardship—there is another virtue associated with the early martyrs that figures prominently in Catholic history, and this is magnanimity in obedience to Christ's command, "Love your enemies" (Lk. 6:27). Jesus' words, "Father, forgive them; for they know not what they do" and Stephen's prayer, "Lord, do not hold this sin against them" have been repeated many times over in one form or another down through the centuries.[46]

A priest before a firing squad during the Spanish Civil War is reported to have asked his captors to untie his hands so that he could use them to bless the soldiers who were lined up ready to do their duty. In response, they cut his hands loose, only to chop them off. Whereupon the priest gave his blessing anyway—with his bleeding stumps. Equally remarkable is the case of Thomas More, already mentioned as an example of cheerfulness. Unable, in good conscience, to sign an oath sanctioning Henry VIII's assumption of papal authority, he was imprisoned and condemned to die on trumped up charges of treason. Yet without the slightest trace of bitterness, he told his accusers that he hoped they might meet "merrily" in heaven to their "everlasting salvation."[47] Edmund Campion, the Oxford-trained Jesuit hanged by Henry's daughter Elizabeth for saying Mass, is another example. Campion must have had More in mind when he forgave George Eliot, the man who betrayed him, and, in so doing, won the conversion of his jailer.

English martyrs of other persuasions may have exhibited similar magnanimity at the time, but, if so, it has gone unrecorded. Foxe's *Book of Martyrs*, a well known account of the death of Anglican leaders during the reign of Queen Mary, is totally devoid of such examples.

We could mention Joan of Arc, Archbishop Oliver Plunket, primate of Ireland (d. 1681), and Paul Miki of Japan, all of whom died the way More and Campion did. During the sixteenth century, the Duke of Guise, scion of France's leading Catholic family, was shot from behind by one of his own soldiers in the pay of Huguenot Protestants. He nevertheless forgave his assassin and, before breathing his last, prayed for the man's salvation.[48] Two centuries later, sixteen Carmelite nuns from Compiegne, along with Louis XVI and his queen, Marie Antoinette, forgave their executioners en route to the guillotine. It was during the same period that Pope Pius VII was held captive and maltreated by a man who called him "an old imbecile." But after Napoleon's defeat at Waterloo and exile to the island of Saint Helena, the pope did what he could to ease the pain of his erstwhile enemy.

In Mexico, Emperor Maximilian was shot by anti-clerical liberals on the aftermath of the U.S. Civil War; Father Miguel Pro suffered a similar fate at the hands of their successors during the 1920s; and in spite of the bitterness of the political climate that led to their execution, both men died uttering words of pardon.

In Italy during the first part of the twentieth century, there lived a girl by the name of Maria Goretti. After sustaining multiple knife wounds in defense of her virtue at the age of eleven and suffering excruciating pain for days on end, she forgave her assailant before dying and touched him so deeply by praying for his salvation that he did a complete about-face spiritually.

Three more examples will suffice. Toward the end of World War II, Monsignor Hugh O'Flaherty, a lawyer with the Vatican's Holy Office, risked his life to hide thousands of Jews and prisoner-of-war escapees. Lieutenant Colonel Herbert Kappler, head of the German Gestapo in Rome, made life as hard as he could for O'Flaherty, arresting and torturing some of his closest associates, and the war within a war went on for months. American troops finally landed. Kappler was arrested, tried for war crimes, and sentenced to life in prison, and the only person to visit him—once a month in a jail located halfway between Rome and Naples—was O'Flaherty. The visits continued for fifteen years, at the end of which Kappler embraced the Faith.

No less inspiring is the story of Pope John Paul II. After being felled by would-be assassin Mehemet Agca and losing six pints of blood, along with twenty-two inches of intestine, he was able to say, "I pray for the brother who wounded me whom I have sincerely forgiven," and later, following his recuperation, he visited Agca in his prison cell. Great-souled John Paul spent part of his youth in Nazi-occupied Poland where ruthlessness was a way of life. But in spite of adverse conditions coupled with tragedy in his immediate family, he gained a reputation for kindness, especially to Jews, and I offer such kindness as a final illustration of Catholic magnanimity.

HITLER'S CHALLENGE

Despite the fierce persecution suffered by Jesus and his disciples at the hands of the Jewish establishment followed by centuries of hostile feeling harbored by the descendants of Abraham—some of it, but not all, justified in response to random acts of Gentile cruelty—a significant number of Catholics chose to act heroically during the Holocaust, and in so doing they saved the lives of an estimated eight hundred thousand Jews.

Some among the Catholic laity risked everything. Aristides de Sousa Mendes, father of fourteen children and a devout Catholic with a crucifix in every room of his house, sacrificed his career in the Portuguese foreign service to save thirty thousand refugees from Nazism, ten thousand of whom were Jews. In Jerusalem, twenty trees are planted in his honor at the Holocaust Museum, and a city square is named after him.[49]

Among clergymen, Monsignor O'Flaherty was one of many. Not all clergymen behaved heroically, but that even a limited number of religious leaders would hazard their safety and social standing for the sake of souls outside the Faith community is rare in any age. Thousands of Catholic monks and nuns endangered their monasteries and convents in order to shelter Jewish refugees. Cardinal Stepinac put his life on the line to combat anti-Semitism in Yugoslavia while, in Hungary, Bishop (later Cardinal) Mindszenty pressed every religious house in his diocese to serve the cause. Germany, too, had its men of courage. In 1934, Bishop Clemens August von Galen of Munster came out with the first in a series of scathing critiques of Nazi racism. Such was the daring and eloquence of the "Lion of Munster" that, during the war, the Royal Air Force dropped millions of pamphlets containing his sermons.

PIUS XII

Pius XII has been vilified for not speaking out forcefully enough on behalf of the Jews. But considering that the deadliest foe of the Nazis, Soviet Communism, was also the deadliest foe of the Church, it is a wonder that he went as far as he did. One could easily argue that for him to have gone further would have been counterproductive.[50] Edith Stein, a Jewish convert and Carmelite nun stationed in Amsterdam, urged the Dutch bishops to condemn Nazi racism, and when they did, the move backfired horribly. Jewish Catholics were singled out for extermination; Stein herself was gassed at Auschwitz; and Pius, on the verge of issuing his own denunciation, thought better of it. "If the protest of the Dutch bishops has cost the lives of 40,000 people," he remarked, "my intervention would take at least 200,000 people to their deaths."[51] Jewish leaders agreed. B'nai B'rith and the American Jewish Congress went so far as to *discourage* such protest because they believed it would only lead to a redoubling of round-ups and deportations. In the end, nine out of ten Dutch Jews were liquidated by the Third Reich, the highest percentage anywhere.

In his Christmas Message of 1942, an intrepid Pius condemned discrimination based on race, and in April 1943, he objected to Slovak persecution of the Jews. When Hitler ordered Budapest to arrest all Jews the following year, the pope protested with such vehemence that Hungarian officials refused to comply, and, as Anne Carroll observes, he did more than merely issue statements:

> When Adolf Eichmann ordered a death march of 20,000 Jews from Budapest to Theresienstsadt for extermination, Cardinal Seredi and the papal nuncio organized relief vehicles to accompany marchers with food and medicine. They carried several thousand blank papal passes and rescued about 2,000 Jews. The nuncio personally hid 200

Jews in his palace ... Pius instructed churches, monasteries, and convents in Rome to take in Jews ... Altogether, 55 monasteries and 100 convents in Rome were hiding Jews. Many Jews found refuge in the Vatican itself, including Dr. Zolli, the Chief Rabbi of Rome, who became a Catholic after the war. The Pope sent letters by hand to Italian bishops calling upon them to hide and rescue Jews. One of the main cities where this was done was Assisi, where the Franciscans coordinated hiding of Jews disguised as religious in cloisters, and printed false identity papers for them enabling them to escape past the American lines. In Italy, in fact, the majority of Jews were saved.[52]

Vatican Radio and *L'Osservatore Romano*, the Vatican newspaper, informed the world of Nazi atrocities in Poland and, in the end, Pope Pius succeeded in saving more Jewish lives than Raoul Wallenberg or Oskar Schindler, both of whom are widely celebrated for their relief efforts. Pinchas E. Lapide, who, as mentioned previously, served as Israeli consul to Italy, concludes that "the Catholic Church saved more Jewish lives during the war than all the other churches, religious institutions and rescue organizations put together. Its record stands in startling contrast to the achievements of the International Red Cross and the western democracies."

Most students of history know that Hitler was a cradle Catholic, but few are aware that he left the Church and hated it all his adult life. In the election that brought him to power, Catholic areas were among the few that voted *against* him, and it was a member of the Church of Rome, Count Claus Schenk von Stauffenberg, who made the most daring attempt on his life.[53]

It is sometimes asked what might have happened during World War II if the role of Catholics and Jews had been reversed. Who can say? There have always been individuals on both sides of the religious divide who reached out to those of other faiths in a spirit of brotherly camaraderie, but Catholic history is replete with such individuals. Gregory the Great, Isidore of Seville, and Vincent Ferrer were notably solicitous, as was Bernard of Clairvaux, who referred to the Jews as the apple of the Lord's eye. Pope Gregory X (1271–76) did what he could to shield them from personal injury and confiscation while Pope Clement VI (1342–52) was the only European leader to stand up for them when they were blamed for the contagion of the "Black Death." Pope Paul III, who organized the Council of Trent, was famously pro-Jewish, and when Isabel expelled the Jews from Spain in 1492, Pope Alexander VI not only welcomed them to Rome, the safest of all European capitals for refugees of any faith; he also prevailed on Naples and Venice to offer additional shelter. Cecil Roth, who held Oxford University's prestigious chair in Jewish history from 1939 to 1964, had the following to say:

> Of all the dynasties in Europe, the papacy not only refused to perse-cute the Jews . . . but through the ages popes were protectors of the Jews . . . The truth is that the popes and the Catholic Church from the earliest days of the Church were never responsible for physical persecution of the Jews and only Rome, among the capitals of the world, is free from having been a place of Jewish tragedy.[54]

Not all pontiffs were well disposed. Whether on account of personal weakness or political pressure, Jewish residents of the papal states were compelled at certain times to live in ghettos and wear distinctive garb. In some cases, they had to sell their real estate and cease doing business with Christians. They were even forced to sit at the feet of Christian preachers, and there were occasions when the Talmud was burned. Such occurrences were rare, however. Far more typical were Sixtus IV's protests against the excesses of the Spanish Inquisition and Leo XIII's support of Captain Dreyfus at a time when France was riding a wave of anti-Semitism. During the 1930s, when Levi-Civita, an eminent Jewish mathematician, failed to receive membership in the Italian Academy, Pope Pius XI nominated him for the Vatican Academy, and after the Holy Father learned that Heinrich Hertz, the German Jewish scientist who discovered Hertzian waves, had fallen on hard times, he came to the aid of his family.[55]

Rabbi David Dalin had it right when he wrote that "during eras of rampant anti-Semitism, the popes in Rome were often the only world leaders to raise their voices in defense and support of the Jews."[56]

Chapter 6

HIGHS AND LOWS
IN PAPAL HISTORY

Popular myths notwithstanding, Pius XII's role in saving Jewish lives during World War II reflected well on his office. At the same time, no organization is perfect, and the papacy, which is human as well as divine, has made its share of mistakes. For much of its history it has been mired in worldly affairs. Commencing with Pepin's Donation in 754, the men who wore the three-tiered tiara ruled an area larger than the Netherlands with centers of culture and commerce at Bologna, Ferrara, and Perugia. They held sway over millions, and statecraft occupied the lion's share of their time. Some excelled at it, others did not. But all were forced to maneuver, and when Italian nationalists appropriated the Papal States in 1870, the Church was better off because it could focus on its *raison d'être*.

Its *raison d'être* is, of course, to witness to the truth, and it's extraordinary that even when Rome's pontiffs were most deeply immersed in secular affairs, they never deviated from the teaching of the apostles. There was a time when all the dioceses of the East and most in the West were Arian in their refusal to recognize the full divinity of Christ, but never Rome. When many of the world's most powerful bishops, including the patriarch of Constantinople, denied the humanity of Christ, the Holy Father held firm.[1] During the sixth century, Theodora, the Monophysite wife of Justinian, installed a pope named Vigilius because he shared her view of Christ as true God but not true man. But the moment Vigilius occupied the chair of Peter, he swung completely around and risked his life for orthodoxy. "Formerly, I spoke wrongly and foolishly," he declared, but now, "though unworthy, I am Vicar of Blessed Peter the Apostle."[2] Most remarkable of all—and this is where the Holy Spirit is most clearly at work—no pope has ever contradicted a predecessor on a matter of faith or morals.

Occasionally, pontiffs have failed to side with orthodoxy, but negligence is not the same as heresy.[3] By the same token, a handful of popes led lives of scandal, but they never allowed it to color their teaching. They never tried to justify their behavior, and approximately a third of Peter's successors have been canonized. This is not a bad record considering the pressures they faced. Some were kidnapped and imprisoned. Others were beaten and slashed. Still others were exiled, executed, or starved to death. One, Agapetus, disappeared mysteriously after confronting an empress. Even within the Church the Holy Father has been rebuked by cardinals and tongue-lashed by saints. St. Bridget of Sweden called Innocent VI "more treacherous" than Judas, "more cruel" than Pilate.[4] Bishops intent on pleasing secular rulers have gone so far as to excommunicate the pope while councils have tried to overrule him.

On the human side, one pontiff resigned to get married, and although none of the popes were ever senile, some held office until they reached their nineties. None apostatized, but greed for preferment and desire for control over ecclesiastical appointments resulted in the installation of thirty-seven schismatic office holders or "anti-popes," the last of whom died in 1449. The worst of these ruptures, known as the Great Schism and lasting thirty years, was the outgrowth of a disputed papal election in 1378. For three decades, different saints backed different claimants as the world looked on in amusement and the faithful were shocked. So parlous was the situation that, long after anti-popes were a thing of the past, skeptics viewed the papacy as on the verge of extinction—Braunbom, for example, in 1640 followed by Mede (Bishop of Halifax) in 1653, Fox in 1666, Jurieu in 1690, Whiston in 1714, and Alix (a Huguenot preacher) in 1716, not to mention Voltaire at the end of the century.[5] After Voltaire came still more prophets of doom. Napoleon dubbed Pope Pius VI "Pius the Last," and when Pius died in prison, French armies did all they could to prevent the election of a successor.

Needless to say, they failed. The cultured and aristocratic Pius VII, who succeeded Pius VI, was a man of mettle. Waving aside Napoleon's demand for an annulment of his brother's marriage to Elizabeth Patterson of Baltimore, Pius persuaded Napoleon to enter into a sacramental marriage with his civil law wife and then refused to close his ports to English shipping. Napoleon retaliated by occupying the Papal States, and when Pius excommunicated him, he thundered: "Does the pope think that the weapons will fall from the hands of my soldiers because of his excommunication?" Little did the Corsican know that in the not too distant future his lieutenants, faced with catastrophic defeat on the plains of Russia, would report: "The weapons are falling from the hands of our [frozen] soldiers."[6] In the meantime, of course, Pius was at the mercy of the mailed fist. Revolutionary soldiers broke into his palace and carried him off on a six-week journey during which his coach overturned and he contracted dysentery. Five years later, his writing materials were confiscated and all visitors were turned away. Yet in spite of this, in spite of being cut off from the world at large, he never ceased pressing for a return of the Papal States, as well as imperial permission to return to Rome.[7]

Scorn for Church prerogative did not end with the French Revolution. Stalin, famous for his jest, "How many divisions has the Pope?" did what he could to destroy the Faith, but he was no more successful than Napoleon. Had he gazed into a crystal ball, he would have beheld one of his successors, Mikhail Gorbachev, going hat in hand to a future pontiff with an admission of Communist guilt. He would also have seen looming alongside Gorbachev the towering figure of Pope John Paul II, whose role in the demolition of the Soviet empire can hardly be overstated.

Egypt's pharaoh is gone, along with the Chinese emperor. The high priest of Judaism has vanished. There is no longer a chief caliph to hold sway over Islam. Only the papacy, which existed long before England, France, or Germany were known as nation states, endures because of the seriousness with which it has taken Jesus' words, "Render . . . to God the things that are God's" (Mt. 22:21). Had it not been for the willingness of many pontiffs to labor long and hard for clerical independence, Christianity everywhere would have become an arm of the state.

THINGS THAT BELONG TO GOD

The Church's battle for religious freedom, ongoing in such places as mainland China, began in the city of Jerusalem and moved from there to Rome. But curiously enough, the first well-documented contest pitting miter against scepter starred

Ambrose, Bishop of Milan, who was neither Roman by birth nor pope. "Palaces belong to the emperor, churches to the priesthood" was his answer when civil authorities ordered him to turn over a house of worship to Arian heretics. Branded a tyrant and told that his head would roll if he did not yield, he stood his ground: "God permit it . . . I shall suffer as a bishop should, and you will act according to your kind." When the Western emperor passed a law to facilitate Arian takeovers, he condemned it out of hand: "I have said what a bishop ought to say. Let the emperor do what an emperor ought to do. Naboth would not give up the inheritance of his ancestors and shall I give up that of Jesus Christ?" Next came the troops. They ringed his basilica and cut him off from food. In the act of teaching his congregation to sing hymns at the time, he went right on teaching. Eventually, a royal legate arrived with an offer to end the impasse if the bishop would agree to have the matter adjudicated by jury. "No," was Ambrose's answer, because the emperor is "in the Church, not over it." At which point, Theodosius, the Eastern emperor, intervened *deus ex machina*, and the crisis passed.

Theodosius was not always on the side of right. In 390, news broke of a massacre in Thessalonica. Seven thousand innocents, including women and children, had been cut down by imperial troops to avenge the assassination of the Roman governor, along with some of his officers. When Ambrose heard of it, he ordered the emperor to do public penance before returning to Holy Communion, and an ominous silence ensued. His flock must have feared for their lives, but the bishop would not give way. He had spoken truth to power, and, in the end, he prevailed. Theodosius did his penance.

On another occasion, the emperor, after bringing his offering to the altar, remained there with the priests, and Ambrose upbraided him a second time: "My Lord, it is lawful for none but the sacred ministers to remain within the sanctuary. Be pleased, therefore, to go out and stand with the rest. The purple makes princes, but not priests."[8] Once more, Milan's bishop emerged unharmed from a royal set-to by the grace of God.

By standing foursquare against imperial intimidation, Ambrose inspired others, most notably the bishops of Rome. A century later, Pope Gelasius I (492–96) enunciated the "doctrine of two swords," according to which the world is ruled by two powers, the temporal and the spiritual, with the former barred from interfering with the latter. The principle stood unchallenged for a time, but eventually Frankish kings began to appoint Church officials and instruct them in their duties. That Charlemagne chaired a number of sessions at an important Church council held at

Frankfurt in AD 794 was a sign of things to come. Laymen would be increasingly involved in the naming of bishops and popes, along with abbots and pastors, and "simony" (the selling of Church offices, so-called from an incident mentioned by Luke in the eighth chapter of Acts) would become more and more prevalent.[9]

TWO STRONG POPES

Although the Church struggled fitfully to regain its independence, it was not until the eleventh century that it made any real headway. Pope Leo IX (1049–54) sponsored the most comprehensive reform program in the history of the Church, riding from Rome to Pavia in northern Italy and from Alsace to Bavaria. Wherever he went he held synods and forced simonists, as well as violators of clerical celibacy, to stand trial. Any cleric, high or low, who had bought his office or lived incontinently was automatically excommunicated. Bishop Kilian of Sutri, a notorious simonist who tried to justify himself, fell dead at Leo's feet, while another malefactor, Bishop Hugh of Langres, was struck dumb. On a visit to Mainz, Leo persuaded the local bishop to expel all of his priests' wives and concubines.

One can well imagine the result of such uncompromising toughness. At one church in Mantua, the Holy Father was met with a shower of stones, spears, and arrows.[10] But Leo was not one to quit, and he had a right hand man by the name of Hildebrand. If he had done nothing else than groom an able successor for the papacy, his reign would be important because Hildebrand, who took the name Gregory VII, carried on admirably.[11]

When Henry IV of Germany (1065–1106) encroached on Church prerogative, Gregory reminded him of the fate of Saul, who refused to listen to the prophet Samuel. Henry turned a deaf ear, and when Rome threatened excommunication, his liege men, knowing that Gregory meant business, charged down the isle of the church where Gregory was celebrating Christmas Eve Mass, struck him on the forehead and tore off his vestments. Gregory's friends rescued him post haste, but Henry was determined to have his way. Calling the pope a "perjurer," a "false monk," a "ravenous wolf," and an "adulterer," he persuaded two dozen German bishops to declare him deposed.

Gregory replied by excommunicating Henry, and for a while the outcome appeared uncertain. Prayer after prayer was offered along the Tiber; letter after letter went out to all willing to listen until eventually there were signs of a shift in popular sentiment. Bishop William of Utrecht, within a month of ex-communicating the pope, was found dead, and this, combined with other factors, worked in Rome's favor. Fewer and fewer attended Henry's meetings, so that before long, it was the emperor's enemies, rather than his friends, who were convening assemblies and mustering troops.

The rest is history. After crossing the snow-laden Alps with his family, Henry reached Gregory at the castle of Countess Matilda in Tuscany (Canossa), and there at the castle gate he knelt, dressed in coarse wool and begging forgiveness. At the end of three days, Henry obtained what he wanted. Almost immediately, however, he reverted to his old ways and a second excommunication was issued. The vituperative ruler now declared Gregory "an undoubted necromancer" under the influence of a "pythonic spirit," and marching on Rome he forced him into exile. The pope found a champion in Robert Guiscard, the redoubtable Norman warrior, but he was thoroughly exhausted, and as he lay prostrate in Salerno, he summed up a lifetime of service in one simple sentence: "I have loved justice and hated iniquity, therefore I die in exile."

In subsequent years, the movement spearheaded by Leo and Gregory made slow but steady progress. Pope Gelasius II (1118–19), elected without the approval of German Emperor Henry V, put a virtual end to lay investiture, but it cost him dearly. He was seized by imperial soldiers, trampled under foot, dragged by the hair, imprisoned, and pelted by stones as he tried to escape down the Tiber. Like Gregory, though, he went down fighting; like Gregory, he died in exile; and like Gregory, his courage bore fruit.[12]

A half century later, Pope Alexander III stood up to Frederick Barbarossa of Germany and Henry II of England—the same Henry who had Thomas à Becket put to death. Then came Pope Innocent III (1198–1216) who declared famously that "the pope judges all and is judged by no one." Innocent excommunicated Emperor Otto of Germany, along with England's King John. In the case of the latter, he took the additional step of issuing an "interdict," which cut the English off from the sacraments. In the end, the emperor ate humble pie and King John took an oath of allegiance to the Church.

The Fourth Crusade, which resulted in the ignoble sack of Constantinople, occurred on Innocent's watch as well, but whatever damage it did was outweighed by a long list of papal accomplishments. Innocent prodded the stubborn Raymond of Toulouse to do penance and take the field against the Albigensian heretics. At the same time, he backed the gallant Simon de Montfort when the odds against Simon's defeating the Cathars in the Battle of Muret were 40-1 (Simon won). He also supported the founding of the Dominican and Franciscan orders, inspired an immensely successful military initiative in Spain that mustered the largest Christian army ever fielded against medieval Islam, and convened the Fourth Lateran Council, which addressed the problem of vacant sees, lagging educational standards, and a demoralized clergy. All of this and more was accomplished in the course of bringing the papacy to the pinnacle of its worldly power.

PAPAL SETBACKS AND TRIUMPHS

In the years to come, there would be occasional throwbacks to the days of Gelasius. When Pope Gregory IX (1227–41) clashed with Frederick II of Germany, he was manhandled by imperial troops. Nearly a century later, France's Philip the Fair levied oppressive taxes on the Church, and when Pope Boniface VIII protested, Philip cut off ecclesiastical revenues. The Holy Father told French legates that "there are two powers ordained by God . . . In no way have we desired to usurp the jurisdiction of the king [but] . . . he is subject to us in regard to sin," and a papal bull, *Unam sanctam*, declared further that "to be subject to the Roman Pontiff is for every human creature a necessity for salvation."[13] Philip was furious at the tone of the bull, and there were consequences. Boniface was visited by armed men and dragged out of bed—one of Philip's knights is said to have struck the pontiff with his fist. An irate populace came to the pope's aid, as had been the case with Gregory, but the psychological blow seems to have been lethal because Boniface died shortly thereafter.[14]

Imperial control over the appointment of bishops was tolerated to one or another degree throughout the period and princes sometimes wielded enough power to fix papal elections. During the early 1300s, when Clement V resided in the French city of Avignon, twenty-three out of twenty-four newly created cardinals were Frenchmen. Clement, who might as well have been a vassal of the French king, interpreted *Unam sanctam* in such fashion as to render it meaningless even as he succumbed to royal pressure for the suppression of the falsely accused Knights Templar.

Any such weakness on the part of the papacy was slight, however, in comparison with the force of its long-term resistance to imperial threats and blandishments. Lay investiture was eventually beaten down, along with the buying and selling of Church offices. Paul III (1534–49), who convened the Council of Trent, was formidable in battling corruption, and he was followed by such like-minded pontiffs as Paul IV (1555–59) and Pius V (1566–72).

Church teaching on the indissolubility of marriage has always been especially difficult to enforce, but not a single pope has ever granted an unwarranted annulment in response to political pressure. As a case in point, Pope Nicholas I (858–867) turned down a petition from Lothaire of Lorraine in the face of death threats coupled with intense lobbying on the part of archbishops and regional councils. "The Holy See," he insisted "does not change its mind." A century and a half later, Pope Gregory V refused to countenance bigamy on the part of King Robert of France, and early in the thirteenth century, the same Innocent III who crossed swords with Emperor Otto and England's King John, set aside a specious annulment granted to Philip II of France. It was better in Innocent's opinion to deny the people of an entire nation access to the Eucharist—he made his ruling stick by placing all of France under interdict—than to permit a king to hold the Sacrament of Matrimony in contempt.[15] In later years, Henry VIII, Napoleon, and Johann Strauss, along with a great many others, applied to Rome for unwarranted annulments. All were denied and we know the outcome. Henry led his nation into schism, Napoleon held the pope prisoner, and the "waltz king" wound up abandoning both faith and citizenship in order to remarry.

The Church's willingness throughout history to risk all in defense of the truth is one of its crowning glories, and it all began when Christ's lead apostle, forced to choose between political correctness and proclamation of the Gospel, asked Jewish leaders "whether it is right . . . to listen to you rather than to God" (Acts 4:19).

GEOGRAPHY, MONEY, MORALS
AND THE EASTERN SCHISM

What a difference between Peter's words and those of a patriarch of Constantinople who proclaimed in AD 754 that the emperors were the "equals of the apostles . . . to perfect and instruct mankind"![16] Such an attitude, in connection with a number of other factors such as geography, would lead eventually to a catastrophic split between the Eastern and Western churches.

If one goes back to the sixth and seventh centuries, Ravenna, the imperial capital in the West, stood at a tolerable distance from Rome, whereas the patriarch of Constantinople lived practically next door to the emperor. The Holy Father may have been within reach of imperial armies, but his main concern lay with Roman mobs, along with local magnates, and this posed less of a threat to Christian unity than the situation on the Bosporus. The Roman Empire also survived far longer in the East than it did in the West. When Pope Leo III crowned the first of the Holy Roman Emperors in AD 800, he could be certain of having a civil ruler pledged to papal independence, and secular power was lodged in areas far removed from Rome.

Geography loomed large if, for no other reason, than the fact that such seats of Eastern Orthodoxy as Constantinople, Alexandria, and Antioch stood in close proximity to Islam, a faith that denied Christ's divinity and banned sacred images. The temptation to yield on these issues for the sake of "unity" or ecumenical outreach may help to explain why Arianism and iconoclasm were so popular in the Christian East.

But even more crucial is that the Church's Eastern sees were wealthier and better schooled than those in the West, and since worldliness is antithetical to asceticism, which includes the practice of clerical celibacy, this was still another obstacle standing in the way of better East-West relations, one that had nothing to do with geography. Worldliness is, of course, conducive to pride, and pride makes it hard to accept subordinate status. As Lord Acton observed, "power tends to corrupt; absolute power corrupts absolutely."[17]

Wealth and power are not always subversive, but if one compares modern Portugal with Spain, Poland with Germany, Ireland (until recently) with England, or North America with its neighbors to the south, it would appear that poorer countries tend to be more vibrant spiritually. Among Anglicans, third world bishops have been stauncher in adhering to biblical teaching than their opposite numbers in Britain and America. None of which is surprising from a Judeo-Christian standpoint. Psalm 34 tells us that the "young lions" (i.e. the rich and powerful) "suffer want" (spiritually). Jesus, who calls the poor blessed, speaks of the deceitfulness of riches, and in the Letter of James we read that God has chosen "those who are poor in the world to be rich in faith."[18]

Finally, it should be said that there was a scandalous deterioration in European morals during the years preceding the final East-West split of 1054. Leo IX (1049–54) stands out as a reformer, but by the time he became pope the damage had been done.[19] Too many priests were unchaste; too many bishops lived opulently; too many popes gave scandal. One pontiff dug up the corpse of his predecessor, dressed it in papal regalia, subjected it to a mock trial, and tossed it into the Tiber after pronouncing a macabre condemnation. Another, Benedict IX (1032–45), abdicated in exchange for a payoff, then attempted a comeback.[20]

THE PROTESTANT REFORMATION

Reviewing what happened at the tail end of the so-called Dark Ages, one is reminded of the years preceding Luther's revolt when pontiffs seemed more interested
in leading armies and feathering the nests of their relatives than in fostering a climate conducive to the salvation of souls. Rome was rife with nepotism by the time
Luther came along. Out of a total of thirteen popes during the period 1431–1534,
only three were unrelated to one or another predecessor. Artists routinely violated
age-old canons of modesty, and not all popes set a good example in their personal
lives. Pope Alexander VI (1492–1503) took a nineteen-year-old married woman as
his mistress, lived openly with her, and threatened to excommunicate her if she returned to her husband. He also attended a party given by one of seven illegitimate
children at which fifty prostitutes are said to have danced in the nude.[21]

Scholars who regard consecrated virginity and priestly celibacy as senseless
or worse—William Lecky, a distinguished nineteenth century Protestant historian, called Catholicism "a war on human nature"—have been quick to seize upon
instances of sexual scandal.[22] If a woman sworn to virginity drove her husband to
infidelity, they have reported it. If a pope admitted to having illegitimate children,
as Julius II did in the early 1500s, they have paid attention.[23] Likewise, if there were
fifteen hundred prostitutes in Rome, a city of only fifty-five thousand, or if a pontiff
was stricken with paralysis while visiting his mistress; if an abbot had seventy concubines and fathered seventeen illegitimate children, it has again been written up.[24]
At the same time, readers have been duly informed if country bumpkins reported
seeing fairies or a Catholic king buried family members alive.

Clearly, the Church of the sixteenth century, like that of the eleventh,
needed reform. Luther, as a case in point, was well within his rights to question
the way in which indulgences were being sold. Deliverance from purgatory is not
for sale, and while the Church as a whole never taught this, some of her priests gave
the wrong impression.

But once one agrees that the Church needed reform, the question is *what
kind* of reform? It is not clear that the revolutionary movements led by Luther,
Calvin, and Henry VIII lifted society to a higher plain spiritually. Three centuries after Luther nailed his ninety-five theses to the door of the castle church in
Wittenberg, Lutheran theologian and historian Adolf Harnack acknowledged that
"since the beginning of the Reformation, one must deplore the relaxed morality of
the German churches and the lack of seriousness in the work of sanctification."[25]

"REFORMATION"?

Not all commentators would agree with Harnack, but there can be little doubt that morality in Protestant areas declined markedly following the break with Rome. Luther set the tone by allowing his protector, Philip of Hesse, to live bigamously. Infanticide, censured by the Middle Ages, reared its ugly head once more, and the principal seats of the Reformation, Germany and England, experienced an unprecedented wave of witchcraft, something that touched France but lightly and Spain not at all. England executed no less than 30,000 women—mostly, it would seem, for offenses involving contraception and abortion—while in Germany, the figure is said to have been in the neighborhood of 100,000. Such figures make the Spanish Inquisition look mild by comparison.[26]

Luther, an ex-monk married to an ex-nun, went to his grave lamenting that Wittenberg, the birthplace of Protestantism, had become "worse than Sodom."[27] Men, he wrote, were "more vindictive, more greedy, more pitiless, more immoral and unrestrained and much more evil than they were [before]."[28] "Under the papacy," he lamented, "the people were, at least charitable, and force was not required to obtain alms. Today, under the reign of the Gospel [i.e. Protestantism], in place of giving they rob each other, and it might be said that no one thinks he has anything till he gets possession of the property of his neighbor."[29] "Why is it," asked Luther's wife, "that in our old faith we prayed so often and so warmly and that our prayers are now so few and so cold?"[30]

Henry VIII, the father of Anglicanism, in his last speech to Parliament, regretted "how much the word of God is abused; with how little reverence it is mentioned, how people squabble about the sense [of Scripture] . . . I am sure charity was never in a more languishing condition, virtue never at a lower ebb, nor God himself less honored or worse served in Christendom."[31] What Henry did not tell Parliament is that he himself was part of the problem. He took Anne Boleyn's sister as his mistress, then impregnated Anne herself before marrying her. He is also the only king in history ever to have received two annulments (both of them from an archbishop whom he controlled), the only Christian monarch to have married six times, and the only one to have executed two of his wives—on charges of adultery! Charles Dickens, in his *Children's History of England*, calls Henry "one of the most detestable villains that ever drew breath" (pp. 281, 297, 306). Philip Melanchthon, another Protestant reformer, agreed with Henry's report to Parliament, as did Erasmus, the most celebrated scholar of the day, and there were things it never mentioned. With moral decline came a decline in culture. "Wherever Luther prevails," observed Erasmus, "the cause of literature and learning is lost."[32]

The indictment can be lengthened. Bigots battened on Luther's anti-Semitism. In one of his tracts he called the Jews "poisonous envenomed worms" whose synagogues "should be set on fire . . . [their homes] smashed and destroyed" and their people "put under one roof or in a stable like gypsies to teach them they are not master in our land."[33] Such language, coming from a prominent religious leader, was unprecedented, and there can be little doubt that Luther's words had consequences. Racism has been closely associated with Prussia and other anti-Catholic regions of Germany, just as it has been a fixture with such groups as the Arians, Deists, and Socinians, none of which were ever in union with Rome. It may be fairly said, in addition, that all of the countries with eugenics laws during the 1930s were Protestant.

Adding to the catalogue of Reformation woes and closely linked with racial prejudice is what John Riddle calls an "intense unprecedented misogyny."[34] One is not surprised to find no female physicians in Anglo-Saxon areas of the world by the late eighteenth century.[35] Luther referred to his wife as his "chain," and John Knox, leader of the Reformation in Scotland, called women "weak," "frail," "impatient," "feeble," "foolish," and unfit for public office. Protestant preachers who opposed the coronation of Mary, Elizabeth's predecessor, claimed that it was contrary to God's word to be governed by a woman.[36]

FACTS AND FIGURES

When it comes to sexual morality, Protestant rates of fornication, illegitimacy, and abortion rose disproportionately.[37] Illegitimacy increased—from 2 percent in 1680 to 6 percent in 1820.[38] The *Journal* of the Statistical Society of London for the years 1860, 1862, 1865, and 1867 put illegitimacy in England and Wales at twice the rate of Catholic Ireland.[39] England may have kept better records; its philanderers may have been less stigmatized. Whatever the case, Ralph Waldo Emerson had it from Carlyle and Dickens at a dinner party that male promiscuity was so taken for granted in England that one could name all the exceptions.[40] By 1867, English prostitution, with over 50,000 professionals on the streets, was, in the words of Lecky, "more prevalent, more degraded, and more irrevocable than anywhere else in Europe."[41]

During the twentieth century, no region has been more notorious for the flouting of family values than Protestant Scandinavia, particularly Sweden, which was the first nation to imprison a religious leader for preaching Bible-based morality.[42] Norway, Denmark, and Sweden were the first to embrace gay marriage, and in present-day Norway, 80 percent of the births are illegitimate.[43] Elsewhere, in what used to be known as Czechoslovakia, Protestant Bohemia had four or five times as many abortions as Catholic Moravia. The Netherlands, another child of the Reformation, was the first country to afford legal protection to assisted suicide, with Australia and the United States not far behind.

The Church of England became the first Christian denomination to approve artificial contraception (in 1930), and after it relaxed its stance on the indissolubility of marriage, divorce rates soared, becoming the highest in Western Europe. Today in England, on any given Sunday, there are fewer Anglicans in church than Catholics. Two thirds of the British population under the age of thirty-five deny the Resurrection, and as religion goes, so goes morality. England is second only to the United States in teen illegitimacy, and when it comes to crime, the British per capita rate in 1995 was ten times that of 1955.[44] America's Episcopal Church, like its mother church in England, now accepts abortion, even as it blesses gay marriage and ordains gays to the priesthood and episcopate. As for divorce rates in the UK and USA, they are among the highest internationally. Comparing Britain and the United States with representative Latin American nations, the Britannica Book of the Year for 1995 listed the number of divorces per thousand persons as: USA 4.6; UK 3; Chile .4; Brazil .5; Mexico .6; Guatemala .2.

Some will argue that because Protestantism has abandoned the principle of marital indissolubility and requires less in the way of child bearing and church attendance, it is better suited to human nature. One could say the same of Judaism and Islam. But the flipside is that human beings thrive on challenge—provided, of course, that it is of the right sort. England's Oliver Cromwell is famous for having gone too far in proscribing drinking, gambling, racing, and theatricals, along with instrumental church music, because when he was overthrown, there was a natural reaction and morals disintegrated.[45] As Oxford educated Ronald Knox observed, "legislation of one sort or another which is designed to stop people being merry . . . makes them dissolute."[46]

THE QUESTION OF HAPPINESS

Happiness is a hard thing to measure. Using sobriety as a yardstick, Protestant England would have to be regarded as better off than Catholic Ireland. Then again, England and Ireland are not representative of the world at large, and if one goes by the number of people committing suicide, the non-Catholic rate following the Reformation was twice that of Catholics. Typically, the Protestant cantons of Switzerland compare unfavorably in their suicide rates with those that are Catholic.[47] People who are traditionally Catholic are less likely to be cold, austere, and forbidding. Ireland, for example, along with "sunny Italy" and Spain, in the days when those countries were true to their past, were full of warmth. Catholic Austria is more light-hearted than Protestant Switzerland, and southern Germany, which again is largely Catholic, is more ebullient than northern Germany, the seat of the Reformation.

Musical rhythm may or may not be a measure of happiness, but to the extent that it is—people who are depressed seldom whistle or sing—the much loved waltz sprang from deeply Catholic Austria, and when it made its debut, many Protestants regarded it as an incitement to sinful passion. High spirited flamenco originated in Spain while the captivating accents of rumba, samba, and tango are native to Latin America.

One last word. We have been speaking of happiness in the abstract, but there were groups whose actual physical welfare was adversely affected by the Reformation. No agency, for instance, remained standing in the wake of Henry's dissolution of the English monasteries that was capable of relieving the destitute, nursing the sick, and offering hospitality. Lecky paid tribute to the monks by whom "the nobles were overawed, the poor protected, the sick tended, travelers sheltered, prisoners ransomed, [and] the remotest spheres of suffering explored." Nothing was more deplorable, in his opinion, than the fact that nuns' convents were "leveled to the dust, instead of attempting to regenerate the whole conventual system of Catholicism." "It is very doubtful," he added, whether "even in the most degraded period [of Catholicism], the convents did not prevent more misery than they inflicted."[48]

Protestant reform was equally hard on peasants facing inflation without an appreciable increase in wages. Because the rising middle class sought to consolidate farm operations for maximum profit, it was not long before individual owners raised rates, converted arable lands to pasture, and began enclosing large areas.[49] People who had been driven off monastic common lands could no longer rent for reasonable sums on a long-term basis, and this created a whole new class of beggars. In the words of William Walsh,

> Another result . . . [of the Reformation] in England had been the reduction of the mass of the people to a state of poverty unknown in

Spain at that time or in medieval England. Not only had the small farmers been dispossessed from monastery lands so that such families as Bacon's could make more money raising sheep; not only did the national and city governments fail to give alms to the poor, the disabled and the insane, who had been cared for by the monks and nuns; not only was the Catholic hospital system in the Middle Ages shattered [along] with the Guilds, which had established an equilibrium of employer and workman; but poor wretches, deprived of a livelihood and of any possibility of finding one, were then punished for their misfortune by inhuman laws, cruelly enforced. The Act of 1573 provided that a beggar should be bored through the ears and whipped, and at the third offense put to death. The Middlesex Sessions Rolls record the branding and whipping of seventy-one vagrants in two months in 1591.[50]

It cannot be denied that much good came from the Reformation. Much good is still coming from it. The Church needed a scourge; it got one in the person of Martin Luther; and the result, beginning with the Council of Trent in the mid-sixteenth century, was a restoration of old-time rigor and discipline. Priests ceased giving the impression that forgiveness was for sale when they ceased accepting alms in exchange for indulgences, and reforms were instituted across the board.[51] It is one thing, though, to be thankful for reform that is long overdue, quite another to overlook the fact that Protestant insurgents threw the baby out with the bath water. There was a price to be paid for flying in the face of biblical blueprints, and, as we shall see in chapter 9, it is a price that is still being paid.

Chapter 7

YOU WILL KNOW THEM
BY THEIR FRUITS

The words of Our Lord that appear at the head of this chapter (Mt. 7:16), are a standing challenge to each and every one of us, but they also apply to the Church as a whole. The true seeker will want to know how Catholicism has contributed to the betterment of mankind. What effect has it had on science and technology? What has it done to enhance the status of women? What role has it played in the elimination of slavery? How has it touched the lives of outcasts generally? In a word, how has it conformed, or failed to conform, to Christian blueprints in the area of social welfare?

SERVICE

Nearly everyone has heard of Nobel Prize-winning Mother Teresa of Calcutta. Her gargantuan relief effort in a predominantly Hindu country made her the premier social worker of the twentieth century. What many fail to realize, however, is that this stooped nun with the winning smile stood on the shoulders of a long line of pioneers who shared her faith. A seventeenth-century priest by the name of Vincent de Paul invented organized charity as we know it, and as early as the eighth century, the pope's soup kitchen was feeding seven hundred mouths a day.[1]

Focusing on specialties in the field of social work, Maria Montessori, another Catholic, is linked unforgettably with education for the mentally challenged, just as one associates Cesare Beccaria with prison reform. When one thinks of lepers one recalls the work of Damien, the hero of Molokai (recently canonized), while, in the case of the deaf, it is the sign language of Abée L'Épée that comes to mind. Another devout Frenchman, Louis Braille, championed the cause of the blind. Even before Braille, a loyal son of the Church by the name of Mozart wrote music for an unsighted pianist, and when it comes to the education of orphans, no one has come even with a brace of priests: Italy's Don Bosco and Fr. Flanagan of Boys Town.[2]

The British journalist and convert G. K. Chesterton once observed that everything worthwhile in Western culture is, by origin, Catholic, and one is hardly surprised given that Western culture was thoroughly Catholic for fifteen hundred years. What is extraordinary is the degree to which the Church, from the very start, was a force for charity and social progress. On the list of Catholic inventions is the orphanage, the nursing home, and the leper asylum, along with the university and habeas corpus.[3] The musical scale, even music itself as we know it today, came into being during medieval times, and canon (Church) law laid the foundation for common and international law. The Franciscans practiced government by election long before it was fashionable, and an archbishop of Canterbury spearheaded the movement for constitutional change that resulted in the Magna Carta.

A whole new attitude toward labor and the laboring man developed under Christianity. The sight of scholarly monks joyfully engaged in manual labor strengthened a work ethic that the modern day West takes for granted but which was non-existent in the classical world. Aristotle viewed manual labor as degrading and tradesmen were contemptible in the eyes of Plato. Roman society, strongly influenced by Greek thought, excluded both of these classes from the Forum every time the high priest offered sacrifice, and certain kinds of manual labor were performed almost exclusively by slaves. The moment St. Benedict and his fellow monks rolled up their sleeves, all of this was a thing of the past, and with the advent of the medieval guilds, workmen were better off than they would be at any other time in history. Expenses related to illness, old age, and unemployment—even to funerals—were underwritten by employers and the guilds for the benefit of apprentices, journeymen, and masters.

Over the centuries, the Church brought warfare under control to a degree unheard of by today's standards. By the time of the Crusades, it was outlawed on Friday, Saturday, and Sunday by the Truce of God, and there were safe havens for refugees (the Peace of God), along with a code of chivalry that required warriors to respect the rights of non-combatants, women, and pilgrims. Long intervals of peace are rare in any age, but Paris remained untouched by invasion or civil strife for five hundred years, enabling Christian civilization to take deep root in central France.

SCIENCE AND AGRICULTURE

Science flourished in a religious ethos that presupposed intelligent design, as compared with the outlook of Hindus, Chinese, Egyptians, and Greeks, whose gods were thought to act capriciously. Each of the above-mentioned groups made important discoveries early on, but eventually they all fell behind. By the end of the Middle Ages, even progressive Islam lagged behind its Western competitors in the race for discovery due in part, perhaps, to its emphasis on divine inscrutability.[4] In the field of optics and mathematics, Roger Bacon (c. 1214–1294), professor and priest, insisted on controlled experiments, and his painstaking observations set the stage for the work of his sixteenth-century namesake, Francis Bacon, who popularized the scientific method under Elizabeth.

Agriculture flourished as well. Benedictine monasteries are said to have been the most efficient economic enterprises known to man. From monastic workshops and drawing boards came one invention after another, including the heavy plow and three-field crop rotation system. Monks introduced revolutionary improvements in farm equipment, water wheels, wool production, and iron smelting. Improvements in printing, stone mining, and spinning came along at a steady clip, and by the 1100s clerics had developed the horizontal axle windmill, the blast furnace, and the steam-driven bellow, along with mechanized paper manufacture.[5]

REMARKABLE INGENUITY

Medieval man fashioned spectacles from glass and built pipe organs of marvelous complexity. A system of dikes was devised; new methods of planting, cultivating, and harvesting were introduced. An entire new face was put upon industries such as fishing, cheese-making, wine production, and bee culture. Giant strides were made in clearing forests, draining morasses, quarrying marble, and mining salt, lead, iron, aluminum, and gypsum. Water power was harnessed and a wide range of machinery made available. Glassworks, cutler's shops, and power mills sprang into existence. Western clock making, the world's most sophisticated, was so highly prized by the Chinese that Peking welcomed missionaries, if for no other reason than to share in modernization, and the Jesuits, ready, as always, to oblige, brought math and astronomy texts, along with their breviaries.[6] Western superiority was marked not only by the ability of crusaders to march thousands of miles and seize strongholds hitherto thought impregnable, but also by the magnificence of cathedrals that continue to draw tourists from around the world.

MORE ON CHARITY

Returning, though, to the theme of Catholic charity, St. Augustine, St. Gregory the Great, St. Hilary, and St. Remi melted down their valuables and sold church property to support the needy. During the twelfth and thirteenth centuries, the Trinitarian monks, along with Peter Nolasco's associates and the Mercedarians, devoted themselves entirely to the work of ransoming prisoners. Throughout the period, they pledged money and, if need be, their lives for the release of captives, and some are said to have rescued thousands.[7]

EDUCATION

Affordable education was another cause close to the heart of the Church. From Charlemagne's schools for the poor and the mandating of free education in cathedral schools by the Third Lateran Council in 1179 to Elizabeth Ann Seton's founding of the parochial school system in the United States, the Catholic assault on illiteracy was relentless. By the end of the Middle Ages, the Orient had only a handful of schools of any type, but not so in the Christian West. England and Wales, with a population of only two or three million, supported approximately 400 grammar schools, a better ratio than obtained in Victorian times. Enthusiasm for education took root when St. Boniface, St. Augustine of England, and St. Patrick established schools in their monasteries, and it was the monks who preserved the literary patrimony of the ancient world, not to mention literacy itself. The Coimbra agricultural school for orphan girls founded by St. Elizabeth, queen of Portugal (1271–1336), is only one of many examples of medieval concern for the lot of unfortunates. It trained young women to raise crops and care for animals so they could marry the sons of farmers, and the queen gave students tillable land from her own estates as wedding gifts. One also finds universities such as Salamanca (Spain's finest at the time of Isabel) welcoming scholarship students.[8]

The Church-sponsored university system fostered lively debate, and because members of the clergy received the best in secular, as well as ecclesiastical, education, they pioneered in such fields as geology, Egyptology, and genetics. Hildegard von Bingen and St. Albert the Great won fame as naturalists.[9] A priest was the first to measure the rate of acceleration of a freely falling body, and the Society of Jesus so dominated the study of earthquakes that it came to be known as "the Jesuit science." Jesuits also invented pendulum clocks, barometers, microscopes, and reflecting telescopes. Thirty-five craters on the moon are named after their scientists, and they led the way in the fields of magnetism, optics, and electricity.[10]

THE "DARK" AGES

Even the years dubbed "dark" running from approximately AD 500 to the end of the first millennium were not without points of light. Lecky, who held no brief for the Church, viewed the period as far superior to the noblest ages of pagan antiquity "in active benevolence, in the spirit of reverence, in loyalty, [and] in cooperative habits."[11] Missionaries by the hundreds laid down their lives in an effort to eradicate entrenched evils such as ritual cannibalism and human sacrifice. Northern Italy was converted, as was France, England, Germany, Hungary, Russia, and Spain (from Arianism). Gregory the Great, Justinian, Benedict, and Hilda of Whitby were anything but "dark." And let us not forget Boniface, Charlemagne, Alfred the Great, Otto the Great, and Stephen of Hungary, who were nothing less than brilliant. Four women—Clotilda (wife of Clovis the Frank), Ingunthis (wife of the Spaniard Hermenigild), Bertha (wife of Kent's Ethelbert), and Theodolinda (wife of Agilulf the Lombard)—converted entire nations by winning over their husbands.[12]

On the negative side of the ledger, education was in decline by the dawn of the seventh century and the priesthood badly in need of reform. Western bishops tended to be worldly and grasping until the arrival of Irish and Anglo-Saxon missionaries. Then, too, the Church made the mistake of aligning itself with the Merovingian dynasty, which quickly fell apart.[13] Morals plummeted and there were frequent outcroppings of cruelty. A contest between rival powers for control of the papacy during the 700s featured such practices as torture, disfigurement, and mutilation. At least one victim was buried alive.[14] The distinguished French historian

Henri Daniel-Rops paints a picture of Christian society on the eve of Islam's rise that is far from flattering:

> To obtain some idea of the state of Byzantine morality in this epoch it is enough to skim through the disciplinary canons of the famous Council "of the Cupola," also called *Quinisextus*. The reader is struck dumb with amazement by the prohibitions which this assembly had to make, and by the errors which it had to denounce: e.g., it was necessary to remind clerks that it was absolutely wrong for them to become proprietors of brothels, and to tell the faithful that sexual intercourse in the church itself profaned the House of God . . . . Immorality seems to have been universal: the Council had to excommunicate religious who had broken their vows [along with] sellers of pornographic pictures and doctors and midwives who specialized in abortion. . . .
>
> Another characteristic of this diseased society is the cruelty of many of the punishments inflicted, not merely on those found guilty in common law, but on political enemies, even upon one's opponents in theological disputes. Practices such as cutting off the nose, the ears, or the tongue, blinding, and mutilations of the vilest kind were commonplace. Capital punishment provided an oft-repeated diversion; during the reign of Justinian II "the noseless Emperor," idle mobs could take their pleasure of beheadings by the hundred. And the abominable way in which even saints, such as Pope St. Martin or St. Maximus the Confessor, were treated is well known.
>
> When the reappearance of various ancient pagan practices is added to all this, particularly those who lent themselves most fully to licentious exuberance—the Saturnalia, the Brumalia in honour of Bacchus, the May-feast or festival of spring, together with the fact that magic, sorcery, and the exploitation of popular credulity were actually more widespread than in pagan times—it is easy to see how thin the veneer of Christianity, which six centuries of faith had impressed on this society, had become. In 717, then Pergamum was besieged by the Arabs, the population indulged in the ritual murder

of a pregnant woman and smeared themselves with their victim's blood; strange aberrations for a world that called itself Christian.[15]

THE CHRISTIAN CHALLENGE

The thing to bear in mind when reading indictments such as this is that moral reform does not occur overnight. It took forty years for a good woman to bring Clovis around, and centuries more were needed for Europe as a whole to embrace Gospel values. The wonder is that it did not take longer, considering the level to which Rome had sunk by time Peter and Paul arrived. The first ten popes beginning with Peter are said to have been martyred, and one can easily see why. Imperial culture was rife with prostitution, adultery, abortion, and infanticide. According to Seneca, women kept track of the years by recalling the names of their husbands—they were married to be divorced. Clement of Alexandria describes the typical society matron as "girt like Venus with a golden girdle of vice" while Juvenal has it that Empress Agrippina, the wife of Claudius, "used to leave the royal palace and go down to serve in a brothel for the sake of sheer lust." Doubtless Juvenal and Seneca were exaggerating, but there is no denying that family life was in a shambles. Children were held in such low regard that the state had to bestow special privileges on couples willing to accept them.[16]

In order to gauge how many obstacles Christianity had to surmount before it could make significant inroads, one need only consider the character of Roman leadership from AD 54 to 68. Emperor Claudius (AD 41–54), who was preceded by the insane Caligula (AD 37–41), was succeeded by the bestial Nero (AD 54–68). After divorcing Octavia to marry his mistress, he had Octavia executed on false charges of immorality. Not content to force his tutor, the exemplary Seneca, to commit suicide, he ordered the murder of Burrhus, prefect of the palace guard, on mere suspicion. Fancying himself an actor, he relished the applause of sycophants and went so far as to stage actual rape scenes. After "marrying" a young man, Sporus, in a state wedding and taking him on a tour of Greece for their "honeymoon," Nero made two unsuccessful attempts on the life of his mother, Agrippina, before succeeding. After which he kicked his pregnant wife to death and died a suicide.

According to Suetonius, one of the most respected of ancient historians, Nero not only started the fire that consumed eighty percent of Rome, but hindered efforts to extinguish it in order to blame the Christians. In the ensuing persecution, believers were used as human torches to light the imperial gardens, and those not burned to death were fed to the animals. The emperor who "fiddled while Rome burned" knifed himself through the neck and is said to have murmured while expiring, "What an artist the world is losing."

FEARFUL ODDS

To build a new civilization on the ruins of an old one requires a modicum of peace and stability, and here again Christianity was up against fearful odds because, after gaining a foothold in the fourth century, it faced constant war. It had to absorb successive waves of Vandals, Visigoths, Huns, and Lombards who were heretical, at best and, at worst, every bit as scabrous as the people they conquered. Muslim warriors plundered Marseilles, seized most of Sicily, and sacked St. Peter's and St. Paul Outside the Walls. The Vikings swept southward from Scandinavia, savaging Paris and obliterating Dorestad, the principal trading centre of the Netherlands. All the way up the Seine River to Rouen they wreaked havoc, demolishing nearly every monastery in sight.[17] Merely to stay alive was difficult in this whirlwind of pillage and rape.

The only reason the Church was able to survive and raise Western society to a certain degree of civility is because of seeds planted early on. During the relatively brief window of opportunity that followed Constantine's victory over Maxentius, it responded to Christ's command to "do it to the least of my brethren" by building hostels for wayfarers (pilgrims and strangers) and stepping up aid to the poor. In Constantinople, for example, Archbishop Chrysostom supported three thousand widows, virgins, foreigners, and sick.[18] Due to Christian influence, crucifixion and other forms of torture were eliminated, along with various kinds of disfigurement such as branding on the face.[19] Infanticide became a criminal offense; the practice of drowning children born sickly or deformed came to an end; foundling hospitals sprouted and along with them homes for the blind and lepers.[20] Fabiola built the first public hospital in the 300s, and in 404 a monk, Telemachus, gave his life to rid Rome of gladiatorial contests featuring murder as entertainment.[21]

In short, the same Church that carried on the tradition of the high priest as God's representative on earth, the Church that embraced the mystery of the Eucharist, that answered Christ's call to evangelize, and that spread rapidly to the farthest reaches of the Empire, effected a slow but steady transformation of popular mores. Polygamy, divorce, abortion, and contraception were gradually cast aside as Jerome inveighed against the practice of "murdering those not yet conceived" and

Augustine condemned the use of "poisons of sterility."[22] Once people came to regard human life as a gift from God, there was little thought of suicide, and the Church's ban on extramarital relations led to the acceptance of matrimony as a union of man and woman dissoluble only at death.[23]

Even Edward Gibbon, the best known historian of the Roman Empire and about as far removed from Catholic sympathies as any Englishman in his position at the time could be, admits that "the dignity of marriage was restored" by the Fathers.[24] Another Protestant, Lecky, describing the Church as "the great enemy of the passions of the flesh," furnishes additional details: "Gays and lesbians, along with others who sold their daughters into prostitution, were excommunicated. No longer did musical girls sing and play at the banquets of the rich. Panderers . . . [had] molten lead poured down their throats, and actresses, on receiving baptism, were permitted to abandon their profession which had become a sort of slavery with vice attached to it."[25]

SEX AND WITCHCRAFT

As might be expected, Christian teaching on sexual morality was a hard sell. St. Columban's denunciation of King Theodoric for keeping concubines led to his expulsion from Gaul. Bishops might threaten excommunication for remarriage after divorce, but it was not until the twelfth century that the practice became illegal. Dante and Aquinas might condemn artificial birth control, Chaucer might depict it as a form of murder, but it did not simply go away. By the dawn of the fourteenth century, the seeds of secular humanism were in the air, Catholicism was losing its grip, and the result was moral fallout.[26] Birth control and abortion became so widespread under the name of witchcraft that they were twice condemned by the papacy within the space of a hundred years—in 1484 by Pope Innocent VIII (*Summis desiderant*) and again by Pope Sixtus V in his bull *Effraenatum* (1588), which decried "magical deeds" and "cursed medicines."[27]

THE RISE OF WOMEN

Nowadays, the word "witch" conjures up thoughts of misogyny. But the Church never harbored an animus toward women. On the contrary, it did all it could to improve their lot. Once it gained toleration under Constantine and began to find its voice politically, daughters were no longer forced into marriage, and masters were no longer free to sleep with slave girls. Pope Innocent I (401–417) considered adultery as great a sin for the husband as for the wife, and, in marked contrast with Jewish tradition, girls were as highly valued as boys.[28] Under the devout Justinian (527–65), mothers were granted guardianship of their children, along with property rights and protection from easy divorce.[29]

In the field of education women fared equally well. Marcella, a young widow inspired by St. Athanasius, gathered a group of friends for the purpose of praying, studying, and doing good works. When they were not learning Hebrew to chant the Psalms in the original, they were studying the New Testament in Greek. Marcella became a pupil of St. Jerome; we have sixteen of his letters to her; and it is clear that she did more than listen. She critiqued his arguments and chided him for his temper. One member of her circle, the brilliant Paula, not only worked as Jerome's research associate but established foundations for male and female religious, while Paula's wealthy cousin, Melania, became a philanthropist. She founded two monasteries (including one for men), endowed many more, and liberated eight thousand slaves.

A few centuries later, two female physicians, Lioba and Walburga, would accompany St. Boniface on his celebrated missionary journey to Germany, and by the end of the Middle Ages women had not only drawn even with men in the field of learning, they were ahead.[30] Many if not most queens of the period were better educated than their husbands, and the list includes Malcolm of Scotland's wife, Margaret, along with the wives of Charles V and Philip II of Spain. The fabulously rich Eleanor of Aquitaine (d. 1204) was more powerful than most kings, and Abbess Hildegard von Bingen (1098–1179) outshone all of her contemporaries with the exception of St. Bernard as an advisor to princes and kings. Hildegard composed chant that is still sung today. She also knew more about zoology and botany than anyone else, put forth the first complete theory of sexual complementarity, and, as Germany's premier physician, wrote a book on diseases.

Both Teresa of Avila (1515–82), the great Carmelite reformer, and Catherine of Siena (1347–1380), the great mystic, earned the title "Doctor of the Church" for their learning, and Catherine, as mentioned earlier, was the most influential person, male or female, of her time. Women taught at prestigious universities (e.g., Salamanca and Alcala) and practiced medicine. Trotula of Salerno is reputed to have written a seminal treatise on gynecology; Sybillina Biscossi, a blind hermitess of the fourteenth century, was famous for her wisdom and learning; but even before Sybillina's time, figures such as Hilda of Whitby ranked among the brightest lights of their age. Caedmon, one of the most celebrated poets of old England, wrote from a monastery run by Hilda, and the great Florentine painter, Fra Anglico, resided in a convent.[31]

WOMEN AS RULERS AND WARRIORS

It may be hard to imagine, but women ruled far more frequently and for longer intervals than they do today. Some served as regents or governed during their husband's
absence. The last great ruler of Italy, Louis II, left his wife Engelburga in charge
of his kingdom for five years (866–71), and from 1056 to 1062, Agnes managed
the Holy Roman Empire as regent for her son.[32] Others ruled in their own right.
St. Bathildis of France (d. 680), who founded religious houses for men, proved to
be an able queen after the death of her husband, and Saint Olga led Russia (Kiev
Rus) for nearly twenty years in the tenth century. After embracing Christianity,
Olga imported Christian missionaries and influenced her grandson, Vladimir, who
was thirteen at the time of her death. Young Vladimir, following in the steps of his
grandmother, converted the entire region from the Baltic to Ukraine.

A bit farther down the road chronologically, four individuals governed
northern and southern Italy in the year 1111, all of them women: Matilda, Adelaide,
Alaine, and Constance.[33] Three centuries later, another woman, Jadwiga, ruled
Poland for fourteen years and, after converting her husband, brought Lithuania into
the fold. Catherine de Medici, who ruled France for three years as regent for her
son, Charles IX (1560–63), exercised almost complete control for another ten years
down to Charles' death in 1574.

Most interesting of all, however, are two extraordinary women who guided
the destiny of their country for thirty and forty years respectively while finding
time to raise large families. One of them, Maria Theresa of Austria (1717–80), made
Vienna the cultural capital of Europe in the eighteenth century. The other, a fifteenth century Spanish queen by the name of Isabel, is a star among stars. Pawning
her jewelry to finance the conquest of Granada, she overhauled Spain's judicial system, appointed the saintly Cardinal Ximenez to reform the Church, and, as part of
her refusal to tolerate slavery in the Canary Islands or the Western Hemisphere, established a supreme court for the protection and education of the American Indian.
Historian Warren Carroll pictures her with "steel armor over her brocaded dress,
riding into robber dens and cleaning them out; or speeding on horseback from city
to city, holding trials and administering the stern justice that was needed to purify
Spain, fearlessly charging alone through mutinous mobs commanding that they put
down their lances and swords; [and] walking barefoot on knife-like stones to praise
God for Christian victories." From childhood on, she could ride and hunt as well as
most men, and as a mother, she did not shrink from leading troops into battle. Mass

was offered daily in her army camps, vespers were sung, and wherever she went there was an end to drunkenness and brawling.[34]

Joan of Arc, who led the armies of France to resounding victory in 1429, was not as singular as one might think. Three centuries earlier, Matilda of Tuscany had led troops into battle, and even before Matilda, during the 600s, a North African woman led Berbers, Jews, and Christians against the forces of Islam. Women fought in the Second Crusade, and one hundred forty years after Joan's execution a woman would lead the Christian charge onto the deck of the Turk's flagship at Lepanto.[35]

This is not to say that martial prowess was central to the medieval ideal of womanhood. Far from it. But that a fifteenth century woman became commander-in-chief of France's armed forces speaks volumes about an era in which there was opportunity without pressure. On the one hand, women could work as tradesmen and hold guild membership with full privileges and livery; on the other, they could stay at home. Society still believed that "the hand that rocks the cradle rules the world," and because industries such as food and clothing were home-based, the role of the woman was, in many respects, more vital economically than that of the man who followed the plow and wielded the sword. Henry Adams, professor of medieval history at Harvard, scion of two American presidents, and the author of *Mont Saint Michel and Chartres*, observed that the woman of the thirteenth century "ruled the household, the workshop, cared for the economy, supplied the intelligence, and dictated the taste . . . [She was] distinctly superior" to men intellectually.[36]

MARY AS MODEL

That devotion to the Virgin Mary reached a crescendo around the time that the status of women rose to an all-time high was hardly coincidental. Professor Adams, who saw the connection, held that such devotion "elevated the whole [female] sex," and Lecky wrote that the cult of the Virgin "ennobled" the fairer sex by "softening the manners of men" and refining the notion of what it meant to be a woman.[37] He did not explain what he meant by "softening," but one thing is certain. Mary's life-long virginity, coupled with the chastity attributed to her spouse, acted as a corrective to the secular view of man as a creature beholden to his baser instincts.[38]

From the time Mary's name first appeared on the walls of the catacombs to the year when Columbus christened his flagship the *Santa Maria*, Marian devotion was big in the West. King Arthur is said to have carried the Virgin's badge into battle when he defeated a pagan army around AD 495, and by the time the people of

England entered the Middle Ages, their land was known as "the Dowry of Mary."[39] On the Continent, King Fernando of Spain (d. 1252) dedicated three of his military field chapels to the Virgin and, as founder of the Castilian navy, he affixed her image to the prow of his flagship. In France, nearly all the cathedrals, beginning with Chartres, were dedicated to her. Louis IX, the only French king ever to be canonized, was a staunch devotee, and Guillaume de Machaut, regarded by many as the father of classical music, composed his finest work, the *Messe de Notre Dame* in her honor.

Farther east, Mary was the patron saint of Constantinople. Her picture hung on the wall of every hut, graced the head of every procession, and later with the rise of Islam in the seventh century, Muslims embraced her too. An entire chapter of the Koran is devoted to her, and to this day the followers of Mohammed venerate her as the woman who remained pure and virginal all her life.

The afterglow of medieval enthusiasm lasted centuries. Michelangelo's most memorable sculpture and the only one on which he ever carved his name depicts Christ in the lap of his grieving Mother (the *Piéta*), and seven years after the Florentine master of marble died, when Don Juan of Austria sailed against a formidable Muslim fleet at Lepanto, all of Europe prayed the Rosary. The banner of the Virgin flew over the mast of Don Juan's ship, every sailor was given a set of beads, and it was with Mary's name on their lips that Christian forces won the battle of the century.[40]

THE EMANCIPATION OF SLAVES

If the Christian cause had floundered at Lepanto, the survivors would have been sold into slavery. Servitude was still a flourishing institution under Islam, and the fact that Don Juan liberated some thirteen thousand Christian bondsmen serves as a pointed reminder that the Christian West differed from the Muslim East in more ways than one. Westerners had begun to gain the upper hand militarily and technologically. At the same time, there was a growing moral difference between the two sides that sprang essentially from religion. Christ started an emancipation movement affecting slaves as well as women. When he said, "The truth will make you free" (Jn. 8:32), he meant not only free from false hopes and moral snares, but also materially free.

The word "abolition" conjures up names like Wilberforce and Stowe, but the movement itself began at the start of the Christian era when at least fourteen slaves were elevated to the office of the papacy, including both of Peter's immediate successors. Calixtus (217–22), another pope with a slave background, insisted on recognizing the marriage of a high-born woman to a freedman, something heretofore illegal, and when Theodosius made Christianity the state religion, the rape or killing of a slave became a capital offense. Slaves also secured the right to marry and raise a family.[41] A century or two later, St. Benedict refused to allow any distinction between free born and freedman; Justinian prohibited the father of the family from selling his children into slavery as a means of paying off debt; and Pope Gregory the Great not only condemned the practice of selling a slave away from his or her family but freed his own slaves.[42]

By the year 1100 slavery was a thing of the past for most Christians, and by the dawn of the fourteenth century it was virtually extinct except in Muslim and schismatic areas of the East.[43] The Church had turned its attention to the elimination of serfdom. And one might add, as an aside, that the evils endured by serfs were more prevalent in heterodox Russia than in Catholic Austria where laborers could not be bought or sold—the policies of Catherine, the so-called "Great," were positively brutal in this respect.

Slavery made a comeback during the Renaissance due to the demands of colonization and a coincidental loosening of the papal grip on crown and gown. Church councils attempted to deal with the problem and there were periodic papal condemnations, but, as always, it was one thing for a pontiff to speak, another for people to listen.[44] Monarchs, too, raised their voices from time to time, but again, without lasting effect. Isabel did all she could to prevent Spanish colonists from enslaving New World Indians, and Charles V took the unprecedented step of suspending all military activity in America pending the results of an inquiry into the conduct of colonial officials. But the results in both cases were inconclusive.

The British became the first to eliminate slavery, and of this they have every reason to be proud. Nevertheless, the motivation behind the act stemmed from a peculiar kind of horror. John Wesley, the founder of Methodism, knew whereof he spoke when he branded slavery in English speaking areas "the vilest that ever saw the sun."[45] If there is anything that stands out clearly in the history of enslavement from the Renaissance to the nineteenth century, it is the disparity between slavery in Catholic areas and slavery elsewhere.

TWO FORMS OF SLAVERY

Max Weber, author of *The Protestant Ethic and the Spirit of Capitalism*, might well have written a sequel entitled, *The Protestant Ethic and Slavery* because a comparative analysis of imperial slave codes reveals striking differences. Unlike their brethren to the North, Latin American chattel could earn their freedom after a reasonable term of service. They also had rights to leisure and reception of the sacraments. There were frequent inspections by the officers of Crown and Church. Colonial governors had to submit to royal investigation at the end of every term, and priests representing secular, as well as religious, authorities insisted on Church marriage, along with guarantees against selling families apart. Slaves in non-Catholic areas enjoyed none of these prerogatives. In fact, there were even instances in which they were *barred* from entering a binding marriage.[46]

Portuguese, Spanish, and French colonizers exhibited remarkably little color prejudice, and again, religion was key. Mexico's Second Audiencia actually urged Spaniards to marry Indian women, and the same holds true for the Portuguese in Goa, the French in Canada, and the Catholics of Maryland. Furthermore, because a father would sometimes free the children of a biracial union, along with their mother, a class of free and relatively prosperous mulattoes emerged in places like Haiti and Cuba.[47]

Anglo-Saxon authorities, by contrast, made miscegenation extremely difficult when they did not prohibit it altogether. After the Philippines was occupied by the United States in 1898, Filipinos visiting North America were shocked to find themselves proscribed from marrying into white society. They shouldn't have been, however. This was long standing American policy both at home and overseas. During the early 1800s, when Latin American freedom fighters enlisted Yankee help in their struggle against Spanish rule, there was a change south of the border: mixed marriage was forbidden.

TWO KINDS OF COLONIALISM

This was not the only way in which the attitude of Spanish sovereigns differed from that of their English counterparts. They would not permit their overseas colonies to be used as a dumping ground for criminals, and they laid great stress on native education. Prize-winning historian William Thomas Walsh describes how Philip II of Spain treated the Filipinos:

He found there a semi-savage people. Instead of exterminating them, as the English were to exterminate the aborigines of North America ... [Spanish officials] patiently taught them Christianity and the arts of civilization, introduced better methods of rice culture, brought Indian corn and cacao from America, developed the growth of indigo, coffee and sugar cane, united the people to the stream of Christian European culture by helping them to learn Spanish, and encouraged their natural love of music. Philip authorized the Jesuits to found a college there in 1585, though it was not opened until 1601. The College of Saint Potenciana for girls was established in 1593. A century and a half after his death, there would be nearly a million Christian souls on the island in 569 parishes. Even in his lifetime, it was evident that Spain had raised a half-savage people to a relatively high standard of civilization, and this not by force or exploitation or political chicanery, but principally by patient labors of priests and monks; by Christian charity. This is indisputable. Philip otherwise could never have held the islands with a garrison of only 400 men to protect them from Sulus, Moslems, and Chinese and Dutch pirates.[48]

Today, the Philippines is the only major nation in the Far East that is Christian, and Spain's record in Manila was not atypical. Within thirteen years of her conquest of Mexico, there were not only schools for children of the poor and an institution of higher learning, Holy Cross College accepted Indians. Nineteen years later Holy Cross was joined by two more colleges, along with a university, and Mexicans of Indian extraction were soon crossing the Atlantic to teach in the universities of Europe.[49] Meanwhile, Portuguese Jesuits established industrial villages or "reductions," as they were called, for the Indians of present-day Argentina, Uruguay, Paraguay, and Brazil. Self-supporting and secure, the reductions offered native Americans a chance to learn a trade and avoid enslavement.

That men like Las Casas, Vitoria, and Montesinos were free to deplore the moral consequences of colonialism is itself significant. Francisco de Vitoria, a Dominican theologian at the University of Salamanca and one of the founding fathers of international law, was outraged by the cruelty and duplicity of Pizarro in Peru. He insisted that the Indians must never be made to suffer so that Spain might prosper, and his writings, along with those of other human rights advocates, had a powerful effect on future generations of scholars, theologians, and government officials.

Prominent among New World champions of the rights of Indians and slaves were Juan de Zumárraga, the first bishop of Mexico; José de Anchieta, S.J., apostle to Brazil and the father of Brazilian literature; Archbishop Turibius of Lima, who abolished slavery; Father Francisco Solano, the Franciscan hero of Indian folk song; Blessed Junipero Serra of California; Diego Vargas of Santa Fe; and three viceroys of New Spain: Mendoza, Velasco, and Buscareli.

Like all nationalities, the Spanish and Portuguese had their share of opportunists. Pedro Margarit, whom Columbus left behind on the island of Hispaniola (modern day Haiti) with instructions to hold the fort, exterminated the natives after robbing and raping them.[50] Unscrupulous owners of plantation fiefdoms called "encomiendas" engaged in other forms of exploitation. But throughout the period there were countervailing forces at work. The encomienda system was abolished, and the Jesuits, whose Indian friends were enslaved when they left Paraguay, had avenues of redress. A papal bull, *Commissum Nobis*, called attention to the brutal treatment of the Guarani tribe, and Jesuit lobbying moved King Sebastian of Portugal to outlaw virtually all enslavement of the colony's indigenous people.[51]

THE BLACK LEGEND

The one problem with the reform movement was that crusaders like Vitoria, in denouncing colonial excesses, tended to exaggerate, and Spain's enemies seized upon their inflated rhetoric to fashion a heavily slanted account of Spanish overseas settlement. "Black Legend" historians, as they came to be known, turned a blind eye to the positive side of Spanish colonialism, focusing almost exclusively on what was brutal and venal. One would never know from what they wrote that Columbus, on reaching San Salvador, was greeted by the remnant of a tribe that had been literally eaten alive by its Carib neighbors or that cannibalism was rife in other areas as well. When Pizarro arrived in Peru, the Incas had just flung the bodies of 20,000 members of a rival tribe into a lake. Mexico's Aztec empire was one of the world's cruelest. Its leaders warred incessantly and, when victorious, they not only loaded their subjects with taxes but demanded victims for "sacrifice." According to Professor Carroll, over eighty thousand men were "sacrificed" in four days during the dedication of a new pyramid-temple in 1487, and not all of them were prisoners of war.[52]

Scholars once assumed that killer diseases such as tuberculosis were brought to America by the Spaniards, but the recent discovery of a body belonging to a Peruvian woman buried a thousand years ago suggests that such germs were already present in the New World when Columbus landed.[53] The Indians were not the sole victims either. Hernando De Soto and most of his party of a thousand men succumbed to diseases contracted from the natives of Florida. But even if one could prove that the *conquistadores* introduced tuberculosis, they had no way of knowing what they were doing given the primitive state of medicine.

THE CHURCH AND SLAVERY

Returning for a moment to the subject of slavery, one of the most frequently asked questions is why the American bishops prior to the Civil War did not speak out against the gross evil one reads about in *Uncle Tom's Cabin*.

We know, of course, that not all slave owners were Simon Legree. Secondly, Catholics were few in number, and what is more, they were looked upon with a mixture of fear and disdain by their fellow Americans. It is debatable, therefore, whether their support would have helped or hurt the abolitionist cause. In addition, there were practical considerations. What would become of a slave if he or she were freed? Masters who educated their slaves and taught them a trade harbored legitimate fears that, once freed, they would wind up unemployed. For Abraham Lincoln and members of the American Colonization Society, the solution was to transport freedmen back to the land of their ancestry. The only problem is that few wished to go. There was also the threat of another uprising such as the one that occurred in Virginia in 1831. By murdering every member of his master's family, along with fifty other whites, Nat Turner took much of the bloom off the flower of the anti-slavery movement.

For these and other reasons, Pope Gregory XVI, in his 1839 letter, *In Supremo Apostolatus*, called for the amelioration of slavery, but he stopped short of requiring abolition except as a long-term goal, and Catholic bishops simply adopted the line of their leader, which was Lincoln's line as well.[54]

No one can charge the Church with a lack of concern for the victims of slavery. Many a saint bore witness to Christ's love by the way he lived. Peter Claver, a Jesuit of noble descent, is famous for having braved the stench of slave holds aboard newly arrived trans-Atlantic galleons in seventeenth century Cartagena to minister to hundreds of thousands of blacks desperately ill from the voyage. So anxious was he to reach his charges spiritually that he went so far as to suck the poison from their festering wounds![55] Two centuries later, Katharine Drexel, a young Philadelphia heiress, displayed courage of a different sort. Founder of a religious order to serve underprivileged blacks, as well as Indians, she donated her fortune to the cause, established Xavier University in New Orleans, and built sixty-two other schools. Xavier was soon turning out 25 percent of all black pharmacists and sending more blacks to medical school than any other college or university in the country. Not all Americans approved. Katharine's sisters were spat upon and their motherhouse set on fire. But this only spurred them on to greater heights. Catholics opened the first free school for blacks west of the Mississippi in addition to the first southern high school for blacks following the Civil War.[56]

To list all the accomplishments of the Church in the field of human welfare would fill volumes. Alcoholics Anonymous (AA), a non-denominational organization, got under way at a Catholic hospital in Akron, Ohio where a nun, Sister Ignatia Gavin, brought addicts in through the back door, pretending to treat them for other ailments. The Catholic Legion of Decency was by far the most powerful moral influence on the American media for three decades (during the golden age of film beginning in the 1930s). Catholics opened New York's first state-certified AIDS treatment center (at St. Clare's Hospital in New York City), and it was a priest, Fr. C. John McCloskey III, who converted America's leading abortion provider, Bernard Nathanson, to the pro-life cause. All told, the Church has done more to combat the slaughter of unborn infants than all other organizations put together.

Suffice it to say that the ecclesiastical organization founded by Christ two thousand years ago and headed by an unbroken line of pontiffs has borne fruit in abundance.[57]

Chapter 8

THE CRUSADES, THE INQUISITION, AND THE TRIAL OF GALILEO

Although we have caught glimpses of Rome's less attractive side in our light-ning survey of ecclesiastic history, the accent, thus far, has been on the positive; and this is as it should be since the world would be much less caring and far more cruel without the Catholic presence. Still, one cannot take the full measure of the Church's character without evaluating the controversial role she played in three highly charged episodes. It is time to look at the Crusades, the Spanish Inquisition, and the Trial of Galileo because there has been a heavy accretion of myth in these areas. In all three cases, there are also deep, fundamental values at stake that call for clarity of thought regarding the role of the historian.

One need not apologize for every outrage committed by every member of the Church over the centuries, though Pope John Paul II, speaking on behalf of the faithful in his Apostolic Letter of November 1994, came close to doing just this in a very real sense when he expressed collective regret.[1] The task at hand is rather to connect the past with the present by reconstructing the ethos of a time long gone and attempting to get inside the mind of the players. We will not be asking, therefore, whether actions taken hundreds of years ago square with current practice. They don't. Human nature remains the same, but the canons of social and political correctness change from one era to another.

Would a modern day prime minister treat conscientious objectors the way Henry VIII treated Thomas More? Would Israel deal with a twenty-first century dissident the way Caiaphas dealt with Jesus? Although George Washington held slaves and Mark Twain used the word "nigger," anyone familiar with American history knows that our first president and the author of Huckleberry Finn were highly progressive by the standards of their day.[2] Likewise when it comes to people and events of the Middle Ages and Renaissance. The Crusades, the Spanish Inquisition, and the trial of Galileo look one way through twenty-first century lenses but quite another when viewed against the backdrop of history.

THE CRUSADES

For the Crusades, one must begin with the year 1008 when the Church of the Holy Sepulcher, the most sacred of all Christian pilgrimage sites, was razed by Ali-al-Mansur Al-Hakim (by 1014, thirty thousand other Christian churches had met a similar fate).[3] In 1064, an unarmed group of German pilgrims numbering seven thousand was so fiercely set upon that less than a third lived to tell the story.[4] And so it went. Deeply etched on the mind of those who took the cross in 1099 was the fact that the Holy Land had been desecrated by Muslims. Christian pilgrims had been murdered.

Such outrages were enough, in and of themselves, to justify the Crusades, all nine of which were defensive, as they aimed to reclaim and secure holy places that belonged as much to the Christians as they did to the Muslims. The First Crusade sought to reprize Jerusalem. The Second was triggered by the Muslim conquest of Edessa, the oldest of Christian cities, and the Third by Saladin's reconquest of Jerusalem. Never was there the slightest intent to use force as an instrument of conversion.

It was rather the Muslims who were the aggressors. Omar ibn al-Khattab, Abu Bakr's successor in the Caliphate and the father of the Muslim calendar, spoke for all of Islam when he declared, not long after the death of Mohammed: "It behooves us to devour the Christians and . . . their descendants as long as any of them remain on earth."[5] By 1099, the year Jerusalem fell to the First Crusade, the Seljuk Turks had conquered the ancient Christian city of Antioch and defeated a Byzantine army at Manzikert (1071), causing the Eastern Emperor Alexius I to look westward for help. Fifty percent of Christendom had been overrun by the Islamic juggernaut by 1099, and while Palestine itself contained a large number of Christians, probably a majority, it was ruled by Muslims.[6]

From a military point of view, the First Crusade was a stunning success. It put Jerusalem back in Christian hands where it remained for a hundred years and secured the fortified cities of Acre, Jaffe, and Ascalon. The goal thereafter was simply to assure the safety of pilgrims, and this was achieved. There were no more closures of Jerusalem of the kind that occurred in 1072, and owing to stubborn Crusader resistance, it took Islam the better part of two centuries to recover all the ground it lost. In the meantime, challenges to the Muslims' homeland deprived them of opportunities elsewhere. There was an easing of pressure on Spain, enabling the Reconquista to go forward; Lisbon and other key cities in Portugal were recaptured; Christianity spread beyond Ukraine to Russia, and the West learned how to build better ships and draw more accurate maps.

ATROCITIES

The other side of the coin is that Christian forces committed occasional outrages. When Jerusalem refused to accept terms of surrender, armies fighting their way into the city slaughtered men, women and children. There is no justification for the taking of innocent life, but it should also be said that fierce reprisals for failure to surrender were standard at the time, and there has never been a war of any magnitude, civil or foreign, without moral lapses.[7] French revolutionaries killed over one hundred thousand men, women, and children in the Vendée, and in the course of drowning thousands at Pont au Baux, *sanscoulottes* tied men and women together naked and cast them into the water in pairs. In Angers, the skins of thirty-two victims were tanned to make riding breeches for officers.[8] Among other abominations, France's atheists crushed pregnant women under wine presses and tossed infants from bayonet to bayonet. Never during the worst days of the Crusades was anything like this ever reported.

More recently, Allied forces fire bombed Dresden and other cities during World War II snuffing out the lives of hundreds of thousands; the United States dropped atomic bombs on Hiroshima and Nagasaki, taking another hundred thousand lives; and American troops since then have been responsible for massacres, rape, and other forms of sexual abuse in Vietnam and the Persian Gulf.

In Constantinople during the Fourth Crusade, there was widespread looting, pillage, and rape—once again a hideous sight. Apologies were offered; a horrified Holy Father excommunicated the sackers, and, where possible, the miscreants were brought to justice. But there is another side to the story. Crusader behavior was not entirely unprovoked. One of the royal princes, after promising to pay the Crusaders enough to enable them to complete their journey to Jerusalem if they restored him to his throne, reneged after Western knights fulfilled their end of the bargain. Then, too, the incident followed decades of anti-Latin action on the part of the East, including an instance of collaboration with Saladin that helped destroy a Crusader army.[9]

What happened on the Bosporus is alleged to have dealt a death blow to Christian reunion, and this is possible. However, the likeliest time for reunion would have been when the West first came to the aid of the East and won resounding victories. Some of the Orthodox did, in fact, return to the Catholic fold out of appreciation for what the Crusaders had done, which was to vanquish a formidable foe without much help from Byzantium.

WHO TOOK THE CROSS?

It is hard to characterize the Crusaders. Many ordinary men put their fortunes on the line and risked grave injury in order to do something noble in the eyes of the Lord. They brought their own horses, mules, and equipment, and few returned home as well off as they left.[10] Among the principals, Bohemond and Charles of Anjou were devious, grasping, and ruthless. Godfrey of Bouillon, on the other hand, along with Raymond of Toulouse and Louis IX of France, were men of integrity and courage. Raymond, in an attack on Muslim-held Tripoli, was outnumbered twenty to one, while King Baldwin I of Jerusalem routed 32,000 Muslims with a force of only 1,160.[11] Later, when Baldwin invaded Egypt, he confronted a populace of millions with a mere two hundred sixteen horsemen and four hundred infantry.[12] England's Richard the Lionhearted was so brave that when he fell from a wounded horse, Saladin sent him two fresh ones, along with a groom! One is reminded of L'Isle Adam, the gallant leader of the Knights of St. John, who made such an impression on Suleiman the Magnificent three centuries later that the sultan ordered his daring recounted in all the mosques of the Turkish empire.[13]

THE DARKER SIDE

Before turning to the Inquisition, we need to mention two other events associated with the Crusades. In the first instance, youngsters recruited to serve as soldiers were sold into slavery by their Muslim captors during the so-called Children's Crusade of 1212, and this is regrettable. In the second instance, a Cistercian monk by the name of Raoul preached genocidal destruction of the Jews, and innocent folks were slaughtered before Hungarian troops came to their aid. Pogroms are, by definition, execrable, and it is clear that much of the motivation on the Christian side boiled down to avarice and greed.

The rationales—justified or not—at the time of these attacks on Jews were many. It is likely that some, if not most, of the victims of intolerance sympathized with Islam, rather than Christianity, at a time when the two sides were locked in mortal combat. Many a Jew hoped for the failure of the Crusade, and Zionist forces were preparing to take advantage of any opportunity that might come their way. The Jewish people, regarding themselves as a superior race were also so resistant to assimilation that they refused to settle in certain towns without being assured of an exclusive enclave or ghetto.[14] Polygamy was not unknown among them, and the Talmud, in unexpurgated form, contained viciously anti-Christian slurs. Mary, the mother of Jesus, was said to have been a harlot and Jesus himself was depicted as condemned to boil forever in excrement.[15] Jewish money lenders sometimes charged unconscionably high rates of interest, and this was doubly objectionable because Christians were forbidden to practice usury on anyone whereas the rabbis prohibited it only in cases where the victims were Jewish.[16]

No sane person would ever attempt to justify the views of Raoul or the madness to which they led. Churchmen like St. Bernard spoke out against anti-Semitism—there is no such thing as a bigoted saint—and there were bishops who sheltered Jewish refugees. The archbishop of Mainz, who sympathized openly with the Jews, had to leave town, and Archbishop Speyer of Cologne, who hanged the ring leaders, did so at the risk of his life.

THE AIM OF THE INQUISITION

Events are best understood within the context of their time, and this is especially true of the Spanish Inquisition, which seems to surface nearly every time the Faith is called into question. Inaugurated by Queen Isabel and conducted by the state from 1472 to 1820, with clerics serving as interrogators, it has been criticized for alleged cruelty and intolerance.[17] Contrary to popular opinion, however, no one was ever burned for being a Protestant, Jew, or Muslim. Jews were free to attend synagogue services and, though forced to leave Spain in 1492, they were not expelled on account of their religion. Muslims, too, were generally free to worship as they saw fit, and again, their expulsion had little to do with the tenets of their faith. The sole purpose of the Inquisition under Isabel was to root out "conversos"—mainly Jews who appeared to be Catholic but, in reality, were not and who held influential political or ecclesiastical posts.[18]

Fear of subversion by a Jewish "fifth column" cannot be understood apart from two other facts. In 1472, the Reconquista had yet to take back the southern, Islamic-controlled portion of the country when the Inquisition got under way. The Peninsula was therefore convulsed in civil war, and the Spanish feared they might wake up one day and find themselves under Sharia law. Secondly, in AD 711, less than a hundred years after the Jews supported the Persian conquest of Jerusalem and assisted in the torture of Christian captives, they had backed the Muslim invasion of the Iberian Peninsula, and after Cordova, Malaga, Granada, Seville, and Toledo fell to the knights of the Crescent, these cities were placed under Jewish control.[19]

STILL ANOTHER REASON FOR THE INQUISITION

This, in itself, would be enough to explain the Inquisition. But there was an even greater threat looming overseas. When Isabel came to power, Constantinople had just succumbed to Turkish (Islamic) military power after a centuries-long struggle. By the time the Inquisition got under way, Muslim armies had come within a hair's breadth of conquering Belgrade, and to the south, the Mediterranean was fast becoming a Muslim lake. In 1480, only six years into Isabel's reign, the Turks overran the mighty fortress of Rhodes and attacked Otranto in Italy, slaughtering twelve thousand out of twenty-two thousand and enslaving most of the rest. Every priest was killed and the archbishop sawed in two.[20]

Islam aimed at nothing less than world conquest, and to Western Europeans in 1492, the future looked bleak, Iberian victories notwithstanding. We know, on hindsight, that Muslim armies would take Hungary in 1526. They would reach the gates of Vienna in1529, and Malta, the last of the Christian strongholds in the Mediterranean, would escape defeat in 1565 by the narrowest of margins. What if Don Juan of Austria had not prevailed at Lepanto in 1571? What if John Sobieski, king of Poland, had not lifted the Muslim siege of Vienna in 1683? Or if Prince

Eugene of Savoy had not bested the Turks in 1697? All Spain knew in the late 1400s was that it was fighting not only for its life but also for the life of the West, and history shows that any nation so engaged will resort to draconian measures.

Abraham Lincoln, in the throes of the American Civil War, suspended *habeas corpus* and jailed political opponents on mere suspicion. During World War II, United States citizens of Japanese extraction were rounded up and, on short notice, shipped off to detention camps for the duration of the war. The alarm aroused by Communism's expansion into Eastern Europe and China in the late 1940s, coupled with Soviet Premier Nikita Khrushchev's famous boast, "We will bury you," was huge. Anyone associated with Communism or communists, even indirectly, during the "Red Scare" was suspect, and there were innocent people who had their reputations destroyed in the course of Congressional investigations. Yet the threat faced by America during these years, accompanied, as it was, by the fear of atomic war and visions of mushroom clouds over New York, was miniscule by comparison with what Christian Spain faced at the time of Isabel.

To be clear, the Isabel who expelled the Jews from Iberia was not *personally* hostile to them. One in particular, Rabbi Abraham Seneor, aided her in her quest for the queenship of Castille, while another, R. Isaac Abravenal, advised her on finance. Still another served as a trusted physician. She welcomed men and women of Jewish descent to her court (including her personal secretary and nearly all the members of her privy council); she forbade the levying of special taxes on their property; and she was happy to build them a synagogue. The problem was that Spain's inquisitorial courts failed in their attempt to check Jewish and Islamic influence on the conversos, and, even more to the point, there was constant feuding between Jews and Christians—feuding serious enough to lead to massacres in Valladolid (1470), Cordoba (1474), and Seville (1478) in spite of Isabel's best effort to keep the peace.[21]

SPAIN IN CONTEXT

Isabel's expulsion policy was not unique either. Edward I, a king whom Dickens calls "wise and great" and who is known as the English Justinian, did the same thing two centuries earlier. Before Edward's time, the Jews were ousted from portions of the Crimea (1016) and the Rhineland (1012). Later, between 1190 and 1454, they were forced to leave France, Switzerland, Austria, Moravia, Bavaria, and Provence (seat of the Albigensian heresy and known as "the second Judea"). In the half century following Isabel's reign, they were exiled from Tuscany, Lithuania, Portugal, Bohemia, and

Saxony (at Luther's instigation). And along the way they had to vacate many cities—Paris in 1182 and, during the 1400s, Cologne, Augsburg, Cracow, Perugia, Vicenza, Parma, Milan, Lucca, and Florence.[22] Spain was one of the few Christian countries willing to have them at the time of Isabel, and this by virtue of a royal indult.

THE QUESTION OF CRUELTY

Shifting the focus to charges of cruelty leveled by critics of the Inquisition, one must bear in mind that burning at the stake, a practice dating back to the time of Moses, was commonplace in England, France, Germany, and Scandinavia, as well as Spain. This was how the English dispatched Joan of Arc, along with others judged guilty of heresy. Treason was, of course, a different matter. Any Englishman convicted of disloyalty was hanged, cut down, and disemboweled. The executioner would cut out his entrails and heart while he was still alive and conscious in many cases, and the carcass would then be drawn and quartered. The ritual seems barbarous by today's standards, but Elizabeth, dissatisfied with the usual procedures, sought new and more horrible methods of torture to ensure even greater suffering.[23] The Catholic poet, Robert Southwell, S.J., was tortured ten times prior to execution in a manner characterized by Southwell as worse than the rack, and what Margaret Clitherow, the mother of three young children, had to endure from English (Protestant) authorities is practically indescribable. They stripped her naked for harboring a priest, then crushed her to death over a three-day period for her refusal to apostatize.

Iberian torture, less used by the Inquisition than by the ordinary criminal courts of Spain, was limited to fifteen minutes and almost never used on the same individual more than twice.[24] A doctor was present to ensure that it did not result in deformity, and because Torquemada, the chief inquisitor, was a champion of prison reform, detention centers were models of humane treatment. Only 2 percent of those brought to trial were tortured, and when torture and/or burning did occur, it had nothing to do with the Auto-da-Fe, a ceremony in which penitents disposed to recant did so publicly.[25] Imprisonment for those who repented was often restricted to a term of house arrest, while some were released on condition that they simply fast or wear penitential garb.

As for the judicial process itself, it was so fair that many of Spain's defendants preferred the Inquisition to normal channels. Under Torquemada, the accused was allowed to draw up a list of enemies whose testimony was automatically excluded, and those falsely accused were promptly released. There were exceptions, to be sure—Pope Leo X excommunicated the Toledo tribunal for violation of due process. But overall, only one to two percent of those tried for treason were executed—two thousand over three hundred fifty years. Furthermore, by uniting the country religiously, the Inquisition, in conjunction with Isabel's reform of the Church, ushered in a golden age of peace and culture, the age of Cervantes. A hundred thousand witches were burned in Germany and thirty thousand in England and Scotland. But the Spanish burned none.[26]

FORCED CONVERSION

That Isabel never forced Spanish Jews to choose between death and conversion bears repeating because such tolerance was not always the rule, either in her country or elsewhere. Spaniards forced Jewish conversion during the seventh century on the eve of the Muslim invasion, and the English did the same five centuries later (in York). The Austrians did it in 1421 (in Vienna), and the Jews themselves were not entirely blameless. John Hyrcanus (c. 175–104 BC) and his son Aristobulus I forced Idumeans in southern Judea, as well as Itureans in the north, to convert to Judaism at the point of a sword.[27] For the Idumeans, it was circumcision or expulsion; for the Itureans circumcision or death. Later, when Bar Cochba led a Jewish revolt against Rome (AD 131–35), he ordered Christians to denounce Christ or die.[28] In 414, Alexandrian Jews massacred Christians wholesale, and in AD 523, the Jewish king of Yemen, Dhu Nuwas, executed three hundred Christians for refusing to convert.[29]

The Islamic record is similar. At Gaza in AD 634, sixty Christian soldiers were captured by Muslim forces and forced to choose between conversion and death. They chose the latter. At Otranto in 1480, eight hundred Christians were tortured and put to death for refusing to convert to Islam—all in violation of the Koran's teaching that "there is no compulsion in religion."[30]

Back to the Christian record, it should be noted that while Catholic heads of state violated peoples' consciences at times, the Church as a church never did. On the contrary, it condemned such practice as early as AD 633 at the Fourth Council of Toledo, and it kept on condemning it. As a case in point, Alcuin, the monk, rebuked Charlemagne for compelling the Saxons to accept Christ as their Savior.

There is a difference, however, between forced conversion, which Rome never sanctioned, and punishment for heresy. During the early centuries, the Church did not approve of harsh measures, even in the case of the latter. But after the Islamic military machine began to roll across North Africa and into Europe, things changed.

In AD 732, the year Muslim armies invaded France, Pope Gregory III approved life imprisonment for heresy, along with execution for *obstinate* heresy (while leaving Jews free to practice as they saw fit).

THE ALBIGENSIAN MENACE

Ultimately, it was the Albigensians or "Cathars" in the eleventh and twelfth century in southern France who, more than any other group, put Christianity to the test. Because they viewed the flesh as evil, they avoided child bearing and rejected marriage. Many who could not live celibately would turn to fornication backed by contraception and abortion. Suicide was common, and the sect was especially dangerous in the eyes of the state because it denied the right of taxation. It even went so far as to foreswear the oath of fealty, which was integral to the feudal system. Cathars mustered armies, lived behind the walls of fortified cities, and condoned stealing so long as no injury was done to members of their own sect. Violence against mainline Christians was so common that St. Dominic took his life into his hands every time he spoke in Provence.[31]

In 1022 King Robert of France executed twelve Cathars, some of them lay and some ecclesiastics. Mobs then entered the picture, forcing the hand of both state and Church. It was no longer safe to detain Albigensians pending trial because an irate populace would likely storm the prison. In 1139, the Second Lateran Council authorized princes to prosecute heretics as a matter of policy, and a hundred years later, Pope Innocent IV sanctioned the use of torture by civil authorities to extract confessions.

PROTESTANT INTOLERANCE

Isabel's reign is commonly viewed as the epitome of intolerance, but this is caricature, not fact. Contemporary Protestants, Jews, and Muslims were as one with Catholics in viewing religious deviance as dangerous to a cohesive society, as well as to the maintenance of religion. In England, heresy was a crime punishable by death up to 1677, and Elizabeth I, fearful of attacks from abroad, quashed every murmur of dissent, political or religious, with a sternness that would have shocked Spain's Torquemada. She executed 124 priests and 57 laymen merely for practicing their faith.[32] North of Spain, on the European continent, Luther urged his followers to attack the pope, the cardinals, and the entire "canker of the Roman Sodom" and wash their hands "in their blood."[33] John Calvin, the founder of Presbyterianism, not only authorized the murder of anyone who stood in the way of Protestant evangelization.[34] He also wrote a book justifying coercion of heretics "by the sword" and, in addition to burning sixty-five nonconformists at the stake in Geneva, he had a woman whipped for praying at a relative's grave.[35]

French Protestants, taking their cue from Calvin, behaved as one would expect.[36] St. Bartholomew's Day 1572 has gone down as a dark day in the history of the Church because thousands of Huguenots (French Protestants) were massacred on the streets of Paris. Less well known is that by 1572, Huguenots in the Low Countries had gutted and sacked Catholic churches in four hundred towns and villages.[37] Thousands of priests and nuns had been murdered. Six weeks before St. Bartholomew's Day, Calvinists captured nineteen priests in the Netherlands town of Gorkum, and, after torturing them for their refusal to renounce the Faith, hanged them.[38]

In France itself prior to 1572 atrocities and sacrileges had mounted until, by one of the Huguenots' own estimates, members of their sect had killed four thousand priests, monks, and nuns, expelled or maltreated twelve thousand nuns, sacked twenty thousand churches, and destroyed two thousand monasteries, along with their libraries and works of art. They desecrated Catholic graves, trampled consecrated hosts, raped nuns, buried Catholics alive, plunged them into boiling oil, tore out their tongues, and disemboweled them alive. Trustworthy reports reached Rome of two hundred priests hurled over a precipice near Saint Séver. To cut off a priest's ears became a kind of pastime, with one leader wearing a scarf of them. Calvinists also introduced the practice of giving no quarter and slaughtering prisoners.[39]

The Hussites of Bohemia were no less savage, and in America, Puritan heirs of Calvin whipped Quakers, cropped their ears, and in at least four instances, executed them.[40] For many years, it was death to be a priest in Massachusetts, and in Maryland, when Protestants regained power after 1689, Catholic children who apostatized automatically received their parents' property. As late as the 1770s, Baptists were still being whipped and jailed by the Anglicans of Virginia.[41]

In sum, intolerance had little to do with Spain. Neither was it confined to Christian circles. Moses had three thousand dissenters put to death in a single day; Elijah executed four hundred fifty false prophets on Mount Carmel; good King Josiah slew heretical priests, along with all priests not properly in the line of Aaron. In the first century BC, Sadducees forced eight hundred Pharisees to witness the slitting of their wives' and children's throats before crucifying them. Sixteen hundred years later, Jews in the Netherlands, not content to arrest Gabriel da Costa

(1585–1640) for heresy, fined him, burned his writings, and scourged him publicly. After receiving thirty-nine lashes da Costa committed suicide. Another Jewish philosopher, Baruch Spinoza (1632–1677), was excommunicated by his synagogue and driven from Amsterdam.[42]

Such things sound almost surreal to those of us blessed with a Constitution that ensures a large measure of freedom. But tolerance is not, in itself, a virtue. It depends on what is being tolerated. Had there been a German Inquisition during the 1920s, Adolf Hitler would never have been elected. With inquisitions in Italy and Russia, Mussolini and Stalin would not have risen to power. There is such a thing as false tolerance, which leads to chaos and despotism. Curiously enough, the twentieth century, least judgmental of all periods from a religious standpoint, has been the most intolerant of ideological opposition, and the tide of narrowness is on the rise as secular humanists seek to throttle a Judeo-Christian moral ethic of four thousand years' standing.

THE TRIAL OF GALILEO

The reader may wonder at this point why we have dwelt so long on the subject of intolerance. If so, the answer is simple: it is integral to a proper understanding not only of the Spanish Inquisition but also the trial of Galileo. There is no way to arrive at a balanced judgment in the case of either without grasping the intellectual milieu. We may feel more in touch with the battle over heliocentrism than with Isabel's prosecution of conversos since the former is one hundred fifty years closer to us, and the issue of science versus religion is still very much alive. But, all things considered, the heliocentrist controversy may actually be harder to understand because of the radical transformation our pedagogical philosophy has undergone in the past hundred years. Education, which used to be religious in orientation, has been secularized to a large degree, and at present much of it is *anti*-religious.

Galilei Galileo was a brilliant Florentine physicist and inventor who championed the Copernican theory of a sun-centered galaxy.[43] In 1616, members of a papal-appointed theological commission condemned heliocentrism as "foolish and absurd" and required that it be taught as theory, rather than fact, since this was all it was at the time. Centuries would come and go before it could be proven beyond all doubt.[44] Pope Urban VIII (1623–44) treated Galileo with honor, granting him six audiences early in his reign and telling him that he was free to write a book on heliocentrism provided it contained arguments against the theory, as well as for it.

Ostensibly, then, the issue was one of intellectual honesty; but below the surface it was far more, for, as we shall see, the Church was concerned about Galileo's tendency to cast doubt on the reliability of the Bible.

At first, Galileo did as the pope directed. He taught theory as theory, and for sixteen years he lectured at Rome, as well as at the universities of Pisa and Padua. But then he went back on his word, presenting heliocentrism, once more, as fact. At this point, the Inquisition ordered him, under threat of torture, to abjure his theory, which he did, and for penance, he was required to recite the seven penitential Psalms once a week for three years and remain under house arrest. He spent five months at the palace of the archbishop of Siena, who idolized him, before returning to his villa outside Florence where he continued to do research, make discoveries, write his greatest book, and receive such visitors as Milton and Hobbes on a comfortable church pension.[45]

There is no question that Catholic theologians erred when they condemned heliocentrism. But to most of the world's intelligentsia, it was Galileo who was in the wrong. His argument based on sunspots was no more impressive to contemporaries than it is to scientists today. He also held mistakenly that planets travel in circles, Kepler's proof to the contrary notwithstanding (they travel in ellipses).[46] Although Galileo invented a new and improved telescope and came up with some important findings—e.g., the existence of mountains on the moon, satellites orbiting Jupiter, and the phases of Venus—he was mistaken on a variety of other points, including the comparative speed of pendulums of different sizes. He also held that the sun is stationary when, in fact, it orbits the center of its galaxy.[47]

THE HISTORICAL SETTING

Did Church leaders extend themselves beyond the area of their competence and jurisdiction? From today's standpoint, the answer would undoubtedly be yes; but not so by the standards of the time. Urban and his theologians were merely living up to seventeenth-century expectations. The Catholic Church, as founder of the university system, occupied a privileged place in research and publication; hence it was viewed as the guardian of education, as well as a natural arbiter of academic disputes. The Church has long since lost its monopoly on education—it still educates, but only as one among many—and so its current position is rather different. Fearful of overstepping the boundaries of political correctness, it now maintains a studied silence on matters of scientific controversy. The shift in power has been so great that it is hard to imagine a time when the present-day dichotomy between miter and mortarboard was unheard of, when schools such as Oxford and Cambridge, Harvard, Yale, and Princeton operated as institutions for the training of clergymen.

Modern-day parallels to the trial of Galileo are few and far between. Hitler's Germany resisted so-called "Jewish physics," and during the days of Stalinist oppression, Soviet insistence on Lysenko genetics led to agricultural disaster. Today's evolutionists do battle with Creationists, along with proponents of intelligent design. For many years, one could not teach evolution. Now it is hard to teach anything else. Still, nothing in our time compares with the way science and religion interacted during the age of Galileo.

Catholic leaders were not alone in critiquing a scientific theory that appeared highly dubious. Luther called Copernicus a "fool," and Melanchthon, another prominent Reformation leader, referred to the Pole's theory as "absurd."[48] Johannes Kepler, a Lutheran astronomer famous for his laws of planetary motion, could not find employment at Protestant Tübingen University because he supported Galileo. He also lost two teaching posts at Lutheran schools and was excommunicated by his church because he taught—correctly, as it turned out—that the moon was a solid body instead of "a lesser light to rule the night." Galileo's works landed on the Catholic index of forbidden books, but Protestants had indexes of their own and thought nothing of expelling university professors for heresy, including Newton's successor at Cambridge. Calvin burned Servetus' edition of the Bible; Henry VIII burned Tyndale's version, and during the 1600s, Oxford University under Protestant leadership burned dozens of volumes, including Hobbes's *Leviathan*.[49]

GALILEO AS THEOLOGIAN

There is also the matter of Galileo's theology. A learned cardinal once remarked that "the intention of the Holy Ghost is to teach us how one goes to heaven, not how the heavens go." He was right, of course, and Galileo agreed, holding that the Bible need not be taken literally when it describes the sun as "standing still" (for Joshua).[50] No one could accuse him of being overly literal in his approach to Scripture. But when he wrote that "we can rather easily remove the opposition of Scripture" to science "with the mere admission that we do not grasp its [Scripture's] true meaning" he was sailing into dangerous waters because he was suggesting the possibility of a conflict between science and Scripture, which the Church has never recognized.[51]

Still more objectionable was his suggestion that the Church's trust in biblical inerrancy be restricted to "articles concerning . . . faith which are firm enough so that there is no danger of any valid and effective doctrine ever rising against them. . . . The authority of the Holy Writ has merely the aim of persuading men of those articles and propositions which are necessary for their salvation and surpass all human reason," and so "no one should fix the meaning of passages of Scripture" except where salvation and the foundations of faith are concerned.[52] In holding that one's confidence in the Bible should be limited to matters of faith and morals, he was flying in the face of hallowed tradition. Indeed, as previously mentioned, the Church, to this day, admits no exception to the rule of biblical inerrancy.[53]

Galileo's pronouncements on scriptural exegesis touched a sensitive nerve because private interpretation of the Bible, the touchstone of the Protestant Reformation, was not something the Vatican wished to encourage, and Galileo, a layman untrained in theology, seemed to be overstepping his authority.[54] Beyond this, in holding that nature is "inexorable and immutable," that she "never transgresses the terms of the laws imposed on her," he seemed to posit a God who sets the universe in motion and leaves it to its own devices.[55] This is the "clockmaker" conception of God popular with Deists, as opposed to the Catholic view that God can and does suspend the laws of nature. What Galileo thought of miracles is not clear, but his teaching on natural immutability lends itself to skepticism. It is a comparatively short step to go from there to Jefferson's expunging of miracles from the New Testament Gospels.

Because the Florentine was ambiguous, because he was hard to pin down, the final summation of the Church's case in June 1633 stopped short of condemning him on theological grounds; but, not surprisingly, it held him to be "vehemently *suspected* of heresy" (italics added for emphasis).[56]

THE ROLE OF CHARACTER

Finally, there is the issue of character. We have focused on Galileo's ideas because they are of paramount importance. But personal makeup is relevant, too, insofar as it affects the political climate. This was a man who took delight in discomfiting his academic peers, on one occasion describing a Jesuit critic he believed he had vanquished as "writhing" like an "injured snake."[57] Had he possessed the humility and intellectual integrity of Poland's Copernicus (1473–1543), who fathered the modern theory of heliocentrism, it is doubtful that he would ever have clashed with

Church authorities. Copernicus dedicated his path-breaking *De Revolutionibus* to the pope, and it was respectfully received once a preface was added, making clear that the author was merely setting forth a hypothesis. Galileo, on the other hand, was neither diplomatic nor honest. He committed perjury at his 1633 trial, took credit for discoveries not his own, fathered illegitimate children, and appeared to ridicule the pope in his book, *Dialogue on the Two Great World Systems*, putting into the mouth of the clown, Simplicio, arguments that the pope himself is thought to have proposed.[58]

In sum, it was wrong of the pope's theological commission to state in its final sentence that heliocentrism is "explicitly contrary to Holy Scripture."[59] Dom Olivieri, head of the Dominican Order and commissary of the Holy Office, issued a formal apology in 1825 for the Church's handling of the Galileo affair, and Pope John Paul II apologized for the impression given that science is not free to operate independently.[60] At the same time, one must distinguish between papal-appointed commissions and the papacy itself. Pope Urban VIII, under whose jurisdiction Galileo was sentenced in 1633, had long contended that the Church would "never condemn" heliocentrism as "heretical, but only as rash," and there is nothing to indicate that he ever changed his mind.[61] Although he allowed the final judgment of the Theological Commission to stand, he did not sign it personally. Lastly, according to Vatican Council I, which framed the Church's definition of papal teaching authority, infallibility operates only when the Holy Father formally addresses the entire Church on matters of faith or morals, and this did not happen in 1633.

Chapter 9

THE CHURCH:
EVER ANCIENT,
EVER NEW

We have given a good deal of thought to the Crusades, the Spanish Inquisition, and the trial of Galileo because textbooks have bent these episodes out of shape. But in attempting to demythologize the past, we must not lose sight of the present. For a half century or more, the spiritual life of the industrial West has been in free fall. Yet people by the millions have poured into the Church—fifteen million in a single year while John Paul II was pope (1978–2005). The indefatigable Pole, who found time to welcome a million visitors a year to the Vatican while traveling seven hundred thousand miles and visiting over one hundred countries, addressed an audience of four million in Manila, and when he flew to the United States, no fewer than two million Bostonians turned out to hear him—in the rain!

John Paul was so magnetic and so holy that people in record numbers chose the consecrated life. During his pontificate, vocations to the priesthood and religious life rose 10 percent annually, and by 2005 the number of seminarians preparing for ordination had increased by 65 percent in Latin America, 125 percent in Asia, and over 300 percent in Africa. More and more Catholics returned to the Sacrament of Reconciliation. When World Youth Day 2000 was held in the Eternal City, the Circus Maximus overflowed with confessionals—two hundred approximately— and major basilicas remained open for Confession until 11 p.m.

Such vitality, inexplicable in merely human terms, has been a hallmark of Catholic history. When a majority of Greeks and Russians left the Church during the eleventh century, Hungarians, Danes, and Normans poured in. Luther and Calvin attracted hundreds of thousands, but New World missionaries under the banner of Spain laid the groundwork for a compensatory influx of millions. Even in areas where the Faith was persecuted, there were always those willing to exchange worldly pomp for the joy of conscious integrity. Sweden's Queen Christina (1626–89) gave up an entire kingdom to follow the dictates of her conscience. And how she must have smiled down from her heavenly perch in the year 2005 when a hundred of her compatriots, including atheists, Pentecostals, Muslims, and Jews (as well as Lutherans) followed her example!

THE CALIBER OF CONVERTS

On the same path as Christina but separated from her by a stretch of two or three centuries, John Henry Newman and Ronald Knox would come from Oxford. From Norway, with everything to lose and nothing to gain, would come Sigrid Undset, Nobel Prize winner in literature. British journalists G. K. Chesterton and Malcolm Muggeridge courted obloquy when they converted, and to their names could be added: Israel Zolli, chief rabbi of Rome; Graham Douglas Leonard, former Anglican bishop of London; William Farmer, one of the world's leading Bible scholars; and media guru Marshall McLuhan. Rabbi Zolli, who entered the Church at the end of World War II, was a renowned expert on the Talmud with many books to his credit. If anyone ever contemplated professional suicide before taking the leap it was he, and the question is why? Why would someone of Zolli's brilliance be attracted to a religion regarded by the academy as little more than superstition?

What is remarkable is that people abandon Catholicism every year as a result of ignorance or backsliding, but virtually all who travel in the opposite direction have been known for their intellectual acumen and virtue. Elizabeth Ann Seton of New York is typical. A devout Episcopalian struck by the soundness of Catholic teaching on the Eucharist, she studied the Faith, entered the Church at the close of the eighteenth century, became a nun, and, after receiving her sister-in-law into the Church, went on to found the parochial school system of America. In the act of converting, she plunged from the highest social standing to the lowest; yet she positively beamed, and over the years Anglicans and Episcopalians of comparable social and intellectual standing have followed in her footsteps. In England, where Catholicism was long regarded as tantamount to treason, twelve thousand converted annually during the 1930s, and since then, well over a thousand Anglican clergymen have gone over to Rome, four hundred on the aftermath of the 1992 General Synod vote to ordain women. Along parallel lines, many Episcopal priests crossed the Tiber, seventy-nine in a single year (2005), and often at great personal cost. One of them became a greeter at a retail store.

THE CHURCH IN AMERICA

In America, an estimated two hundred thousand converted during the five-year period 1992–97. Considering that the Church normally requires a preliminary year of study and that anti-Catholicism is "the deepest bias in the history of the American people," according to historian Arthur Schlesinger Sr., such a figure is impressive. A black pastor from Detroit brought fifty congregants with him, while a Pennsylvania minister with a degree from Yale Divinity School delivered a fold of seventy.[1]

Sad to say, a great many American nuns have abandoned their vows in recent years, but the same period has seen the birth of a host of dynamic new religious orders, among them the Sisters of Life and the Franciscans of the Renewal. Dominican teaching sisters in traditional habits are booming, with one Michigan-based group receiving more postulants than it can comfortably accommodate. Also on the intellectual front, the *New Oxford Review*, a Catholic journal of commentary and opinion, was founded by converts of Episcopal and Anglican background. Catholic Answers, another recent entry, has mushroomed into the largest apologetics organization in the nation, if not the world. Although the media has never been sympathetic to the Faith—Paul dubbed Satan "the prince of the power of the air" (Eph. 2:2)—there have been significant gains even on the devil's own turf. Catholic radio stations have increased in number from only a dozen in the year 2000 to well over a hundred.

Individuals have moved mountains. Mother Angelica, a simple nun raised in a humble home, was able, with two hundred dollars, to launch EWTN, a religious broadcasting station that within a decade of its founding in 1981 became the largest enterprise of its kind in the world, reaching a hundred million viewers in over a hundred countries.[2] Another American, Fr. Paul Marx, OSB, launched Human Life

International in the 1980s, and within seven years HLI had twenty-two offices on five continents supporting pro-lifers in one hundred four nations on a budget of less than one percent of Planned Parenthood.

THE CHURCH ABROAD

Overseas, the French Community of St. John founded in 1975 by Père Marie Dominique has over eight hundred monks, and Opus Dei, a religious organization established by the Spanish saint Josemaría Escrivá in the 1920s to sanctify the laity, now has something on the order of eighty-five thousand members in sixty countries. It operates scores of residences and cultural centers, along with dozens of universities, colleges, and technical schools. The Missionaries of Charity, Mother Teresa's order, had four thousand sisters in the field when she died in 1997, and since then another thousand have joined. At last count they were operating 757 hospitals, clinics, hostels, and youth centers in 134 countries.[3] In Calcutta alone, they saved over three thousand children from abortion and took in over forty thousand homeless. AIDS patients, lepers, and the mentally ill—all have felt the touch of their loving hands.

Firepower of this kind demands explanation. Where did Katharine Drexel and her fellow founders and foundresses find the strength to give themselves totally to the Lord? From whence did Fr. Damien derive the grace to sacrifice his life for a colony of lepers? Robert Louis Stevenson said of the Belgian saint's work on Molokai:

> I have seen sights that cannot be told and heard stories that cannot
> be repeated. Yet I never admired my poor race so much nor (strange
> as it may seem) loved life more than in the [Catholic] settlement
> [on Molokai].

Damien, he declared, was "a man with all the grime and paltriness of mankind, but a saint and hero all the more for that."[4]

Catholic history is rich in Drexels and Damiens. In the fourth century, St. Catherine of Alexandria turned down marriage to a Byzantine emperor rather than apostatize; subsequently, after the emperor married, she converted the empress and two hundred soldiers, all of whom gave their lives for the Faith. The spiked wheel used in her execution fell apart before it could do her harm, and so powerful were her arguments that they brought fifty pagan philosophers into the fold.[5]

AUTHORITY IS KEY

The key to such dynamism, I submit, is a special kind of assurance, which brings us back, full circle, to the notion of blueprints. Matthew tells us that Jesus' listeners were astonished because he taught with unparalleled authority.[6] "No man ever spoke like this man!" they exclaimed (Jn. 7:46). The harshest rebukes of Jeremiah and Ezekiel were nothing in comparison with the way Jesus smote scribes, Pharisees, elders, and priests with the rod of his mouth.[7] One look from the Savior was all it took to send hardened soldiers sprawling to the ground (Jn. 18:6).

Today, if one seeks the equivalent of John the Baptist's chastisement of Herod Antipas or Christ's rebuke of the Samaritan woman (for living with a man not her husband), there is only one place to go: Rome.[8] Popes in recent years have stood up to fornicators and contracepters, abortionists and euthanists, militant homosexuals and radical feminists. The Archbishop of Canterbury and the Eastern Orthodox patriarchs are considerably less outspoken because Protestantism is based on the principle of private interpretation of Scripture, which, as seen earlier, breeds disunity. Choose three men who are unfamiliar with Scripture, ask them to read the New Testament and tell them to decide, on the basis of what they have learned from their reading, how many sacraments Christ instituted. One will say seven, another four, and the third none.[9] Protestants have split into scores of thousands of competing sects, and such splitting will continue because they lack consensus on the meaning of the Word.[10] Without authority, there is division—on everything from doctrine to the proper form for religious services.[11]

THE IMPORTANCE OF UNITY

Again and again, Scripture touches on the need for unity. When Korah, Dathan, and Abiram asked Moses what right he had to exalt himself "above the assembly," all three were struck dead.[12] Miriam, on questioning her brother's mandate, contracted leprosy.[13] Centuries later, Jesus said he was building a "church," not "churches" (plural), and by making Peter the head of this Church and praying at the Last Supper that all might be one, he established the basis for an unbroken line of command that has lasted two thousand years.[14] Peter and Paul had their differences, but neither questioned the need for unity. Peter condemned private interpretation, warning against "false teachers among you, who will . . . bring in destructive heresies," while Paul, for his part, said the same thing in different words.[15] "Take note," he wrote, "of those who create dissensions and difficulties, in opposition to the doctrine which you have been taught; avoid them."[16]

If one consults the Patrologia, one will find St. Ignatius of Antioch (d. 107) calling unity "the greatest of goods" and warning that to follow a schismatic leader is to lose one's soul.[17] St. Irenaeus writes that Christians have "but one soul" and "one mouth."[18] Two centuries later, Augustine calls schism a "sacrilege," holding that "there is no just cause for severing the unity of the Church."[19]

Dissidents there have always been. As early as the first and second centuries, various heresies flourished under the name of Gnosticism. By the seventh century when Islam burst upon the scene, there were over a hundred heretical groups in the Middle East, ranging from Eucratites and Pepuzians to priestesses who called themselves Christians and confected the Holy Eucharist with infants' blood.[20]

The Church countered these centrifugal tendencies by coming out with a catechism known as the *Didaché* or "The Teaching" (c. AD 60–100). Quoted by the Church Fathers and written, most likely, by Peter as Bishop of Antioch before he moved to Rome, "The Teaching of the Lord to the Gentiles Through the Twelve Apostles" (its full title) covers everything from sacraments and prophecy to liturgy and morals in sixteen chapters. As mentioned earlier, it contains injunctions against birth control (the taking of "potions"), abortion, infanticide, and sodomy. Wednesdays and Fridays were days of fasting, and the faithful were bidden to "keep away from every bad man."

Over the years, the Church continued to put out catechisms. The Council of Trent published one in the sixteenth century and in 1994 Pope John Paul II produced an eight hundred-page compendium of Church teaching that not only contains nothing contrary to the *Didaché*, but quotes it.[21] Bible-based and historically documented, the latest version lays out, in reasoned form, a Church position on virtually every conceivable topic, and its worldwide acceptance is one of the leading indicators of the unity Catholicism enjoys relative to other groups.

Papal encyclicals are another means of strengthening the faithful. When the Lambeth Conference of the Anglican Church voted in 1930 to approve artificial contraception and other denominations followed suit, Pius XI responded with *Casti Connubii* (1930).[22] Thirty-eight years later, notwithstanding a climate of opinion in the industrial West that was distinctly contraceptive and a papal commission's vote *in favor* of contraception (sixty to four), Pope Paul VI affixed his name to an encyclical that not only upheld traditional teaching on sexual morality, but also foretold with stunning specificity the catastrophic results of a contraceptive mentality. *Humanae*

Vitae (Of Human Life) foresaw a decline in chastity, a rise in conjugal infidelity, a rapid rise in abortion, the growth of a movement to legalize euthanasia, forced sterilization by totalitarian governments, and a surge in violence against women. Human bodies, it warned, would be treated as machines—to wit, *in vitro* procedures and surrogate motherhood. Every one of these predictions has come true.

The spectacle of a single individual bereft of worldly power breasting a tidal wave of criticism, much of it from within his own fold, was something to behold. *Humanae Vitae* drew a clear line of demarcation and, over time, it won converts because of the contrast between Paul VI's firmness and the position taken by other religious leaders. Once Protestants yielded to popular pressure on contraception, it was only a matter of time before they would yield willy-nilly on abortion and same sex marriage. The Episcopal Church voted to ordain men who are openly homosexual, and Sweden's Lutherans installed a registered lesbian as Bishop of Stockholm. Small wonder that President George W. Bush described Catholicism as "a rock in a raging sea."[23]

HOLINESS AND UBIQUITY

Converts, like fish, must be caught by the head, and many of them are impressed by two thousand years of papal firmness on faith and morals, interpreting it as a sign of infallibility. Some are more apt to be touched by reasons of the heart. On entering a Catholic church for the first time, they may be struck by the atmosphere of hushed silence, accompanied by the scent of candle smoke and the aroma of incense announcing the Real Presence of Christ in the tabernacle.

Others are impressed by the sheer ubiquity of the Church. In remote villages, as well as a rising number of airports and shopping malls, Mass and confession are available on a regular basis. Priests bring solace and comfort to prison inmates, as well as to patients in hospitals and nursing homes. They appear at the scene of fires. They lead soldiers into battle (all the military chaplains who have received the United States Medal of Honor since the time of the Civil War are Catholic). They even minister to circus troupes!

CATHOLICITY AND DEMOCRACY

For those who value diversity, Catholicism is uniquely international. The Messiah was to be "a light for the nations," and, in keeping with Jesus' decision to dispatch his apostles to the farthest reaches of the world, all races and nations have found a home in Rome. In cities like New York and Los Angeles, Mass is offered in dozens of languages.[24] Priests of African origin are currently assisting American pastors, and Mexico, which has twelve thousand men studying for the priesthood, is sending missionaries to Europe.

Still another feature of Catholicism that conforms to Gospel specifications is its democratic openness. Jesus set the example by dining at the home of a leper; Peter stayed with a humble tanner; and Mary Magdalene, a woman "from whom seven demons had gone out," served the apostolic band alongside Joanna, a woman of the court. Matthew, a despised tax collector, took his place beside John the Evangelist, who, like John the Baptist, had priestly connections; and later, Paul, a member of the Jewish elite, would instruct his flock to "associate with the lowly." On the Tiber, as in Corinth and Jerusalem, there was a social amalgam, and the tradition continues.[25] Every Sunday, university professors and millionaires rub shoulders with nursemaids, cleaning ladies, and policemen. One of India's bishops hails from the nation's lowest class, and while the majority of popes, like the majority of political leaders, come from the middle and upper classes, there are many exceptions. Adrian IV (1154–59), an Englishman, was the son of a laborer. Sixtus V (1585–90), who did more than any other pontiff to give Rome its architectural tone, began as a swineherd. Pope St. Pius X (1903–1914), who has been declared a saint, rose from the peasantry, and John XXIII (1958–1963), the father of Vatican II, was the son of a tenant farmer (as well as one of fourteen children). More recently, Popes John Paul II and Benedict XVI were raised by fathers who made their living in the military and constabulary.

THE GRACE OF CONFESSION

Unconfessed guilt weighs heavily on the human soul judging from the number of people who have recourse to the psychiatrist's couch, and so it is not surprising that certain converts have been attracted to the Faith by the beauty of the Sacrament of Reconciliation, formerly known as Penance. It costs nothing, is available weekly (daily in cities), and those in need can approach a clergyman at any hour of the day or night, certain that what they say in private will remain confidential—two Czech priests, John Nepomucen (c. 1340–1393) and Jan Sarkander (1576–1620), gave their very lives to preserve the seal of confession. One must, of course, do penance and strive to amend one's life; but today's penances are relatively light compared with the Middle Ages when a prescribed course of action might take months or even years to complete.

Catholics may dispense with the Sacrament in situations where it is unavailable provided they resolve to avail themselves of it at the first opportunity. They may also confess directly to God unless their sin is mortal (i.e. deadly). There is much to be gained, however, from a regular examination of conscience followed by an admission of minor faults, along with major ones, to a good confessor. In this way one engages the devil at the outer perimeter of one's defenses, and the enemy finds it harder to reach the citadel.

By enabling the penitent who is truly sorry to return to life's battlefield with justice as a shield (Eph. 6:14) and "the hope of salvation" as a helmet (1 Thess. 5:8), confession is to the soul what a shower is to the body or an oil change is to the automobile. In the process of cleansing, it imparts a wonderful feeling of lightness, and those who go down on their knees and say "sorry" to God, firmly resolved to change their lives, derive an added benefit: they find it easier to say "sorry" to their spouses and business associates.

The whole idea of getting right with God by means of auricular confession sounds very Catholic, but the Anglican C. S. Lewis went weekly to confession (of a non-sacramental kind) during his most productive years, and Lutherans of the Missouri Synod are returning to the practice after being away from it for centuries. It is one of the twelve steps of Alcoholics Anonymous, and according to Carl Jung (1875–1961), the founder of analytic psychology, it satisfies a deeply felt human need. Out of thousands of patients seen by Jung over the years, only five or six were practicing Catholics.

There is a scriptural basis for all of the seven sacraments (see Appendix B), and for Reconciliation we have Christ's words to his apostles on rising from the dead: "If you forgive the sins of any, they are forgiven; if you retain the sins of any, they are retained." Obviously, no priest can decide whether a sin should be "retained" or forgiven unless it is confessed, and it is difficult to mistake Jesus' intent when in pronouncing these words he breathed upon his disciples, signifying that sacramental forgiveness is life-giving. The only other time God ever breathed on man was when he blew life into Adam![26]

There is also Tradition dating back to the early Church. The *Didaché* (AD 60–100) exhorts Christians to confess serious sin before receiving Communion, and Tertullian (c. 150–230) urges his readers "not [to] hesitate to make use of the remedy [of penance]." Knowing that some were "inclined to draw back" because they found themselves confessing the same faults over and over again, he assured them that "medicine must be repeated for repeated sickness."[27]

As an aside, one of the most frequently prescribed "medicines" in days of old was fasting, and this, too, is featured in Scripture. We have Jesus' command: "The days will come, when the bridegroom is taken away from them, and then they will fast" (Lk. 5:35). The Lord himself fasted for forty days, and we have the added example of Moses, David, Elijah, Judith, and Anna the prophetess, not to mention Paul, who fasted frequently.[28]

Like confession, fasting fosters humility and stiffens the will by subordinating passion to reason. Those who engage in it express solidarity with Jesus in his Passion; and because they save on grocery bills, they are better able to give to the poor. They are also healthier physically because fasting removes toxins from the body; and again, Catholics are not alone. Jews fast on Yom Kippur, Muslims do so during the month of Ramadan, and the discipline is not unfamiliar to Protestants— Dr. Bill Bright, founder of the Campus Crusade for Christ, called for fasting, and long before Bright's time, during the early days of the Republic, four out of the first five presidents proclaimed days of fasting and prayer.

In short, fasting is a moral good hallowed by tradition. Still, modern man winces at the thought of any kind of mortification not undertaken in the name of sports. Every day, runners suffer heart failure; football players sustain concussions. Every year, high school students die by the dozen of bodily injury. Olympians have been known to abstain from marital relations for six months to a year in order to win a gold or silver medal. Such people are lauded for their "commitment." Yet when spiritual athletes mortify themselves to gain a prize more precious than anything awarded by Olympic committees, they go down as fanatics.

LOVE OF LIFE

Returning, though, to the question of why people of the present age convert to Catholicism, natural law and the Word of God are heavily on the side of an organization that bears witness to the value of human life. In the Old Testament, Jeremiah tells us that God knew him before he formed him in his mother's womb (Jer. 1:5), and in Luke's Gospel, an unborn infant, John the Baptist, leaps at the approach of another unborn infant, Jesus (Lk. 1:44). Again and again, the question raised by the prophet Isaiah comes back to haunt a nation that has witnessed a holocaust of fifty million babies: "Can a mother forget her infant, be without tenderness for the child of her womb?" (Is. 49:15. CE). Verse after verse in the New Testament tells of Christ's tender love for children, unmatched in the annals of religious founders.[29]

He embraced them, blessed them, and held them up as models of trust and humility. On one occasion, taking a child and placing it by his side, he said, "Whoever receives one such child in my name receives me . . . it is not the will of my Father who is in heaven that one of these little ones should perish."[30]

It matters not whether a child is handicapped, illegitimate, or unborn. If he is conceived by Catholics who take their faith seriously, he is safe. Nor does it matter how many siblings he has. The Church reserves a special place on her honor role for parents of large families, believing, in the words of Mother Teresa of Calcutta, that "the child must be something very special if God himself became a child." When parochial schools were staffed by sisters, they charged less for each successive sibling, then waived tuition altogether after the third or fourth; and even today, there are schools where this is true.

Catholics, who make up 25 percent of the US population, furnish the lion's share of the nation's anti-abortion leadership. Hundreds of non-profit pregnancy centers owe their existence to Catholic action, and Church members who pray and offer counsel outside aborturaries have saved thousands of lives while suffering taunts and, in some cases, receiving jail sentences. Joan Andrews Bell, arrested twenty-five times for her work on behalf of the innocents, spent three and a half years in prison, much of it in solitary confinement, for trying to warn expectant mothers of the devastating psychological effects of abortion. Catholics are closing hospitals and orphanages rather than bend the knee to political correctness, and a small but significant number who are engaged in such fields as medicine, pharmacy, and the law have sacrificed their careers in response to Jesus' assurance that "he who loses his life for my sake will find it" (Mt. 10:39).

A CHURCH OF MIRACLES

A last point worth mentioning in connection with Catholic drawing power is the Church's steady witness to the power of divine intervention. It is only logical to assume that the stream of miracles that began at Creation, that continued under Moses, and that reached a climax with the advent of Christ is ongoing. Jesus promised his followers they would work signs, and they did.[31] Peter and Paul raised the dead and made miraculous escapes.[32] Centuries later, the venerable Ambrose and erudite Augustine vouched for similar marvels in their time, and the ministries of saints such as Patrick and Boniface were studded with wonders.[33] St. Dominic, who is reliably reported to have cured hundreds, raised at least three from the dead. No less than 873 miracles are documented in the case of Vincent Ferrer. St. Bernard and the Curé of Ars left behind amazing records as well, and in our own time, hundreds of cures are reliably attributed to Padre Pio, who bore the stigmata. Well might the modern day Catholic say, as Moses did: "What great nation is there that has a god so near to it as the LORD our God is to us?" (Deut. 4:7).

Three more miracles furnish as clear an indication of ongoing divine intervention as anything else in two thousand years with the exception of Fatima, as mentioned in chapter 1, and they occurred in three very different countries: the United States, France, and Mexico.

THE STAIRS AT SANTA FE

Nuns in the late nineteenth century erected a chapel in Santa Fe, New Mexico, and there today one will see a handsome spiral staircase built in answer to nine days of community prayer by a mysterious individual who charged nothing for his work, declined to give his name, and never used a single nail, screw, or drop of glue. To this day, architects and engineers marvel at the sight of a free-standing, self-supporting structure that, in the course of two 360 degree turns, rises twenty feet to the choir loft. They have no idea how it can remain sturdy after almost a century of use, and when a respected forest technologist analyzed the wood in 1996, it was found to be unique.[34]

LOURDES

Soon after the Santa Fe staircase was built, a Nobel Laureate in medicine by the name of Alexis Carrel visited Lourdes, a lovely French village nestled in the foothills of the Pyrenees. Here the Blessed Virgin appeared in 1858 to a devout peasant girl named Bernadette Soubirous. After asking for prayer and penance, Mary directed the girl to dig in the ground with her hands until water from a hidden spring began to flow—water that would grow from a mere trickle to thirty-two thousand gallons per day.

When Carrel went to Lourdes, he was on the verge of becoming a world-famous pioneer in the suturing of blood vessels and preservation of tissue. But a practicing Catholic he was not, until he examined a woman with tubercular peritonitis in its final stage. Her abdomen, swollen to the size of a late-term pregnancy, was rock solid, and she was so weak that her hometown physician feared for her life en route to the shrine. Before Carrel's very eyes, the tumor, after contact with the miraculous waters of the Grotto, shrank so dramatically that within the space of an hour it was gone. So moved was the young medic that in addressing the Lyons University Medical School he said he could not rule out the possibility of divine intervention. His words were met with chilling silence followed by a cry of "Get out!"

The other half of the story concerns a Jew by the name of Franz Werfel, who was amazed at the stringency of the requirements for certification of cures. Hundreds of alleged miracles were reported every year at Lourdes, but only a small fraction met the criteria for official filing, and of these, only a handful were formally endorsed. Dossiers in Werfel's time were reviewed once a year by a panel of twenty doctors from all over Europe, and then, as now, the patient's malady had to be (a) incurable, (b) organic or caused by injuries, and (c) demonstrably serious based on verifiably trustworthy documents. In addition, the cure itself had to be sudden or instantaneous with a total renewal of bodily functions observable over a period of five years.

Werfel was even more impressed by the fact that four days after dying a painful death at the age of thirty-five from tuberculosis of the bone, Bernadette's body was found to be odorless and well preserved. In the course of canonization proceedings thirty-nine years later, the body was exhumed and found, once more, to be incorrupt. Following reinterment, the devil's advocate objected that embalming had never been *officially* ruled out, and so it was that in 1925, seven years after the first exhumation, a second confirmed the absence of artificial preservatives.[35] Werfel later wrote a book about Lourdes which became a movie—*The Song of Bernadette*. By this time Dr. Carrel, *persona non grata* at Lyons, had accepted a position at New York's Rockefeller University, and his riveting memoir, *The Voyage to Lourdes* (1950), left little doubt that an angel similar if not identical to the one that worked cures in Jesus' time at the Pool of Bethesda was still active.[36]

Apparitions such as those reported at Lourdes and Fatima are often thought of as Catholic, but a more accurate term would be "Judeo-Christian" because Jacob wrestled with an angel, and an angel visited Daniel. In the New Testament, Mary sees Gabriel, just as Paul sees the risen Lord, and both he and Peter are rescued by angels.[37] Lourdes recalls what happened at the Pool of Bethesda, while Fatima reminds one of the solar miracles worked by Joshua and Isaiah. Seven centuries after Daniel's companions survived Nebuchadnezzar's white hot furnace, Bishop Polycarp of Smyrna (AD 155) resisted burning at the stake, and Christian martyrs at Tyre escaped the jaws of ravenous beasts much the way Daniel did.[38] Lastly, one can compare Lourdes and Fatima with the wonders worked by Moses in Egypt. In all three cases, a luminous sign of the presence of God quickly lost its appeal.[39] Once Moses' people reached the desert, they forgot all about the wonderful things that happened in Egypt, and soon after Bernadette and Lucia witnessed to the power of divine intervention, it was business as usual in France and Portugal. The only miracle known to have converted people en masse—six to nine million in seventeen years—occurred at Guadalupe on the outskirts of Mexico City, and this, once again, is a story.

GUADALUPE

In the year 1531 the Blessed Mother appeared to an Indian by the name of Juan Diego. After appealing for prayer and mortification, she asked that a chapel be built on the spot for the glorification of her Son, and as a sign of her presence, she instructed Juan to gather flowers out of season on a rocky hill where they were not normally found. Being a man of faith, he did as he was told, wrapping the flowers in his cactus cloak or "tilma." Then, armed with his special bouquet, he approached the bishop with the request for a new church. Bishop Zumárraga was a true friend of the Indians, but he remained skeptical until Juan unfurled his tilma which, to the utter amazement of all, bore a brilliant portrait of the Virgin, perfectly proportioned, and magnificent in detail. The world's foremost experts on pigmentation cannot determine what material was used in place of paint because ultra red testing has ruled out anything of an animal, vegetable, or mineral nature, and synthetics were unknown at the time. Whatever the substance, it never penetrated the canvas; and yet there is no evidence of a primer. One more enigma. Most curious of all, cactus cloth normally decomposes within twenty years; but Juan's tilma, exhibited in the open air and exposed to candle smoke and the touch of human hands and for over a hundred years, has been on display for *nearly half a millennium.*

In 1921, a terrorist concealed a bomb in a vase of roses and detonated it below the tilma. The force of the explosion bent a nearby bronze crucifix nearly in half. But Juan's cloak, along with its glass case, was miraculously spared, and it remains as radiant as ever. More recently, an environmental systems engineer with a degree from Cornell University, using a digital process employed by satellites and space probes, succeeded in magnifying the image twenty-five hundred times its normal size, and what he found was incredible. In the pupil and iris of each of the Virgin's eyes are imprints that portray figures closely resembling those of a period painting. An Indian is shown unfolding a tilma and there is an elderly man with a white beard, presumably Zumárraga. The figures are also differently proportioned depending on the eye in which they appear, which is exactly how real eyes reflect objects put before them.

One can even make out optic blood vessels and nerves so microscopically small that they could never have been inserted by human hands.[40]

Catholics might well echo the words of the Psalmist, "The LORD has done great things for us" (Psalms 126:3), as there is no Jewish Guadalupe, no Islamic Lourdes, and no Protestant Fatima. To be sure, one can be a Catholic in good standing without believing in Marian apparitions; but it is far more logical in the above-cited instances to believe than not to believe. Going strictly by the evidence, it would appear that Jesus' promise of miracles, like his promise of Petrine power, was for all time, and if this is so, then it is on the pages of Catholic history that Christ's promise is most strikingly fulfilled.[41]

MORE ON MARY

The irony of ironies is that at the very time Marian devotion was growing in Mexico and other parts of Latin America, it was waning in Protestant areas. But interestingly, it never entirely disappeared even among the followers of Luther and Calvin. George Washington hung a striking portrait of the Blessed Mother in the busiest room of his home, and Sir Walter Scott died praying a *Stabat Mater* composed by a Franciscan monk. A half century later we find Wagner's hero, Tannhäuser, begging Mary to deliver him from the power of Venus, while the opera's heroine, Elizabeth, does likewise, and both prayers are answered.

Add another fifty years and Harriet Beecher Stowe will bring back rosaries from Europe. The author of *Uncle Tom's Cabin*, along with the Quaker proprietors of the Mohonk Mountain House in the Catskills, will hang Madonnas on the walls of their homes, and John Singer Sargent, one of the foremost Protestant painters, will execute murals for the Boston Public Library that illustrate the fifteen mysteries of the Rosary. Edvard Grieg will compose an *Ave Maris Stella*, George Bernard Shaw will call upon Mary to save him, and Henry Adams, a convert to the Episcopal Church, will profess "adoration" for one who, in his words, "remains the most intensely and most widely and most personally felt of all characters divine or human or imaginary that ever existed among men ... No other has even remotely taken her place."[42]

Although Catholics are not required to develop a personal relationship with Mary, the results of such devotion have been spectacular. Pope John Paul II, in union with the world's bishops, consecrated Russia to the Immaculate Heart of Mary, and within five years, the Berlin Wall, which had been an immovable fixture of Marxism for over a generation, came tumbling down. In 1990 Marian devotion fuelled an insurrection in Lithuania that jolted the Red Army. After losing thirteen killed and hundreds wounded in a single day, freedom fighters began chanting, "Maria, Maria," and from that moment on they were invincible.[43] Lithuania's victory inspired the people of Estonia, and from there the movement spread to Latvia. By December 1991, the Soviet Union was officially dead, and it was on the feast day of the Queenship of Mary, August 22, 1992, that Lenin's statue was toppled in Moscow's Red Square, recalling Mary's prophetic words to the children of Fatima on July 13, 1917: to wit, that Russia would "spread her errors throughout the world," but "in the end . . . the Holy Father will consecrate Russia to me and she will be converted and a period of peace will be granted to the world." Once again religious icons were fashionable, and one, in particular, outsold all others: that of the Madonna and Child.

Orthodox believers continue to celebrate feast days honoring Mary, along with her parents Joachim and Anne, and she remains a force even in the secular West. The flag of the European Union, designed by a man who prayed the Rosary daily, features twelve stars on a field of blue. Blue is the Marian color, and the stars represent Mary's crown as described in the Book of Revelation (12:1).[44]

CONCLUSION

In my work as a street evangelist I am sometimes asked how it feels to be Catholic at a time when the American Church is at low ebb spiritually. "No different," I answer, "than it must have felt to be Catholic in pre-Cluny France or the England of Henry VIII." Along with its highs and lows, the Church has had its share of scapegraces beginning with Judas—Christ himself predicted that scandals were "sure to come," and "woe to him by whom they come!" (Lk. 17:1). But to judge an organization by its delinquents is to judge it wrongly, and when I shudder at the human side of an organization that is divine in origin, I simply recall three things that I know to be true beyond any shadow of doubt: Jesus of Nazareth claimed to be God, he made good on this claim by rising from the dead, and there is one and only one Church that meets all of the specifications laid down by the Gospel.

In the final analysis it is a matter of reason. Catholics do not assent to the doctrine of transubstantiation because it lifts the soul. They accept it on the strength of John 6 and other biblical passages. They do not rely on papal teaching because they shrink from doing their own thinking. Matthew 16:18–19, along with the testimony of early Church leaders leaves them no choice, and they are conscious of the broad sweep of history. There is not a single papal teaching in two thousand years that conflicts with anything found in Scripture. No pontiff, however dissolute, has ever set aside the teaching of another.[1] No occupant of the chair of Peter has ever accepted money or political favor in exchange for an unwarranted annulment. No individual who has ever been canonized, no seer whose claims have ever been recognized, no pilgrimage site that has ever been approved, no relic that has ever been endorsed by the Holy Father has failed to stand the test of time.

This is not to say that Catholics have nothing to learn from people of other faiths. Many of our separated brethren are exemplary in the way they study the Word of God and spread it. Ours is a society awash in consumerism, and the Amish emphasis on simplicity serves as a useful corrective. At a time when many are obsessed with preventive medicine, Christian Science places a wholesome reliance on God's Providence. Muslims bear witness to the need for modesty. Jewish insistence on strict observance of the Sabbath acts as an antidote to cavalier disregard of the Third Commandment, and the Jewish passion for education, coupled with a willingness on the part of those who are observant to wear the yarmulke and display the mezuzah, is edifying. Without exception, I respect men and women who strive with all their heart, mind, and soul to live by the light of their conscience.

Still, I would not have written this book if I didn't believe that those who harken to Catholic teaching will draw down the full panoply of God's grace. By deepening their relationship with Christ through the sacraments, they will experience true joy and lasting peace. No relief is greater than that felt by a penitent who hears a priest intone the words, "I absolve you from your sins in the name of the Father, and of the Son, and of the Holy Spirit." The Catechism (1449) reflects the consensus prayed for by Jesus and insisted on by Paul; and in the area of spiritual reading, few things this side of Scripture can compare with the lives of the saints.

The true seeker will be drawn to Catholicism because, with all of its failings, it has displayed a consistency in its teaching, a holiness in its saints, and a record of charitable work that is unique. There is a warmth about it that echoes the Lord's tenderness; there is a rigor about it that mirrors his stepped up demands; there is a timelessness about it that reflects the enduring nature of God's Word. Most of all, it makes sense, which gives it universal appeal, for to be human is to think, and to think is to believe.

NOTES

INTRODUCTION

1. John 8:58 (Confraternity edition of the Bible).

2. John 3:16; 8:51; 11:25–26; 14:6 ("I am the way . . . "). On the need to keep his commandments, see Matthew 7:21–23; Luke 6:49; John 15:10; 15:22.

3. Matthew 4:17; Mark 1:15; 2:5; John 20:22–23.

4. Plato's *Republic*, Book (361e in some editions) as cited by Cambridge historian Henry Chadwick in *The Oxford Illustrated History of Christianity* (1990), 21. Although the Greeks did not crucify, the Persians, Egyptians, and Romans did. As early as 615 BC the king of Persia crucified three thousand political opponents; and so, the Greeks of Plato's time would have been well aware of what they commonly referred to as "impaling." In the *Republic*, Socrates' interlocutor Glaucon is reporting what the "eulogists of injustice" say: "the just man who is thought unjust will be scourged, racked, bound—will have his eyes burnt out; and at last, after suffering every kind of evil, he will be impaled: Then he will understand that he ought to seem only, and not to be, just" (Jowett's translation). The word *anaskinduleuein*, translated as "impaled," is rare, and later authors took it to mean crucified (as translated by Allan Bloom). The passage enjoyed a wide currency among Christian writers, e.g., in the Acts of Apollonius (martyred in the AD 180s) in which Apollonius says, "Among the Greeks someone has said, 'The just man is whipped, beaten, bound, blinded in both eyes, and after he has suffered every evil, crucified.'" For a discussion of this idea as used by Christians, see Klaus Doering, *Exemplum Socratis : Studien zur Sokratesnachwirkung in der kynisch-stoischen Popularphilosophie der frühen Kaiserzeit und im frühen Christentum* (Wiesbaden, 1978) 145. My thanks to Professor Christopher Jones of Harvard University for much of the above information.

5. John 8:46.

6. For instances in which Jesus foretold his crucifixion, see Matthew 26:2; Mark 8:31; John 8:28; 12:32.

CHAPTER 1

1. For religion and health, both physical and mental, see Cornelia, "Churchgoing May Aid Health," *New York Times* [Science Watch Section] (November 4, 1997), 14; *Catholic Digest*, (February 1992): 1–2; Harold G. Koenig, Harvey Jay Cohen, Linda K. George, Judith C. Hays, David B. Larson, and Dan G. Blazer, "Attendance at Religious Services, Interleukin-6, and Other Biological Parameters of Immune Function in Older Adults," *The International Journal of Psychiatry in Medicine*, vol. 27, no. 3, (1997): 234 and 247; also H. G. Koenig, compiler, *Research on Religion and Aging: An Annotated Bibliography* (Westport, Conn: Greenwood Press, 1995); Harold George Koenig, *Is Religion Good for Your Health?* (Binghamton, NY: The Haworth Pastoral Press, 1997); Thomas W. Graham, Berton H. Kaplan, Joan C. Cornoni-Huntley, Sherman A. James, Caroline Becker, Curtis G. Hames, Siegfried Heyden, "Frequency of Church Attendance and Blood Pressure Elevation," *Journal of Behavioral Medicine*, vol 1, no. 1 (March, 1978): 37–43; David B. Larson, Harold G. Koenig, Berton H. Kaplan, Raymond S. Greenberg, Everett Logue, and Herman A Tyroler, "The Impacct of Religion on Men's Blood Pressure," *Journal of Religion and Health*, vol. 28, no. 4 (Winter/ December, 1989): 265–78; George W. Comstock and Kay B. Partridge, "Church Attendance and Health," *Journal of Chronic Diseases*, vol. 25, issue 12 (December,1972):665–72; William J. Strawbridge, Ph.D., Richard D. Cohen, MA, Sarah J. Shema, MS, and George A. Kaplan, Ph.D., "Frequent Attendance at Religious Services and Mortality Over Twenty-Eight Years," *American Journal of Public Health*, vol. 87, no. 6 (June, 1997): 957–61.

2. See Patrick Glynn, *God the Evidence* (Rocklin, CA: Prima Publishing, 1999), chapter 3. The following prayer attributed to Reinhold Niebuhr is at the core of the Alcoholics Anonymous program and has been for decades: "God grant me the serenity to accept the things I cannot change; courage to change the things I can; and wisdom to know the difference; living one day at a time; enjoying one moment at a time; accepting hardships as the pathway to peace; taking, as He did, this sinful world as it is, not as I would have it; trusting that He will make all things right if I surrender to his Will, that I may be reasonably happy in this life and supremely happy with him forever in the next. Amen."

3. Knight-Ridder News, "Nation's Leaders Must Recognize Religion's Power," American Family Association *Journal*, vol. 20, no. 4 (April 1996): 9; William Waters, O.S.A., "Staying Together: The Basics," *Catholic Digest* (August 1994): 79.

4. Ari L. Goldman, "Religion Notes: Churchgoers as Answer to I.R.S. Prayer," *New York Times* (April 20, 1991): 10; Samuel G. Freedman, "Atheists' Collection Plate, With Religious Inspiration," *New York Times* (April 3, 2010): A15.

5. For the Christian obligation to correct erring brethren, see Matthew 18:15–18; Luke 17:3; 1 Thessalonians 5:14; 1 Timothy 5:1–2; Titus 3:10. For the obligation to shun free thinkers and public sinners, see 1 Corinthians 5:9–13; 15:33; 2 Timothy 3:2–6.

6. Acts 2:46 (Christians prayed daily in the temple following the Ascension).

7. On the speed of light, see "World-Wise," *Wall Street Journal* (July 20, 2000): 1 (author unlisted).

8. Blaise Pascal, *Pensées* (New York: Pantheon, 1965 ed.), 29–31.

9. On the long-term fate of Babylon, see Isaiah 13:19–22; Jer. 51:26. For the return from Babylon and Isaiah's naming of Cyrus one hundred fifty years before he ruled Persia, see Isaiah 44:24–28; 45:13; Ezra 1. Some have alleged that Isaiah's prediction regarding Cyrus was interpolated (i.e. inserted after the event). But this is unlikely. See Warren Carroll, *The Founding of Christendom*, 1st ed. (Front Royal, **VA:** Christendom Press, 2004),121–22, 127–28, 139.

    Zephaniah prophesied of Nineveh that it would be overthrown and turned into a wasteland, also that flocks would eventually lie down there (2:13–15), and this is what happened. In the case of Babylon, Isaiah and Jeremiah were much more specific: it would be overthrown and never again inhabited; shepherds would not rest their flocks there. Instead, it would be home to jackals, hyenas, owls, and goats (Isaiah 13:19–22). Jeremiah added that its use as a rock quarry for cornerstones and foundation work would end (Jeremiah 51:26). Interestingly, both cities were eventually destroyed and for centuries they remained desolate. Nineveh, a modern suburb of Mosul, is used for sheep grazing. Babylon is still in ruins. The Arabs shun it as a habitation. Its soil, too poor for flocks or herds, is used to make brick, and its stone is burned to lime to make mortar. See Douglas Geivett and Gary Habermas, eds., *In Defense of Miracles* (Downers Grove, **IL**: IVP Academic, 1997), 219–20.

10. For Memphis, see Ezekiel 30:13–15 (in the King James, Douay-Rheims, RSV, and Jerusalem translations). Thebes, for its part, was sacked by Assyrians, as well as Persians, and eventually destroyed under Caesar Augustus. Rome left only a few small villages standing in its vicinity. But its stone work survived, and today its statues, many of them gigantic, constitute the greatest assemblage of monumental ruins in the world. See Geivett and Habermas, eds., *In Defense of Miracles*, 220–21; also Karl Keating, *The Usual Suspects* (San Francisco: Ignatius Press, 2000), 58–59.

11. Geivett and Habermas, eds., *In Defense of Miracles,* 221.

12. Michael and Jana Novak, *Washington's God* (New York: Basic Books 2006), 225.

13. For Rembrandt, see Christopher White's biography, *Rembrandt* (New York: Thames and Hudson, 1984), 14. It is worth noting, in the same connection, that Thomas Kinkade, America's most collected living artist, affirms the values of faith and family.

14. For Haydn and the Rosary, see Rosemary Hughes, *Haydn* (London: 1962), 47, 106, and for Mozart, see Wallace's translation of his letters, Lady Wallace, trans., *The Letters of Wofgang Amadeus Mozart* (New York: Hurd and Houghton, 1866), vol. 1, 214. Felix Mendelssohn was a devout Lutheran, Antonin Dvorak a daily communicant, and Franz Liszt, who was schooled for the priesthood, took minor orders. If one visits Liszt's home in Budapest, one will see his well-worn kneeler, rosary, and Bible. Robert Schumann was not notably religious, but neither is he on a level with Bach, Haydn, Mozart, or Beethoven, and he wound up in a mental ward after attempting suicide.

15. Robert Burns, Scotland's greatest poet, was religious—see William Barclay, *The Gospel of Matthew* (Philadelphia, PA: The Westminster Press, 1975), 1:227, 240; Barclay, *The Gospel of Luke*, (Philadelphia, PA: The Westminster Press, 1975), 66. Longfellow wrote of the Sabbath, "O Day of rest! How beautiful and fair. How welcome to the weary and the old! Day of the Lord and truce to earthy care. Day of the Lord as all our days should be!" He also wrote a play

about Judas Maccabeus, the great defender of the Jewish faith, and spent many years translating Dante's *Divine Comedy* (the first American to do so), along with the work of St. Teresa of Avila.

Samuel Johnson, Jane Austen, and Charlotte Brontë wrote prayers, as did Robert Louis Stevenson, who penned "The Celestial Surgeon" and conducted family worship services every morning (Barclay, *Matthew*, 1:222–23). Wordsworth, who became a high Anglican toward the end of his life, described the Virgin Mary as "our tainted nature's solitary boast." The Alcott family was again religious, and Harriet Beecher Stowe, wife and daughter of ministers, as well as the sister of nine clergymen, wrote a book on women in the Bible. Finally, Alfred Lord Tennyson wrote that "more things are wrought by prayer than this world dreams of." See Barclay, *Matthew*, 2:321; Barclay, *The Letters of James and Peter* (Philadelphia, PA: The Westminster Press, 1975), 132.

16. For Sophocles, see Dorothy Sayers, *The Man Born to be King* ((London: Victor Gollancz Ltd, 1st ed., 1943), 2. Plutarch and Josephus were also priests, and Plato, who described man as "a plant of heavenly, not earthly growth," spoke in the opening lines of his *Republic* of going to the temple to pray (see L'Estange, ed., *Josephus*, 1775 edition, III, 330, 344). Dante was a Third Order Franciscan, and the furnishings of the Cervantes home in Valladolid bear eloquent witness to the Christian commitment of Spain's greatest writer. One might also mention J.R.R. Tolkien, whose *Lord of the Rings* is regarded by many as the greatest work of the twentieth century. A convert to the Catholic faith, he was a daily communicant and, as an Oxford don, was instrumental in C.S. Lewis' conversion to Christianity.

17. By midlife, Newton was a "recondite theologian," according to biographer James Gleick. Although he rarely attended church, he was intensely scrupulous, morally speaking, and, to quote Gleick again, he "researched and wrote the history of the church again and again [while teaching science at Cambridge]." He also "indulged a particular fascination with prophecy," set down "a set of fifteen rules of interpretation and seventy figures of prophecy," calculated and recalculated the time of the Second Coming, studied in detail the description of the Temple of Jerusalem, collected Bibles, and compared translations in Greek, Latin, Hebrew, and French. He also sought out and studied the early fathers of the church, along with the lives of saints and martyrs (see Gleick, *Isaac Newton*, [Pantheon, 1st ed., 2003], 3–4,7, 21, 107–109, 112). Newton felt that in being a mathematician he was doing God's work, and he saw in his discoveries a reflection of the creative genius of God's handiwork, remarking that "this most beautiful system of sun, planets, and comets could only proceed from the counsel and dominion of an intelligent and powerful being" (Gleick, 111; Dinesh D'Souza, *What's So Great About Christianity*, [Washington, D.C: Regnery Publishing, 2007], 97).

18. Blaise Pascal, who discovered the laws of atmospheric pressure, was ardently Catholic; Johannes Kepler wrote a book on religion; and the first American astronauts to enter lunar orbit, in their moment of triumph, read a passage from Genesis that ends with the words: "And God saw that it was good." On Einstein, see Anthony Flew's reply to Richard Dawkins, *First Things* (December 2008), 21; also *Wall Street Journal* (December 24, 1997), p. A10 ("the more I study science, the more I believe in God"); *Encyclopaedia Britannica*, vol. 18, p. 156.

19. One thinks also of Florence Nightingale, the "lady with the lamp," one of nursing's pioneer geniuses, who described the human body as the "living temple of God's spirit."

20. See E. Michael Jones, *Degenerate Moderns* (San Francisco: Ignatius Press, 1993) and Paul Johnson, *Intellectuals* (New York: Harper and Row, 1988).

21. One could draw similar conclusions looking at such groups as explorers, warriors, and athletic coaches. Greece's greatest warriors, the Spartans, arrived late at Marathon owing to their participation in a religious festival (Warren Carroll, *The Founding of Christendom*, 179), and Prince Henry the Navigator of Portugal, who opened up the route to India and paved the way for Christopher Columbus, was devout, chaste, celibate, and ascetical. The great admiral of the ocean sea—his name stands for "Christ bearer" (Christopher) and "dove" (Colombo in Italian)—felt that God had entrusted him with a special mission, and in preparation he visited the shrine of Our Lady of the Pillar in Zaragoza. He refused to dispense with the customary Sabbath rest, which kept him from making better time during his voyage. He also required that his sailors attend Mass, confess their sins to a priest, and pray the Rosary. Finally, he called his first fort in the New World "Trinidad" in honor of the Trinity (see Samuel Eliot Morison's splendid biography, *Admiral of the Ocean Sea* [Boston: Little, Brown, 1942], 42–43, 163–65, 197–99, 217–18, 341).

    William of Normandy, the Frenchman who conquered England in 1066, received Communion with great devotion before sailing, and once he subdued his cross-Channel antagonist, an immoral man who had broken his word to William, he enforced clerical celibacy and undertook a massive reform of the English church beginning with his appointment of the holy Archbishop of Canterbury, Lanfranc. William also erected Westminster Abbey as part of a nationwide program of church building with the Norman arch as its trademark, and agreed to forego marriage to Matilda of Flanders when Pope Leo IX ruled against its validity.

    What more can one say? Three centuries later, England's Henry V, hero of the Battle of Agincourt, ordered that all glory be given to God, and Joan of Arc, greatest of all female captains, was nothing if not religious. Anyone who studies the life of Saladin, Islam's hero of heroes, will find an individual unusually devout. In Europe, Gustavus Adolphus, the most distinguished general of his age, prayed twice daily for his soldiers and gave a book of Lutheran hymns to each of his soldiers. Admiral Nelson, hero of the Battle of Trafalgar, died with words of God on his lips, and Marshall Foch, the great World War I general, was also deeply religious (for Nelson, see Warren Carroll, *The Revolution Against Christendom* [Front Royal, Va: Christendom Press, 2006], 314). Napoleon, a man who was anything but religious, lacked humility, and his life ended in humiliating defeat.

    Football is a form of warfare, and again the paradigm holds. Tom Landry, legendary coach of the Dallas Cowboys, was deeply religious, as was Don Shula of the Miami Dolphins and Vince Lombardi of the Green Bay Packers, winner of five national championships (the latter two were daily communicants).

22. Both in the morning and at night, Washington knelt to read the Bible and pray. While in London, on his way to acquiring hundreds of books on religion, he bought a pocket edition of the Psalms. Later, as commander of American troops during the Revolution, he made church

attendance mandatory and refused to tolerate profanity or obscenity. He was also sympathetic to Catholics, remarking that "to be insulting" toward their religion "is so monstrous as not to be suffered or excused" (see Michael and Jana Novak, *Washington's God*, 15, 30, 66, 89, 93–98, 122, 127, 159, 163).

Abraham Lincoln, raised on the Bible, was not notably religious during his years as an attorney. But the stress of civil war, coupled with presidential responsibility, brought him back to God. One of the most spiritual of presidents, he recommended Bible reading, delivered a sublimely religious Thanksgiving Proclamation in 1863, and, as his last presidential act, approved the words "In God We Trust" for American coins.

Queen Victoria, mother of nine, issued a proclamation calling it her duty to "maintain and augment the service of Almighty God, as also to discourage and suppress all vice, profane practice, debauchery, and immorality" (Gertrude Himmelfarb, *The Demoralization of Society* [New York: A. A. Knopf, 1996], 28). To foster strict Sabbath observance, she prohibited the playing of cards and other games in public or private on Sunday, forbade the sale of liquor or the presence of patrons in taverns during church services, and commanded all her subjects "to attend with decency and reverence at Divine Service on every Lord's Day." Abortion had been illegal in England since 1803 (twelve years after it became illegal in France) but Victoria tightened the law by dropping the distinction between "quickened" fetuses, whose presence could be felt in the womb, and those that were "unquickened." Her reign saw a marked decrease in crime, violence, drunkenness, illegitimacy, and broken families, as well as the flowering of an immense number of charitable organizations and Britain's arrival at the pinnacle of world power.

Ronald Reagan, one of the most spiritual of American chief executives, did a great deal of praying and, as president, published a major attack on abortion (Peggy Noonan, *When Character was King* [Penguin, 2002], 98).

Surveying the larger picture, Justinian, a sixth-century Eastern Roman Emperor, was an amateur theologian who knew his Bible and had studied his faith. Even though he was hampered by a Monophysite wife, his aim was to create a truly Catholic Eastern Empire (H. W. Crocker III, *Triumph* [New York: Forum, 2001], 102). Charlemagne, King of the Franks and Emperor of the Romans, was the son of a devout Catholic father and mother, as well as the nephew of a monk. He was also a daily communicant who fasted, spent long hours in prayer, attended evening vespers, and read the Bible daily. Despite questionable early marriages, along with the forced conversion of the Saxons, he was an exceedingly upright man who enforced church attendance, insisted on respect for the Sabbath, and fostered almsgiving, along with monastic discipline. Education advanced notably during his reign, and militarily he was everywhere victorious.

The list is long! Otto the Great did for Germany what Charlemagne had done for France, and again, he was extremely religious, receiving Holy Communion and praying the Divine Office daily. In France, Louis IX, a canonized saint, ended serfdom, personally meted out justice under the royal oak at Vincennes, and ranks as probably the greatest of all French kings. Isabel, one of the greatest, if not *the* greatest, of Spanish monarchs, was known for her piety. Among her many accomplishments, she raised five children, relieved the poor, reformed the Spanish Church, brought justice to citizens of every class, supported Columbus, fought vigorously for the rights of the American Indian, and completed the Reconquista (the reconquest of Spain from the Moors).

Another extraordinarily devout woman, Maria Theresa of Austria, found time to raise sixteen children while subduing formidable enemies and bringing peace and security to her people. Her reform program, enough in itself to earn her a place in history, made school mandatory for all children from the ages of seven to twelve, introduced music as a staple of the curriculum, built thousands of new schools, reduced taxes on the poor and, for the first time, taxed noblemen. She also limited peasant labor, instituted a new and faster system of courts, personally heard many grievances, and balanced the budget. Cursing and working on the Sabbath were forbidden, and by the time she died, Vienna was the cultural capital of Europe.

23. According to some estimates, the number of Cambodians slaughtered by Pol Pot was as high as a third of the nation's population. For mass murders and atheism, see Dinesh D'Souza, *What's So Great About Christianity?* 17.

24. Isaiah 55:8.

25. For God's command to Joshua to exterminate the Canaanites, who knew of Moses' miracles yet refused to convert (Joshua 2:8–11), see Deuteronomy 7:2, 16, 22–23; 20:16–18; Numbers 31:7, 13–18; Joshua, chapters 6, 9, 10 (especially 10:40), and 11. For Canaanite immorality and God's warning, see Leviticus 18:24–25; 1 Kings 14:24; 21:26; Wisdom 12:4–5; 8–10; and Warren Carroll, *The Founding of Christendom*, 219. The Amorites were again very immoral and God destroyed them too (see 1 Kings 21:26; Amos 2:9). Were the Amalekites as immoral as their neighbors? One would have to assume so, as Saul was commanded by Samuel to destroy them root and branch (1 Samuel 15:3). Lastly, it should be noted that the Book of Sirach (39:30) specifically defends the extermination of the morally scabrous.

26. Cardinals Richelieu and Mazarin, French prime ministers during the Thirty Years War, were anything but religious. Confined mainly to Germany, military action was driven by a mix of territorial, dynastic, and religious issues. Catholic France bankrolled Protestant Sweden, then joined the Protestant cause against the Catholic Hapsburgs of Austria. As for the so-called "Wars of Religion" in France (1562–98), Philip Hughes had it right when he wrote: "the political Calvinist came into existence to thwart the political Catholic." See Hughes, *A Popular History of the Catholic Church* (New York: Macmillan Pub Co, 1962 paperback), 192, 195. See also Carlton Hayes, Marshall Baldwin, and Charles Cole, *History of Europe* rev. ed. (New York: Macmillan Pub Co,1956), 544.

27. See, for example, Matthew 5:39, 43–44; 6:14–15; Luke 17:4; Exodus 23:4–5; Proverbs 25:21–22.

28. On Sunday school, see Frederick W. Marks III, *Velvet on Iron: The Diplomacy of Theodore Roosevelt* (University of Nebraska Press, 1979), 91. On TRs advocacy of weekly churchgoing, see *Theodore Roosevelt's Nine Reasons Why A Man Should Go To Church*, (New York: Roosevelt Memorial Association, undated). For his repeated use of such terms as God, Lord, devil, evil, sin, wicked, and good, not to mention biblical quotes, see his *Fear God and Take*

Your Own Part (New York: George H. Doran Company, 1916), 55–58, 139, 165, 170–72, 186, 191, 204, 210, 343.

CHAPTER 2

1. For weekly assembly, see Leviticus 23:2–3; for fasting, Matthew 9:14–15.
2. See Deuteronomy 15:11 and Matthew 26:11 for biblical predictions.
3. Sirach 18:9; Isaiah 65:20.
4. See Matthew 5:36; 6:27.
5. See Matthew 6:19; 13:29.
6. See 2 Kings 19:35; Isaiah 37:36; Robert B. Strassler, ed., *The Landmark Herodotus* (New York: Pantheon, 2007), 183–84, 184n. (Book 2, Section 141 of Herodotus' *Histories*); also Josephus, *Antiquities of the Jews*, X, 1, 5 in Sir Roger L'Estrange, trans., *The Works of Flavius Josephus* (Philadelphia: W. T. Bradford, 1773–1775).
7. Josephus says that Jesus was put to death for predicting the destruction of the temple, but he also supports the Gospel statement that jealousy on the part of Jewish leaders had a lot to do with the crucifixion. See L'Estrange, trans., *Josephus*, III, 11–12; Josephus, *Antiquities*, book 18, chapter 4, *ibid*; G. A. Williamson, trans., *The Jewish War* [Slavonic edition] (London: Penguin, 1970), 396–400; G. A. Williamson, *The World of Josephus* (Boston/Toronto: Little, Brown, 1965), 308; Henry St. John Thackeray, *Josephus: The Man and the Historian* (New York: The Jewish Institute of Religion Press, 1929), 131–134, 139–40, 144. For the reliability of Josephus, see Frederick W. Marks, "Jewish Light on the Risen Lord," *New Oxford Review* (April 2006): 38–43.
8. For the results of radiometric dating, see Amos Frumkin, Aryeh Shimron, and Jeff Rosenbaum, "Radiometric Dating of the Siloam Tunnel, Jerusalem," *Nature* [London], vol. 325, issue no. 6954 (September 11, 2003): 169–71; also News Notes: "Hezekiah's Tunnel Confirmed" (citing Michele Shabin, Religion News Service), *The Wanderer* (September 25, 2003): 3.
9. On Greek and Roman writers, see Warren Carroll, *The Founding of Christendom* (Front Royal, VA: Christendom College Press, 1985), 44. On geology, see Edith Deen, *All the Women of the Bible* (Edison, New Jersey: Castle Books, 1955), 20.
10. On Moses' ability to write, see Williamson, *The World of Josephus*, 60. On Abraham and the Canaanite cities, see Carroll, *Founding*, 44, 82.
11. For the Hittites, see O. R. Gurney, *The Hittites* (London: Allen Lane, 1975). Skeptics doubted that Adam really lived to be nine hundred thirty years of age as recorded in Genesis 5:5. But archaeologists unearthed Greek and Roman records that contain references to life spans of hundreds of years. The historicity of the Book of Judith was also in question until 1846 when at Behistun diggers found a monument to Darius the Great that shed new light on the subject. The voice of the naysayers is still audible, but less so as time passes.

Two more examples will suffice. For a long time there was no evidence for the existence of the Assyrian king, Sargon. Consequently Isaiah's reference to him was regarded by many as a "fable" (Isaiah 20:1). Then came excavations at Nineveh in the latter part of the nineteenth century that uncovered numerous inscriptions bearing the king's name. Likewise in the case of Sennacherib's ill-fated expedition to Jerusalem followed by his assassination (2 Kings 18–19). Doubt reigned until telltale Babylonian inscriptions were discovered.

12. See Mark 4:38. Also Marie-Christine Ceruti-Cendrier, "The Gospels—Direct Testimonies or Late Writings?" *Homiletic and Pastoral Review* (January 2005): 50.

13. In like vein, scholars questioned Luke's reference to a Roman proconsul in Cyprus. For years the island had been ruled by a propraetor, but documentation was eventually found showing that at about the time Luke was writing his Acts of the Apostles, the island was taken over by the Senate and a proconsul replaced the propraetor. A marble inscription with the words "Apostolou Paulou" was also found confirming Paul's presence in Cyprus. See *Catholic World Report* (October 1999): 4.

14. In 1988, carbon 14 testing of a sample of its cloth seemed to suggest a fabrication date of AD 1200 at the earliest, and since there was no solid documentation supporting its prior existence, many assumed it was a medieval forgery. Carbon 14 tests can be misleading, however. The *Journal of Radio Carbon* reported instances where the dating was skewed by margins of five hundred, one thousand, or even fifteen hundred years. In the case of the Shroud, there is even greater reason for skepticism. Carbon 14 testing on fabric that has been dyed, patched, or touched by fire is unreliable, and the testing was done on a very small sample about the size of a postage stamp taken from an edge of the Shroud that had been patched four times after fire scorched it and melted its silver container (fire adds carbon isotopes, a process called carbonizing). The Shroud was also dyed in order to conceal the patching. Finally, bacteria fungus and other microorganisms had attached themselves to the linen material over the years producing a lamination effect that had been overlooked.

University pathologists and criminologists, along with professors of chemistry, medicine, physics, and botany have examined the Shroud, and all agree that it was *not* a medieval forgery. Its distinctive three-over-one, herring bone twill weave of hand-spun linen led a world authority on ancient textiles to pinpoint the location and time of manufacture as the Dead Sea area during the period 40 BC to AD 70 (see Janice Bennett, *Sacred Blood, Sacred Image* (Littleton, Colorado: Libri de Hispania, 2001), 86–88, 94–96). The costliness of the material supports the tradition that it was purchased by the wealthy Joseph of Arimathea, and the Shroud's blood stains indicate nail penetration through the wrists, rather than the palms. We know now that the bone structure of the palm could not have withstood the strain of crucifixion. But the images of the crucified Christ familiar to men of medieval times showed nails through the palms, and so this, most likely, is what forgers would have depicted. There is also the fact that the cubit was the most common unit of measurement at the time of Jesus, and the Shroud measures exactly 2x8 cubits (14'3" x 3'7").

The evidence for authenticity keeps on accumulating. First of all, traces of calcite gravel have been discovered in the foot area of the Shroud, and such gravel is found in only two geographical locations: (1) a remote region of Africa, and (2) the vicinity of the Sheep Gate that leads from Jerusalem to Calvary.

Secondly, forensic scientists, including Jews and other non-Catholics, have found pollens and microscopically small bits of flowers, along with flower imprints, that square with Scripture's account of burial in a garden tomb (John 19:41). Several of the floral images are of plants that grow nowhere else but the Holy Land—certain types of chrysanthemum, for example, along with rock rose and bean caper. Furthermore, the geographical location of the plants in question overlaps in the vicinity of Jerusalem. Out of fifty-eight species of plants, twenty-eight are from the Holy Land while the rest are from Eastern Turkey and Constantinople (Istanbul). One can therefore be certain that the Shroud did not originate in western Europe, as assumed by the carbon 14 testers.

Thirdly, floral evidence supports the entire history of the Shroud, as we know it, inasmuch as it confirms its having been in three locations: (1) Palestine, (2) the eastern portion of modern-day Turkey close to the ancient Christian city of Edessa; and (3) Constantinople. According to Eusebius and other early scholars, the apostle Jude, also known as Thaddeus, took the Shroud to Edessa in response to a request for a Christian healing from the fatally ill King Abgar (see Barclay, *Matthew*, 1:82; Carroll, *Founding*, 409). The king was miraculously cured and his kingdom converted to Christianity. The Shroud then surfaced in Constantinople, only to vanish and reappear in Lirey, France in 1354 after French-led knights sacked Constantinople. There is an account of the Shroud being in Constantinople in the tenth century and in 1203, Robert de Clary, a crusader, reported, while in Constantinople, that it was on display weekly at a monastery. In 1247, King Baldwin II sent his cousin Louis IX a piece of the Shroud, and the entire Shroud is thought to have been brought to Europe by the Knights Templar.

Fourthly, investigators working with computers from the Viking Space Mission at the Jet Propulsion Laboratory in Pasadena, California, ascertained that the Shroud's image was not made by pigments, and hence could not have been painted on the linen, and this squares with the fact that the image rests on the outer fibers of the cloth forming a layer thinner than the width of a human hair. Fifthly, scientists at the U.S. Air Force Academy in Colorado Springs, Colorado photographed the face of Jesus as it appears on the Shroud, placed it in a VP8 computerized image enhancer that had been designed for the Mariner Space Program, and found that the picture contained encoded information which produced an uncanny three-dimensional image. It seems that the image on the Shroud contains X-ray information that could never have been duplicated by a forger, medieval or ancient.

Finally, and perhaps most impressive of all, there is the blood of the Shroud. In the first place, it has the X and Y chromosomes of the male. Secondly, the degraded nature of the DNA indicates ancient blood, again proof against medieval skullduggery. Thirdly, its high concentrations of bilirubin are suggestive of intense trauma—see Rich Rinaldi, "Turin Shroud Dated to 1st Millennium," *National Catholic Register* (August 15–21, 1999): 1; Rich Rinaldi, "Shroud Data in Line With Gospel Account," ibid. (August 22–29, 1999),: 1; Shafer Parker, "Shroud of Faith?" ibid. (October 6–12, 2002): 1; also Rodney Hoare, *The Turin Shroud is Genuine* (London: Souvenir Press, 1974). Fourthly, and most telling, the blood is type AB, which is common to only 3.2 percent of the world's people, almost all of whom are native to

Palestine. AB happens, at the same time, to be the blood found on the face cloth or Sudarium said to have wrapped the head of Jesus when he was taken down from the Cross and that has been on display in Oviedo, Spain, since the seventh century. The pollen on the Sudarium even matches that found on the Shroud, and the blood of the Eucharistic miracle at Lanciano, Italy, is also AB. Lanciano is where the host and wine used at Mass turned into visible flesh and blood around the year AD 700.

Could the Shroud have been fabricated early in the Christian era with sham artists substituting another crucified corpus for that of Christ? Again the answer must be no because even if charlatans had thought of procuring costly cloth, adding flowers, and ensuring that the corpse was properly wounded on the knees and temple, how could they have produced—or even *thought* of producing—the scorched effect mentioned earlier?

In closing, let it be said that Catholics are not required to accept the authenticity of the Shroud any more than they are required to believe in the miracles of Guadalupe, Lourdes, and Fatima. But the evidence on its behalf is overwhelming.

15. There must have been an influx of energy that overcame the strong force binding protons and neutrons together and left behind a disproportionate amount of carbon 14.

16. Hermas was the author of *The Shepherd* (c. AD 144–50.).

17. Hegesippus' five-volume history of the early Church written in the first half of the second century is no longer extant—see G. A. Williamson, trans., *The History of the Church by Eusebius* (London: Penguin, 1989), 4:8. Another example of a source unavailable to modern scholarship is Papias' *Explanation of the Sayings of the Lord*, possibly the first Christian Bible commentary. Eusebius quoted from this and many other works that have been lost. See Maisie Ward, *The Authenticity of the Gospels* (New York: Sheed and Ward, 1956), 13–14; William G. Most, *Catholic Apologetics Today* (Rockford, Illinois: Tan Publishers), 49.

18. How likely is it that Matthew would borrow from others when it came to a matter as personal as his own call to follow Christ? Note that his version is nearly the same as those found in Mark and Luke (Matthew 9:9; Mark 2:14; and Luke 5:27–28).

19. John 19:35; 21:24 (for repeated claims). Eusebius tells us that John came from a priestly family. See also Carroll, *Founding*, 292–93; William Barclay, *The Gospel of John* (Philadelphia: Westminster Press, 1975), 2:229.

20. For Jesus' wrath, see Mark 8:33. For the mother-in-law, compare Mark 1:29–31 with Matthew 8:14–15 and Luke 4:38–39. For anger and indignation, compare Mark 3:5 and 10:14 with parallel passages in Matthew (chapters 12 and 19) and Luke (chapters 6 and 18) that say nothing about the way Jesus looked or felt. See also Mark 6:6 (he "marveled because of their unbelief"), as compared with parallel passages in Matthew and Luke (chapters 13 and 4 respectively). For references to Jesus sighing, see Mark 7:34 and 8:12 (found only in Mark).

21. Luke 4:23. Noted Bible commentator William Barclay detects medical expertise in the way Luke describes the cure of a withered hand, also in his use of a verb that suggests clinical observation, and finally in his choice of a noun that implies symptoms of insanity. See William Barclay, *The Gospel of Luke* (Philadelphia: Westminster Press, 1975), 52, 72, 86.

22. See L'Estrange, trans., *Josephus* (*Antiquities*), III, 11; also Carroll, *Founding*, 392; and Most, *Catholic Apologetics*, 148 (referring to Celsus' objections).

23. Sanhedrin 43a and 67a (Jesus is said to have hung on wood on the eve of the Passover and there is reference to the release of Barabbas—for use of the word "wood" in place of "cross," see Acts 10:39; 13:29); 43a and 107b (on his miracles); 104b (re: the Egyptian sojourn). See T. Herford, *Christianity in the Talmud*, 736. All of the above is taken from the unexpurgated edition of the Babylonian Talmud published before 1578, which refers to Mary as a hairdresser, as well as a harlot, and brands Jesus as illegitimate (Sanhedrin 67a and 106a).

24. Hilarin Felder, *Christ and the Critics* (London: Burns, Oates and Washburne, Ltd., 1924), 2:294–95.

25. Lee Strobel, *The Case for Christ* (Grand Rapids, Michigan: Zondervan, 1998), 60; J. Edward Kosmoszewski, M. James Sawyer, and Daniel Wallace, *Reinventing Jesus* (Grand Rapids, Michigan: Kregel Publications, 2006), 71. For the *Odyssey*, see Norman Geisler and Abdul Saleeb, *Answering Islam* (Grand Rapids, Michigan: Baker Books, 1993), 232. The oldest surviving copies of Tacitus and Suetonius date to the ninth century; the oldest copy of Josephus is a product of the eleventh century; and five hundred years separates the originals of Herodotus and Thucydides (which have been lost) from the oldest surviving copies. We have only three manuscript copies of the complete Tacitus (which is incomplete). For Thucydides it is twenty, for Herodotus seventy-five, for Josephus one hundred thirty-three, and for Suetonius two hundred. See Mark Roberts, *Can We Trust the Gospels?* (Wheaton, Illionis: Crossway Books, 2007), 30–31.

26. N. G. M. Van Doornik, S. Jelsma, A. Van de Lisdonk, *Handbook of the Catholic Faith* (Garden City, New York: Image Books, 1956), 79–80; Kosmoszewski, Sawyer, and Wallace, *Reinventing Jesus*, 71, 75–77, 82–83, 104–106, 117.

27. See Karl Keating, *What Catholics Really Believe* (San Francisco: Ignatius Press, 1992), 40–44.

28. See Marie-Christine Ceruti-Cendrier, "The Gospels—Direct Testimonies or Late Writings?" *Homiletic and Pastoral Review* (January 2005): 46–52; Keating, *What Catholics Really Believe*, 40–44.

29. Marie-Christine Ceruti-Cendrier, "The Gospels—Direct Testimonies or Late Writings," *Homiletic and Pastoral Review* (January 2005): 47–48. Around 1980, Fr. José O'Callaghan identified a papyrus written in Greek that was found in cave Number 7 in Qumran, the "7Q5," as being a fragment of Mark and another papyrus from the same cave as being a fragment of 1 Timothy. According to Ceruti-Cendrier, "the first reaction of theologians was to hide this discovery and not to tell anything about it . . . [and] when, twenty years later, the German Protestant papyrologist Carsten P. Thiede brought the manuscript out and declared it to be authentic in *The Earliest Gospel Manuscript* (Carlisle, Cumbria: Paternoster Press, 1992), the outcry against its authenticity was enormous" (p. 48).

30. Acts 1:1; Luke 1:1.

31. Doornik, Jelsma, and Lisdonk, *A Handbook of the Catholic Faith*, 60.

32. Lee Strobel, *The Case for Christ*, 43; *Jewish Encyclopedia* (c. 1901 edition), 12:19. A twentieth century London edition of the Talmud (1935–52) ran to eighteen volumes. Still a lot to memorize.

33. Warren Carroll, *The Building of Christendom* (Front Royal, Virginia: Christendom College Press, 1987), 57 on Chrysostom.

34. James Davison Hunter, *The Death of Character* (New York: Basic Books, 2000), 39.

35. Maisie Ward, *The Authenticity of the Gospels*, 8. Even today it is thought that millions of Muslims have the entire Koran memorized—see Mark Roberts, *Can We Trust the Gospels?* (2007), 81.

36. Tacitus, *Annals*, 15:44 in A. J. Church and W. I. Brodribb, trans., *The Complete Works of Tacitus* (New York: Random House, 1942).

37. Mark 9:33–34.

38. John 5:19; 12:50; 14:28. Paul's letters, written during the decade AD 55–65, are a clear indication that the apostles preached Christ's divinity.

39. Matthew 20:23; 26:39.

40. Warren Carroll, *Building*, 190.

41. Isaiah 28:15, 17; 33:15; 59:3–4, 14–15; Sirach 20:23–24 ("better a thief than an inveterate liar"). See also Micah 6:12; Zephaniah 3:13, as well as the Ten Commandments ("Thou shalt not bear false witness").

42. Barclay, *Matthew*, 1:158.

43. Tacitus, *History*, 5:5 in Church and Brodribb, trans. *Tacitus*.

44. Barclay, *Matthew*, 1:337; Barclay, *John*, 1:120–21; Deuteronomy 4:2; Josephus, *Contra Apionem* (Book 1) in L'Estrange, trans., *Josephus*, 3:277–78.

45. Proverbs 30:5–6.

46. Josephus, *Contra Apionem*, book 1 (trans. by L'Estrange, 1775), 3:277; Barclay, *Matthew*, 1:337.

47. The Mosaic law prescribed the death penalty for unauthorized touching or gazing at sacred objects, most especially the Ark (Numbers 4:15, 20). Seventy men were struck dead for their refusal to reverence it (1 Samuel. 6:19), and at least one individual was cut down simply because he tried to steady it in transit when the oxen stumbled (2 Samuel 6:6–10).

48. Acts 5:5–10.

49. Aristedes' *Apology* (c. AD 125). See Avery Cardinal Dulles, *The History of Apologetics* (San Francisco: Ignatius Press, 2005), 31.

50. 1 Peter 2:1; 3:10; Ephesians 4:25; 5:9–10; 6:14.

51. John 17; James 1:18, 21.

52. Revelation 22:18–19.

53. See John 8:32; 14:6; also John 1:17; 4:24; 8:44; 16:13; 19:35; 21:24; 1 John 2:21.

54. John 18:37–38.

55. Carroll, *Founding*, 453; William Edward Hartpole Lecky, *History of European Morals From Augustus to Charlemagne,* (London:Longman's Green, 1869), 1:451.

56. Ibid., 460; William Barclay, *The Letters of John and Jude* (Philadelphia: Westminster Press, 1976), 2:144.

57. *Catechism of the Catholic Church*, 2480. Pliny is quoted by W. Paley, D.D., in *The Evidences of Christianity* (New York: King Publishers, 1824), 354.

58. Compare Matthew 6:9–13 with Luke 11:2–4.

59. Compare Matthew, chapters 5–7, with Luke 6:17–49.

60. See Rev. Mario Romero, *Unabridged Christianity* (Goleta, California: Queenship Publishing, 1999), 104–105 (taken from Bruce Metzger and Michael Coogan, eds, *The Oxford Companion to the Bible*, 573). The order of the meal was as follows: (1) Thanksgiving prayer, (2) first cup of wine blessed and consumed, (3) bread blessed and consumed, (4) second cup of wine blessed and consumed, (5) lamb sacrificed and eaten, (6) third cup of wine blessed and consumed, (7) Psalms sung, (8) fourth cup of wine blessed and consumed. According to Rabbi Hayim Donin, there was a final serving of matzo between the conclusion of the dinner and the blessing of the third cup of wine. See Haym Donin, *To Be A Jew* (New York: Basic Books, 1972), 233–35.

61. See, for example, Gleason Archer, *New International Encyclopedia of Bible Difficulties* (Grand Rapids, Michigan: Zondervan, 1982) and Norman Geisler and Thomas Howe, *When Critics Ask* (Grand Rapids, Michigan: Baker Books, 1992). Although these works are colored at certain points by Protestant theology, the authors have made a signal contribution to scholarship.

62. See Archer's *Encyclopedia*, 68–69 (one account is chronological, the other thematic).

63. Compare Matthew 27:5 with Acts 1:18 and consult Archer's *Encyclopedia*. Matthew tells of an earthquake (Matthew 27:51), and it is possible that a jagged portion of an uprooted tree fell on Judas after he hanged himself, tearing open his stomach.

64. What Old Testament prophet uses such a wide array of searing epithets (i.e. "fool," "fraud," "hypocrite," "swine," "liar," "viper," and "whited sepulcher") to describe the people of his generation or condemns whole towns, not to mention whole classes of people (e.g. lawyers, scribes, Pharisees, Sadducees, elders, and chief priests)? What Old Testament prophet ever took a whip to his people as Jesus did (in the temple)? Or promised the destruction of Jerusalem as the wages of depravity? Or condemned hard-hearted listeners to hell? See Frederick W. Marks, "How New is the New Testament?" *Homiletic and Pastoral Review* (December 2000): 18–25.

65. See Frederick W. Marks, "The Case for Hell, Fire, and Brimstone," *Homiletic and Pastoral Review* (March 1996): 17–24.

66. That the Nathaniel of John's Gospel is called Bartholomew in the synoptic Gospels and that Luke refers to Thaddeus as Jude poses no problem because Jews often had more than one name. Saul and Paul were one and the same, as were Matthew and Levi, John and Mark (Acts 12:12, 25), Thomas and Didymus (John 20:24), Barnabas and Joseph (Acts 4:36). Simon was, of course, called Peter, and in the Old Testament Daniel was known as Belteshazzar (Daniel 4:19), Hoshea was called Joshua, and several famous figures had their names changed—e.g. Abram to Abraham, Sarai to Sarah, and Jacob to Israel. Later, Ignatius of Antioch was called Theophorus in a letter to Polycarp.

67. Maisie Ward, *The Authenticity of the Gospels*, 26.

68. Robert D. Smith, *Comparative Miracles* (St. Louis, Missouri: R. Herder, 1965), 131–32; Geisler and Saleeb, *Answering Islam*, 174.

69. Ward, *Authenticity*, 30.

70. Most, *Catholic Apologetics Today*, 7.

71. For more on the weakness of "Q" theorizing, see David Dungan, *A History of the Synoptic Problem* (New York: Doubleday, 1999).

72. The term apocrypha, which means "hidden away," was originally used by Jerome. Only later did it acquire a different connotation, suggesting something fictional. Church councils at which canonicity was decided were held at Hippo, Carthage, and Rome.

73. When Jesus spoke of "the tradition of men" (Mark 7:7), he was quoting a version of Isaiah 29:13 found only in the Septuagint. See Steven L. Kellmeyer, "Counting the Canon," *This Rock* (June 1998): 22. Matthew alone has over one hundred quotations from the Septuagint— see Victor Claveau, *Bible Sabotage* (Angels Camp, CA: The Evangelization, 2006), 22. When Jesus said, "Come to me all who labor . . . take my yoke upon you," the phraseology was reminiscent of Sirach (compare Matthew 11:28–29 with Sirach 51:23, 26). Although the New Testament does not quote from the actual deuterocanonical books of the Septuagint, neither does it quote other Old Testament books such as the Song of Songs, Ecclesiastes, and Judges. It also quotes numerous non-canonical books. Jude, for example, quotes the *Book of Enoch*, along with *The Assumption of Moses*. Hebrews alludes to *The Ascension of Isaiah*, and Paul quotes the writings of pagan poets (in Acts 1, 1 Corinthians, and Titus). Finally, there are a great many references to the deuterocanonical books that stop short of being direct quotes—e.g., for Mary's Magnificat: Tobit 13:7 and Baruch 5:7. For the "Our Father": Sirach 23:4–6; 28:2; 51:10. For the spirit of the Beatitudes: Sirach 10:29; 11:1, 12–13; 35:17. And for Paul's spiritual armor, compare Ephesians 6:13–17 with Wisdom 5:17–20.

74. For perpetual priesthood, see Sirach 45:7, 13, 17, 24–25. For purgatory and prayer for the dead, see 2 Maccabees 12:42–46.

75. Jones, *Degenerate Moderns* (San Francisco: Ignatius Press, 1993), 246.

76. See Sirach 15:11, 15, and 21:1.

77. Sirach 16:12; James 1:12, 22; 2:14–17, 19, 24, 26.

78. See John 14:16; 16:13 for the guidance of the Holy Spirit. The Eastern Orthodox and non-Chalcedonian Oriental churches have also accepted these books as part of their canon.

CHAPTER 3

1. Matthew 25:31–46; 28:18–20; John 10:18; 20:28.

2. Compare Exodus 3:14 with John 8:58. The literal rendering of John 8:24 is: "You will surely die in your sins if you do not believe that I am" (see Alfred Marshall, *The Interlinear NIV Parallel New Testament in Greek and English* [Grand Rapids, Michigan: Zondervan, 1976], 397; also the *New American Bible* version).

3. Matthew 9:2–3; John 8:46; 20:23.

4. John 14:6 ("I am the way, and the truth, and the life").

5. Mark 2:28; John 10:30; 14:9.

6. Matthew 11:29;12:6, 41–42; Luke 11:31–32. For the denials of Peter and Paul, see Acts 3:12; 14:14.

7. John 8:58; 17:5; Luke 10:18. See also John 1:1, 10, 15 ("he was before me"—even though John was older than Jesus); 17:24.

8. John 5:18; 10:33; 19:7.

9. See Matthew 26:63–67. For the meaning of "you have said so," compare Matthew 26:64 with Matthew 26:25 (where Jesus replies "you have said so" to Judas' question, "Is it I, Master [who will betray you]?)" See also Luke 23:3 (Jesus replying "You have said so" to Pilate's question, "Are you the king of the Jews?").

10. John 2:9 (water to wine); Mark 6:49 (walking on water); Luke 22:51 (severed ear); John 4:50 (distance curing); Matthew 8:26 (calming a storm). For raising the dead, see Mark 5:42; Luke 7:15; John 11:44.

11. Mark 2:2–12 (paralysis); Luke 17:11–19 (leprosy); Mark 3:22–27; 5:1–20 (mental illness).

12. Mark 1:23–27 (unclean spirits); Mark 5:21–34 (hemorrhage); John 9:1,7, 32 (blind); Matthew 9:33 ("never was anything like this . . . ").

13. Mark 3:5 (withered hand); Mark 6:34–44 (five thousand); Matthew 17:23–27 (temple tax).

14. Mark 11:12–14, 20 (fig tree); Mark 7:31–37 (deaf and dumb); Luke 4:30 (passing unseen); Luke 5:1–11 (catch of fish); Luke 13:10–17 (woman bent over); John 5:1–9 (thirty-eight years helpless); Luke 14:2–4 (man with dropsy).

15. See chapters 7 and 8 of Exodus; also Matthew 12:24 (Beelzebul). For the Talmud, see Sanhedrin 104b, 43a, 107b.

16. Isaiah 53:5 (scourged); Psalms 22:17 (mocked); Isaiah 50:6 (spat upon); Psalms 22:17 (pierced in hands and feet—compare with John 19:33–37); Zechariah 12:10 (thrust through—compare with John 19:34); Isaiah 53:5 (suffering for our sins); Isaiah 53:3 (counted among the wicked); Psalms 22:18 (lots cast); Numbers 9:12 and Psalms 34:20 (not a bone broken assuming Jesus is "the just one"). Compare with John 1:29 (the Passover Lamb); Psalms 16:10 (no corruption).

17. See the Septuagint—the Greek translation of the Hebrew by seventy-two rabbis—for the meaning of the Hebrew word 'almâ in Isaiah 7:14. See also Zechariah 11:13 compared with Matthew 27:3 (on thirty pieces of silver); Genesis 49:10 (on Judah); 2 Samuel 7:12 (on David); Isaiah 11:4 (on "rod"); Isaiah 7:14 (on Emmanuel); Isaiah 9:6 (on his name being God); Isaiah 49:6 (on the Gentiles); Isaiah 61:6 (on the universal priesthood).

18. One scholar, Alfred Edersheim, puts the count at 456. See Shoeman, *Salvation is from the Jews* (San Francisco: Ignatius Press, 2003), 79, note 9.

19. Matthew 26:34; Mark 14:13–16, 18; John 21:6.

20. Mark 10:34 (mocking, spitting, and scourging); Matthew 26:2 (crucifixion). For Jesus' prediction of the fall of Corozain, Bethsaida, and Capernaum, see Luke 10:13–15. For those regarding the destruction of Jerusalem and its temple, see Luke 19:41–44; 21:24. For Jesus' foreknowledge of his suffering, death, and Resurrection, see Matthew 12:39–40; 16:4, 21;

17:9, 22; 20:18–19; 26:12, 32; 27:63–64; Mark 8:31; 9:9, 31; 10:33–34; 14:58; Luke 9:22; John 2:18–19, 21; 12:32.

21. John 16:13; Acts 5:9; 13:11; 23:3. The Sicarii assassins targeted Romans and Roman sympathizers. Ananias' death is confirmed by Josephus. See Robert Smith, *The Other Side of Christ* (Avon-by-the-Sea, New Jersey: Magnificat Press, 1987), 59.

22. For Jesus' New Covenant, see Matthew 26:28 and Mark 14:24. For the uniqueness of his miracle working (i.e. working wonders in his own name), compare Matthew 9:27–29. with Exodus 11:4 (Moses' style).

23. Compare Exodus 33:12–13 and Jeremiah 4:3 with John 14:6.

24. Matthew 10:37.

25. Luke 19:41 (weeping); Luke 22:42 (begging the Father's help); John 8:42 ("I proceeded and came forth from God").

26. Just before submitting to arrest, trial, and execution and fully aware of what was to come, he "gave thanks" to God the Father (Matthew 26:27; Luke 22:19).

27. Acts 3:15 (Peter); Colossians 2:9 (Paul); Jude 6; Revelation 1:8 (John).

28. Oliver Barres, *One Shepherd, One Flock* (New York: Random/Bantam, 2000), 117.

29. God is just (Psalms 72:1–4; Ezra 9:15 and 2 Timothy 4:8), as well as merciful (Psalms 111:4), and it was prophesied that the Messiah would govern with justice, as well as mercy (Isaiah 11:4–5; Psalms 72:1–4 and 12–13). See also Sirach 5:7 and 16:12.

30. John 8:1–11; see also Luke 23:40–43.

31. Luke 19:41 (weeping over Jerusalem); Luke 23:34 (forgiveness of his executioners).

32. John tells us that Judas, as treasurer of the apostolic band, stole from the common purse (12:6). See also Matthew 26:50.

33. Matthew 18:2; 19:13–15; Mark 9:36; 10:13–16; Luke 1:44; 9:47.

34. Mark 5:21–43; Luke 8:40–56.

35. Luke 10:25–37.

36. Matthew 19:30; 26:13; Mark 14:9. For evidence that Mary of Bethany and the penitent woman of Luke 7:36–50 are one and the same, see Frederick W. Marks, "John the Clarifier," *Homiletic and Pastoral Review* (July 2007): 13–15.

37. Luke 19:1–10 (for Zacchaeus).

38. Matthew 19:21; Mark 10:21 (generosity enjoined); Acts 2:44–45 (holding all in common); Matthew 26:11; John 12:8 (warning about the enduring nature of poverty). Needless to say, early Church deacons also distinguished between the poor who were worthy and those who were not. See 2 Thessalonians 3:10 (no work, no welfare).

39. For mass cures, see Matthew 4:24; 8:16; 12:15; 14:35–36; 15:30–31; 19:2; Mark 1:32–34; 6:53–56; Luke 4:40–41; 9:11. For his forgiveness of sins, see, for example, Matthew 9:2 and Luke 7:48.

40. Isaiah 11:5.

41. For "sin no more," see John 5:14; 8:1–11.

42. Matthew 10:33; 12:36; 16:27.

43. Matthew 25:31–46.

44. Isaiah 11:4; Luke 11:46 (lawyers); Luke 20:45–47; Matthew 5:20; 23:27 (scribes); Matthew 5:20–21; 23:27, 29–30 (Pharisees); Matthew 21:45–46 (chief priests).

45. John 17:12.

46. Matthew 16:23.

47. Jesus, as quoted by Luke (10:28), echoes the Old Testament: i.e., love God with your whole heart, soul, and strength, and love your neighbor as yourself, and "you shall live."

48. Matthew 24:51; 25:41, 46.

49. Luke 19:44 (on Jerusalem); John 8:23–24 (dying in sin). For the meaning of the expression "die in your sins," see 1 Corinthians 15:16–20.

50. Luke 10:15. This is one of forty odd occasions on which the word "hell" appears in the New Testament.

51. John 2:15.

52. Luke 11:39–40, 44; Matthew 23:15, 17, 19, 23, 25, 29, 32; John 8:55.

53. Matthew 7:6. For pejorative use of the word "dog" among early Church leaders, see Philippians 3:2; 2 Peter 2:22; Revelation 22:15.

54. On lust, see Matthew 5:28. On remarriage after divorce, see Matthew 5:32; 19:3–9; Mark 10:7–12; Luke 16:18.

55. Compare Luke 9:61–62 with 1 Kings 19:19–21 (Elijah allowed it).

56. John 11:34–37 (weeping over Lazarus).

57. John 10:18, 39; 13:12; 21:9–12.

58. See, for example, Matthew 8:4; 9:30; Mark 3:12.

59. Who but a man of sound mind could have said such things as: "You will know them by their fruits"; "Where your treasure is, there will your heart be also"; "If any one strikes you on the right cheek, turn to him the other also"; "Man shall not live by bread alone"; "Blessed are the meek, for they shall inherit the earth"; "He who finds his life will lose it, and he who loses his life for my sake will find it" (Matthew 5:39; 7:16; 10:39; Luke 4:4; 12:34).

60. John 10:38.

61. John 3:2; 9:16.

62. Numbers 14:26–35 (for Jewish rebellion); Luke 19:44.

63. For Peter's teaching on the impartiality of God, see 1 Peter 1:17 and Acts 10:34–35. For Paul, see Romans 2:11.

64. See Deuteronomy 10:17 and Psalms 98:9.

65. Matthew 14:1–2.

66. Acts 14:11. See also Edward Gibbon, *History of the Decline and Fall of the Roman Empire* (London: Penguin, 2005), 550–51.

67. Mark 16:14 (a passage found in the vast majority of Greek New Testament manuscripts).

68. Luke 24:7, 12; John 20:9.

69. For Jesus' appearances, see Matthew 28:9–10, 16–18; Mark 16:9–11; Luke 24:13–32, 34; John 20:19–29; 21:1–22; Acts 1:1–9; 9:1–9; 26:12–18; 1 Corinthians 15:5–8 (five hundred at once). For his appearance(s) to Paul, see Acts 18:9; 22:18; 1 Corinthians 9:1.

70. Janice Bennett, *Sacred Blood, Sacred Image*, 66–67.

71. Acts 12:19. Thirty Roman guards and one thousand Jewish onlookers were at the tomb according to Josephus. See Williamson, trans., *The Jewish War* (Slavonic edition), 400.

72. Acts 16:27–28; 27:42.

73. John 20:6–7. John tells us that he and Peter found a head cloth wrapped up and separate from the other burial cloths.

74. Acts 7:60–8:3.

75. See Acts 9:1–9; 22:6–9; 26 (entire); 1 Corinthians 15:8; Galations 1:13–17.

76. The early Church believed at least as far back as Origen that Pilate's wife, Claudia Procula, converted to Christianity. See Origen Hom. in Mat XXXV. The Greek Orthodox celebrate St. Procula's feast day on October 27. See *Harper's Bible Dictionary* (New York: Harper and Row, 1973), 559.

77. For the Copts, see Crocker, *Triumph*, 27; Barclay, *Matthew*, 2:359. According to Eusebius, Pilate was forced to commit suicide during the reign of Emperor Caligula (Gaius), who was insane and hostile to Christianity—see Williamson, trans., *Eusebius*, 43.

78. Pilate's story is an interesting one. According to Josephus, he interrogated Jesus long before Good Friday in response to Jewish charges of Christian treason against Rome. Josephus reports that Pilate let Jesus go after this preliminary hearing because he did not regard the Nazarene as a threat, and also out of gratitude for a cure received by his wife, Claudia Procula. See Williamson, ed., *The Jewish War* by Josephus (Slavonic edition), 399–400. This is, of course, consistent with the way Pilate and his wife are portrayed in the Gospels, both of them anxious to secure Jesus' release (Matthew 27:15–25). "I find no crime in him," declares the procurator, and, failing to appease the mob, he nonetheless insists on writing over the Cross, "King of the Jews," rather than "This man said, 'I am king of the Jews,'" as requested by the priests (John 19:19–22).

79. See Williamson, trans., *Eusebius*, 38–39; Barclay, *Matthew*, 2:360; L'Estrange, *Josephus (Antiquities)*, 3:18. Pilate's alleged report is not extant despite Rev. W. D. Mahan's spurious claims to have found it in the Vatican Library during the nineteenth century—claims so convincingly packaged that they continue to mislead rank and file readers.

80. Williamson, trans., *Eusebius*, 38–39. Tiberius' nomination was evidently rejected by the Senate. Lecky disputes the contention of Tertullian, and therefore of Eusebius, that Tiberius nominated Jesus for a place in the Roman pantheon of gods, but he gives no reason except to cite Gibbon, and Gibbon's reasons are unpersuasive (see his *History of the Decline and Fall of the Roman Empire*, (London, Penguin, 1994), 1:550). According to Gibbon, (1) Tiberius was contemptuous of religion and thus would not have wanted Jesus in the pantheon of Roman gods. (2) A servile Senate would not have disobeyed its master. (3) Gibbon wonders how Tiberius could have protected the Christians from the severity of laws that were not passed until many years after Tiberius' death, as claimed by Tertullian. (4) He also wonders how the memory of such extraordinary events, escaping the notice of Greek and Roman historians, could have been visible only to the eyes of an African Christian who composed his apology one hundred and sixty years after the death of Tiberius.

Gibbon's skepticism is unconvincing. First, Tiberius' religious laxity would have made him *more*, rather than less, likely to want a Jew added to the Roman pantheon of gods. Secondly, while the Roman Senate may have been servile on many occasions, it could have acted independently in this particular case owing to intense Jewish pressure—the Jews, who had influence, were about to gain additional power under Caligula and Nero—and since Tiberius may not have lobbied very hard, one can easily imagine the Senate going its own way. Thirdly, while Tiberius may not have been able to shield Christians from the severity of laws passed under Nero that criminalized Christianity, he could have protected them from laws requiring them to partake of food sacrificed to the emperor as a god and exempted them from military service—they could not, in good conscience, join the army owing to their unwillingness to recognize the emperor as a god, something required of all soldiers. Fourthly, it is not surprising that Greek and Roman historians do not refer to Pilate's report or Tiberius' nomination. They have almost nothing to say on the subject of Christianity which, after the time of Nero, was a capital offense. As for an African being an insider, Gibbon seems to have forgotten that Augustine was African. The canon of the Bible was largely settled by African councils, and Alexandria, the largest and most cultured Greek-speaking city in the Roman world was African. It was easier to reach Rome from certain places in North Africa than from many places in Italy.

81. Matthew 27:51; Mark 15:33.
82. For the Gospel account, see Matthew 27:51–52; Luke 23:45. For Josephus, see Williamson, trans., *Jewish War*, 400; also Alfred Edersheim, *The Life and Times of Jesus The Messiah* (London: Longmans Green, 1884), 2:610–12. For the *Gospel of the Hebrews*, see Carroll, *Founding*, 391–92.
83. For the Talmud, which dates the opening at AD 30, see Yoma 39a and b and Rosh Hashanah 31b. For Josephus, see Williamson, trans., *The Jewish War*, 292, 348–49. Tacitus' reference to the "prodigy" of a mysterious opening of "the doors of the inner shrine" [of the temple], which he juxtaposes with an allusion to Jewish messianic prophecy, is cryptic and undated but nevertheless suggestive (*History*, 5:13). See also Carroll, *Founding*, 375.
84. See Jacobus de Voragine, *The Golden Legend* trans. by William Granger Ryan (Princeton University Press, 1993), 2:237–38. Eusebius mentions earthquake activity in Bithynia (i.e. present-day Turkey), and Orosius places it in Rome on the day Jesus died. See also Stanley Jaki, *The Bible and Science* (Manassas, Virginia: Christendom College Press, 1996), 195.
85. Voragine, *Golden Legend*, 2:237–38.
86. See F. F. Bruce, *Jesus and Christian Origins Outside the New Testament* (Grand Rapids, Michigan: Eerdmans, 1974), 30–31; Strobel, *The Case for Christ*, 85; Geisler and Saleeb, *Answering Islam*, 230–31; Gary Habermas, *The Historical Jesus* (Joplin, Missouri: College Press Publishing, 1996), 196–97; Jacobus de Voragine, *The Golden Legend*, 2:237–38 (on Eusebius); Jacques-Bénigne Bossuet, *Discourse on Universal History* (1976 translation from the French, University of Chicago Press), 71. Phlegon confuses the issue somewhat by giving AD 33 for the crucifixion, instead of AD 30, which is more likely as it was a year with a noon as dark as night (so dark one could see the stars twinkling).

87. L'Estrange, trans., Josephus (*Antiquities of the Jews*), 3:11; Williamson, trans., *The Jewish War* (by Josephus), 38–39. As mentioned in note 15, some scholars have claimed that portions of Josephus' work were inserted by Christian propagandists after the fact. But even among Josephus' own people, no one possesses a single copy of his work, manuscript or otherwise, that does not affirm the Resurrection. For more on Josephus, see Frederick W. Marks, "Jewish Light on the Risen Lord," *New Oxford Review* (April 2006): 38–43.

88. For the Talmud, see Yoma 39a and b; Rosh Hashanah 31b; also Shoeman, *Salvation is from the Jews*, 130–32. According to the Talmud, the scarlet thread *always* turned white during the period of forty years when Simeon the Righteous was high priest. Thereafter, the miracle was intermittent until AD 30, after which it never again turned white.

89. For murder in the temple, see Giuseppe Ricciotti, *The History of Israel* (Fort Collins, Colorado: Roman Catholic Books, 1955), 2:142. Among the handful of high priests who stand out for their excellence are Samuel, who anointed David; Onias mentioned in 2 Maccabees 15:12; Simon, son of Jochanan (mentioned in chapter 50 of Sirach); and Simeon "the Righteous" mentioned in the Talmud (Yoma 39a) who reigned virtuously for forty years. For a typical lament by one of the prophets over the scandalous iniquity of the Jewish people, see Baruch 1:15–3:8.

90. Samuel Phineas, the last of the high priests, came to power through political intrigue and was not even in the line of Aaron, as required by Mosaic Law.

91. See Paul Glynn, *Healing Fire of Christ* (San Francisco: Ignatius Press, 1999), chapters 13, 14 (on Zola and Lourdes), especially 174–75, 181, 184–989. Dr. Boissarie, *L'oeuvre de Lourdes* (Paris: P. Téqui, 1907) contains a whole chapter on Zola's falsification of facts. See also Joris-Karl Huysmans, *The Crowds of Lourdes* trans. by W. H. Mitchell (London: Burns, Oates and Washbourne ltd., 1925).

92. Well before October 13, the children were interrogated by skeptical ecclesiastical authorities, as well as by hostile civil officials, who threatened them with torture and death for refusing to take back their story. See John De Marchi, *Fatima from the Beginning* (Farima: Missoes Consolata, 2002), which contains photos of newspaper articles; also Louis Kondor, ed., *Fatima in Lucia's Own Words: Sister Lucia's Memoirs* (Fatima: Secretariado dos Pastorinhos, 2003); William Thomas Walsh, *Our Lady of Fatima* (Garden City, New York: Doubleday, 1954); and John Young, "The Importance of Fatima," *Homiletic and Pastoral Review* (August/ September 2000). For Portuguese newspaper accounts, see *O Seculo*, October 15, 1917 written by its Masonic editor ("a spectacle unique and incredible . . . the sun resembles a silver plate . . . one would say that an eclipse had occurred . . . crowd . . . pale with fear . . . the sun trembles . . . makes abrupt movements never seen before and outside all cosmic laws, the sun 'begins to dance,' as the peasants say . . . "); *O Dia*, October 17, 1917 (e.g. "the silver sun . . . seen to whirl . . . people fell on their knees in the muddy ground . . . the light turned to a beautiful blue"). For interviews of hundreds of eyewitnesses, see John Haffert, *Meet the Witnesses* (Spring Grove, Pennsylvania: Amerian Society for the Defense of Tradition, Famiy, and Property, 2006). An atheist on the faculty of Columbia University also wrote a vivid description of the miracle, according to Fr. Edwin Gordon (letter to the author dated September 24, 2004), and there is

a massive volume in Portuguese containing a treasure trove of information yet to be translated into English.

93. Jeremiah 17:9.

94. Wise, who spoke at Carnegie Hall on December 20, 1925, is quoted by his biographer, Melvin Urofsky, in *The Voice That Spoke for Justice* (State University of New York at Albany, 1982), 194–95.

CHAPTER 4

1. For a detailed discussion of this point, see Frederick W. Marks, "How New is the New Testament?" *Homiletic and Pastoral Review* (December 2000).

2. Matthew 5:17–18; 23:2–3; John 10:35.

3. See Marks, "How New is the New Testament?" cited above, 21–23.

4. Malachi 2:16; Matthew 19:3–6; Mark 10:6.

5. Matthew 19:12; Luke 18:29.

6. See Roy Varghese, "Ten Hard Facts About the Doctrine of Perpetual Virginity," *Homiletic and Pastoral Review* (June 2006): 45. When Moses was about to come into God's holy presence on Mount Sinai and receive the Ten Commandments, he asked Jewish males to honor the occasion by staying away from their wives (Exodus 19:15). David and his followers refrained from marital intercourse for two or three days before consuming the sacred Loaves of Proposition (1 Samuel 21:4–6), and similar abstinence was enjoined during the Maccabean rededication of the temple.

7. See, for example, John 5:1; 7:2–10; 10:22–24.

8. Compare Matthew 21:13 with John 2:14–15. See also Mark 11:17; Luke 19:46; Isaiah 56:7 (on God's house as a "house of prayer").

9. Matthew 8:4; 23:3; 23:23 ("you tithe mint and dill and cummin, and have neglected the weightier matters of the law, justice and mercy and faith; these you ought to have done without neglecting the others"); Luke 17:14. When Jesus himself broke the law on such matters as hand washing and healing on the Sabbath, he was, of course, acting in his capacity as God.

10. All of the angels of the Bible, including the Seraphim mentioned by Isaiah, are male.

11. For the good shepherd, see Ezekiel 34:11, 23–24; Sirach 18:13. For the Magnificat, see 1 Samuel 2:1–10; Isaiah 26:4–6; Baruch 5:7; Psalms 33:11; Tobit 13:7. For the Lord's Prayer, see Sirach 23:4–6, 10; 28:1–2; 51:10; Psalms 119:29. For the Beatitudes, see Sirach 10:29; 11:1, 12–13; 35:17; Psalms 37:11 (re: meekness); 126:5 (re: mourning); Proverbs 28:11. Paul's comparison of spiritual weaponry to military armor (Ephesians 6:13–17) is traceable to Isaiah 59:17; Psalms 141:8; 144:2; and Wisdom 5:17–18.

12. Leviticus 19:18.

13. Compare Matthew 7:12 with Leviticus 19:17–18. See also Proverbs 25:21; Exodus 23:4–5.

14. Luke 24:53; Acts 2:46; 4:1–2; 18:4; 19:8–9; 20:5.

15. Acts 18:18; 21:26; 24:17; 2 Timothy 3:16. Paul was paraphrasing verses 151–52 of Psalm 119 ("All thy commandments are true. Long have I known from thy testimonies that thou hast

founded them for ever") when he said that "Jesus Christ is the same yesterday and today and for ever" (Hebrews 13:8).

16. For less direct language on the perpetuity of the priesthood, see Jeremiah 33:18. For Jesus as high priest, see Hebrews 2:17; 3:1; 4:14; 5:5 (Jesus was and remains "the" high priest of Christianity; but he delegated his priestly power to Peter and Peter's successors who would exercise it on earth after the Ascension). For Jesus as the "Lamb of God," see John 1:29.

17. For daily prayer in the temple, see Acts 2:46.

18. See Exodus, chapters 35–39; Sirach 45:8.

19. See Ezekiel 37:28.

20. Exodus 39:25; Sirach 45:9.

21. Leviticus 23:3 (on weekly assembly). According to *Harper's Bible Dictionary*, the high priest used to approach the Ark of the Covenant through a cloud of incense. See also Luke 1:9; Psalms 141:2; Judith 9:1; Wisdom 18:21; Keating, *The Usual Suspects* (San Francisco: Ignatius Press, 2000), 72.

22. Luke 1:11.

23. For Solomon kneeling, see 1 Kings 8:54; for Daniel, see Daniel 6:10. For Jesus, Peter, and Paul, see Luke 22:41; Acts 9:40; 20:36; 21:5.

24. Eusebius, *History*, 5:5. For James, see William Barclay, *Letters of James and Peter* (Philadelphia: Westminster Press, 1976), 12–13.

25. See, for example, 1 Kings 2:13–20 (for Bathsheba's throne next to that of Solomon and her influence as queen mother); 14:21; 15:9–13; 2 Kings 24; Jeremiah 13:18; Josephus, *Antiquities*, IX.10.3;11.2; 3.1; X.4.1; 5.2; 6.3.

26. On the meaning of "blessed" see James R. White, *The Roman Catholic Controversy* (Minneapolis, Minnesota: Bethany House, 1996), 203. For general background, see the *Jerome Biblical Commentary* (1st edition), New Testament section, 122; and for the meaning of the Greek word "*kecharitomene*," compare Karl Keating, *Catholicism and Fundamentalism* (San Francisco: Ignatius, 1988), 269 with James R. White's *Roman Catholic Controversy* (Ada, MI: Bethany House, 1996), 202.

27. John 2:4; 19:26.

28. John 12:32. See also John 3:14 and 8:28.

29. Exodus 28:1–3; Deuteronomy 17:8–13; David Goldstein, *Letters to Mr. Isaacs* (St. Paul, Minnesota: Radio Replies Press, 1943), 12; James Cardinal Gibbons, *Faith of Our Fathers* (Rockford, Illinois: Tan, 1980), 63–64.

30. See Leviticus. 21. Moses referred to the high priest as "the priest who is chief among his brethren" (21:10). For other references to the high priest, see 2 Kings 12:10; 22:4, 8; 23:4.

31. *The Jewish Encyclopedia* (1905), 11:42. This would seem to be borne out by comparing Luke's description of those who wished to condemn Paul to death ("all the Sanhedrin") with Josephus' description of those who condemned James the Lesser ("the sanhedrin of judges" with a small "s"). See Acts 22:30; Josephus, *Antiquities*, XX.9.1 (1774 edition).

32. Acts 14:23.

33. Titus 1:5.

34. Acts 13:3; 1 Timothy 4:14.

35. Acts 6:6; 8:17.

36. Acts 6:6; 8:14–17; 19:6.

37. Acts 15:1–2, 22.

38. For "the Lord himself" see Ignatius to the Ephesians in W. A. Jurgens, ed., *The Faith of the Early Fathers,* 3 vols. (Collegeville, Minnesota: Liturgical Press, 1970–1979), 1:18. See also ibid., 1:17, 19–20, 23, 25. Peter, Paul, and James refer to priests as "elders" in the New Testament letters (e.g., 1 Timothy 4:14; 5:17; Titus 1:5; James 5:14; 1 Peter 5:1). This is because the earliest Christians were overwhelmingly Jewish and, by Jewish law, a priest had to be biologically descended from Aaron. After AD 70, when the Jewish priesthood ceased to exist, elders could be called by their proper name because there was no longer any competition or confusion as to what was meant by the "priesthood."

39. For Origen, see Paul Stenhouse, *Catholic Answers to "Bible" Christians* (Kensington, N.S.W., Australia: Chevalier Press, 1993), 1:38. For Irenaeus, see Jurgens, ed., *Faith,* 1:89.

40. Matthew 16:18–19. Some Protestant commentators have interpreted this passage to mean that Christ intended to build his Church on *himself,* and they cite, as evidence, Paul's words, "and the Rock was Christ" (1 Corinthians 10:4). Others hold that Jesus promised to build on *Peter's faith or confession of faith.* But none of this makes sense in view of the promises made to Peter; and, as David Currie points out, Nathanial made the same confession without being given keys or binding authority (John 1:49). Still other Protestants have a problem with translation. The oldest manuscript copies of Matthew, all of which are in Greek, use two different words with two different meanings for "rock" (i.e. "Thou art *Petros* and upon this *petra* I will build my church"). *Petros* means small rock while *petra* connotes one that is massive. Critics of the Catholic interpretation of Matthew 16:18–19 seize upon this difference in Greek to buttress their position that Jesus did not promise to build on Peter. Again, though, the objection is unconvincing because Jesus spoke Aramaic, not Greek, and Aramaic has only one word for rock: *kepha* (*cephas* in Greek). When the Aramaic was translated into Greek, *petra* could not be used in reference to Peter because the word is feminine. Karl Keating points out, in addition, that God is the only person in the Old Testament called "rock"—the word was never used as a proper name. See Keating, *Catholicism and Fundamentalism,* 205–206, 209–211; David Currie, *Born Fundamentalist, Born Again Catholic* (San Francisco: Ignatius Press, 1996), 75–76.

41. Isaiah 22:20–22.

42. See Frederick W. Marks, "Thou Art Peter," *Homiletic and Pastoral Review* (December 1992): 8–16.

43. John 21:15–17.

44. See, for example, Matthew 10:2; Mark 3:16; Luke 6:13; and Acts 1:13.

45. Luke 22:31–32.

46. Acts 1:15–26.

47. See Acts 2:14; 3:6–7; 4:8–9; 9:36–43.

48. Acts 5:14–15.

49. Acts 5:1–11.

50. See Galations 1:18–19.

51. Acts 15:7 and 12.

52. See, for instance, John 21:7–8; Acts 1:15–26; 5:29; 15:6–12.

53. 2 Peter 3:16.

54. 2 Peter 1:19–20.

55. 2 Peter 2. Although the authorship of the second letter of Peter has been called into question, skepticism falls flat when weighed against Tradition. If the author was someone other than Peter, this "someone" would presumably have been close enough to the lead apostle to speak on his behalf, and Peter would undoubtedly have passed on its content.

56. For evidence that Peter was in Rome, see 1 Peter 5:13 (among the early Christians, Rome was known as "Babylon"). Also pertinent is Paul's Epistle to the Romans (people whom he says he has yet to visit but whose faith is known throughout the world)—see Romans 1:8, 10–15; 15:22–24. Peter, known to have traveled with Mark the Evangelist, mentions Mark's presence in Rome (1 Peter 5:13), and this is corroborated by Paul, writing later from a Roman prison (Colossians 4:10). See also Ignatius of Antioch's Epistle to the Romans 4:3 (c. AD 110). Ignatius writes: "Not as Peter and Paul did I command you . . . They were apostles and I am a convict." All the Church fathers who touch on the subject connect Peter with Rome (see *This Rock* [January 1997]: 30–32 for a list of such Fathers and quotations from each). Lastly and most importantly, Rome is the only city that lays claim to Peter's tomb.

57. Carroll, *Founding*, 460–61 (on Polycarp).

58. Mike Aquilina, *The Fathers of the Church* (Huntington, Indiana: Our Sunday Visitor Press, 1999), 32.

59. Carroll, *Founding*, 465.

60. On Josephus' claim, see *Contra Apionem*, book 1, section 7 in L'Estrange, trans., *Josephus*. On Irenaeus' lists, see *Adversus Haereses*, 3:5 quoted by Stenhouse, *Catholic Answers*, 1:37; also John Milner, *The End of Religious Controversy* (New York: Edward Dunigan and Brother, 1855), 170–71.

61. St. Irenaeus, *Against Heresies*, 3,3,1–2.

62. Compare Matthew 16:18–19 with Isaiah 22:21–22.

63. After defeating his adversaries, Solomon tried to restore unity by banishing one priest and retaining the other. But after Solomon's death, the banished priest took ten out of twelve Jewish tribes with him, resulting in the establishment of a second Jewish nation complete with its own chief priest, and from then on, the kingdoms of Judah and Israel were continually at loggerheads.

64. John Laux, *Church History* (Rockford, Illinois: Tan, 1989), 161–62.

65. St. Cyprian's Epistle LIV *To Cornelius on Fortunatus and Felicissimus* cited by Herbert Thurston, S.J. and Donald Atwater, eds., Butler, *Lives of the Saints* (New York: P. J. Kennedy and Son, 1956), 3:563.

66. Augustine Sermon no.131, 10; Laux, *Church History*, 135 (on Ambrose). See also Augustine to Glorius et al. (AD 397 or 398) in which he speaks of "the Church of Rome, where the primacy

of the apostolic chair has always flourished" in *Fathers of the Church: The Apostolic Fathers* (Christian Heritage, 1947), 187.

67. Carroll, *Building*, 62.

68. *Ibid.*, 118, 127.

69. Eamon Duffy, in his history of the popes, is even more specific: "Till the reign of Stephen [254–57], the Roman church's primacy had been gladly conceded." See Duffy, *Saints and Sinners: A History of the Popes* (New Haven: Yale University Press, 1997), 16.

70. Carroll, *Building*, 170 (for the bishop of Patara); Currie, *Born Fundamentalist, Born Again Catholic*, 95 (for Agapitus).

71. Ibid., 64, 352.

72. Ibid., 355.

73. Ibid., 324.

74. John the Baptist was the first man in the service of Christ to give his life for the Faith, died, fittingly enough, for the principle of marital indissolubility. See Matthew 14:4; Mark 6:18.

75. See Frederick W. Marks, "John the Clarifier," *Homiletic and Pastoral Review* (July 2007): 10–17. Modern Scripture scholarship has failed to uncover anything by way of evidence that would justify overriding Tradition. It is Mark who clarifies Matthew rather than the reverse on (a) the question of the mount ridden by Jesus when he entered Jerusalem in triumph— Matthew describes it as an ass "and" a colt, which is confusing (Matthew 21:7) while Mark makes it clear that Jesus rode a single animal, not two, and so we know that Matthew was simply identifying the ass as a colt (Mark 11:1–7); (b) regarding the matter of divorce, Matthew records what Jesus had to say about men divorcing their wives, but not what the Master had to say about women doing the same to their husbands (5:32; 19:9). Mark fills in (10:12); (c) it is hard to imagine Matthew borrowing from Mark or Luke when he tells the story of his own call to discipleship (the phraseology is the same in all three synoptics). It should be said, in addition, that not all who are eminent in the field of modern Scripture scholarship cast doubt on Tradition. See William Most, *Catholic Apologetics Today*, 54, 179 for the exceptions, including William Farmer, who puts Matthew first in order of composition. For the Fathers on indissolubility, see William A. Jurgens, ed., *The Faith of the Early Fathers*, nos. 119 (Justin), 420 (Clement), 506–507 (Origen), 611b (Council of Elvira), 1308 (Ambrose), 1351 (Jerome), 1388 (Jerome), 1861 (Augustine), 1863 (Augustine), 1864 (Augustine), 1867 (Augustine). In his otherwise excellent *Fundamentals of the Catholic Dogma* (Rockford, Illinois, Tan, 1960), 464, Ludwig Ott claims that Basil allowed remarriage after divorce in cases of adultery, but Ott's point is unsubstantiated. Basil writes, "She that left her husband is an adulteress if she went to another man. But the husband she abandoned is to be pardoned, and the woman who cohabits with such a man is not condemned." According to the notes that accompany Basil's Letter no.188 in the four-volume 1955 edition of Basil's collected writings (part of the larger set, *The Fathers of the Church*), "St. Basil clearly does not mean here that the man who, being illegally dismissed by his [adulterous] wife, cohabits with another woman is blameless. Pardon is granted only to the guilty. He simply states that the custom does not authorize the imposing of the canonical penance for fornication." Most likely, too, the word "condemned" at the end

of the sentence does not refer to condemnation in the eyes of God but rather to condemnation in the sense of civil prosecution and punishment for adultery. Basil, in the same letter (no.188), says that a wife is not warranted in leaving her husband even if he beats her, loses his money, or proves unfaithful. If the father of eastern monasticism writes so strongly against "leaving," one cannot expect to find him tolerant of divorce and remarriage. Then, too, in his *Morals*, Rule 73, Cap. 1, he refers to Matthew 19:9 without admitting any exceptions to the rule of "no remarriage after divorce" (see Basil's *Ascetical Works* in *The Fathers of the Church*, 1950, p. 189).

76. William Barclay, *The Letters of the Galatians and Ephesians* (Philadelphia: Westminster Press, 1976), 171; Lecky, *History of European Morals*, 2:317.

77. Liddell and Scott's *Greek-English Lexicon* (New York: Oxford University Press, 2002) supports the RSV's use of "unchastity," but "fornication" is preferred by: C.D. Yonge's *English-Greek Lexicon* (London: Longman's Green, 1887), George R. Berry's *Interlinear Literal Translation of the Greek New Testament* (Grand Rapids, Michigan: Zondervan, 1958), and Alfred Marshall's *R.S.V. Interlinear Greek-English New Testament* (London: Bagstar, 1968).

78. In chapter 5, we shall see that St. Augustine insisted on hewing to the literal sense of Scripture except where "reason makes it untenable or necessity requires." Clearly, this is not such a case. The phrase in question could be taken to mean that people who have come together through fornication do not have to stay together (the Mosaic Law—Deuteronomy 22:28—required fornicators to marry). Pressure to marry arising from fornication or cohabitation could be considered a ground for annulment because those who tie the knot out of a sense of duty, rather than love, may lack the freedom necessary for such a contract to be binding. Among the better known renditions of the so-called "Matthean exception" or escape clause, which, properly interpreted, is neither an exception nor an escape are: Douay-Rheims ("except for fornication"); King James ("except it be for fornication"); New American Bible ("lewd conduct is a separate case"). As an aside it should be mentioned that certain commentators take *porneia* to mean canonically unlawful sexual union. According to James Drummey, "in the community to which Matthew was writing, there were persons who appeared to be married, but were actually in illicit unions according to the Mosaic law (cf. Leviticus 18:6–18) which forbade marriages between persons of certain blood and/or legal relationships" (*Who Do You Say That I Am?* [Norwood, MA: C.R. Publications: 2009], 88).

79. The RSV version, for example, uses the phrase "except for unchastity" (Matthew 5:32 and 19:9). Note that Jesus prohibits remarriage after divorce not only for husbands but also for wives, which was a possibility in Roman society, and even among Jews, if the woman resorted to legal maneuver (Mark 10:11–12).

80. Compare Matthew 19:9 with Matthew 15:19; 1 Corinthians 6:9; Galations 5:19; and Hebrews 13:4 in George P. Berry, *Interlinear Literal Translation of the Greek New Testament* (New York: Hinds, Noble, and Eldridge, c. 1897) and Alfred Marshall, *The Interlinear NIV*.

81. See Shammai, two volumes by William Barclay: *The Gospel of Mark* (Philadelphia: Westminster Press, 1975), 239, and *The Gospel of Luke*, 212. For Jesus' words, see Matthew 19.

82. Clement of Alexandria (in *The Instructor of Children*, AD 91), Lactantius (in *Divine Institutes*, AD 307), Chrysostom (in *Homilies on Matthew* and *Homilies on Romans*, AD 391), Jerome

(*Against Jovinian*, no. 49, and Letter 22, no. 13 dated 393 and 396 respectively), Augustine (*Marriage and Concupiscence*, book 1, chapter 17 [15]; *Against Faustus*, AD 400;and *The Good Marriage*, AD 401), and Caesarius (*Sermons*, AD 522). For these and other citations, see *This Rock* Magazine (January 1996), 40–42.

83. Genesis 1:28; 9:1, 7; 35:11. See also Exodus 1:7, 12; Deuteronomy 7:13; Psalms 127:3–5; 128:3, 6.

84. Genesis 38:9–10.

85. See Deuteronomy 25:8–10 (the Jewish penalty for refusal to raise up issue in such a case was not capital punishment). Classical Jewish commentators all agree that the punishment inflicted on Onan was a reprisal for the *method* of refusal—namely, his calculated wasting of seed. See Brian Harrison, "Onan's Real Sin," *This Rock* Magazine (April 1997): 40–42; also John F. Kippley, "The Sin of Onan: Is It Relevant to Contraception?" *Homiletic and Pastoral Review* (May 2007): 16–22.

86. Matthew 19:4–5.

87. See Galations 5:20; Revelation 9:21. Although Romans 1:26–27 is a condemnation of sodomy, Paul bases his condemnation on the fact that same sex relations are unnatural. "Natural" relations are thus the norm. See also John A. Hardon, S.J., *The Catholic Catechism* (Garden City, New York: Doubleday, 1975), 367. For evidence of the intimate connection between contraception, "magic," and witchcraft down through history to the Renaissance, see John Riddle, *Eve's Herbs* (Cambridge, Massachusetts: Harvard University Press, 1997), 8, 14, 64, 67, 84, 108, 111–12, 133, 136. Riddle is summarized in note 27, chapter 7.

88. For the *Didaché*, see Jurgens, ed., *Faith of the Early Fathers,* 1: 2.

89. Acts 13:4–12.

90. John 11:11–14; Matthew 16:5–12; Mark 10:17–27. For additional explanations offered to puzzled listeners, see Matthew 15:15–20 and Mark 7:17–23 ("whatever goes into a man from outside cannot defile him"); John 10:1–18 (re: the sheepfold gate) and John 16:1–24 (re: "A little while and you will see me no more").

91. "Offended," "scandalized," "upset," or "shocked" depending on the translation.

92. Matthew 26:26–27.

93. 1 Corinthians 10:16; 11:27–29.

94. Ignatius Letter to the Smyrnaeans 7:1; Justin Martyr's *First Apology*, 66.

95. Gibbons, *Faith of Our Fathers*, 243–44.

96. For Jesus' bridal imagery, see Matthew 9:15; Mark 2:19; Luke 5:34; John 3:29. For St. Paul's use, see 2 Corinthians 11:2. For John, see Revelation 21:2.

97. See Mark 7:33; John 9:6 (for Jesus' use of his spittle).

98. John 14:16; 16:13.

CHAPTER 5

1. 2 Timothy 3:16. See also Matthew 24:35 ("my words will not pass away").

2. St. Augustine is quoted by Pope Leo XIII in *Proventissimus Deus*, his Encyclical on the Study of Sacred Scripture (November 18, 1893), section 15. For Leo's words, see sections 14 and 20. Pope Benedict XV (1914–22), in his *Spiritus Paracletus*, section 21, also defended the historical trustworthiness of the Gospels.

3. After examining König's allegations of error, the Vatican II's Theological Commission ruled that all three were based on ignorance of Jewish custom and history. Accordingly, the notion of inerrancy was not restricted to matters of salvific faith, as the cardinal urged (the vote was seventeen to eleven after papal intervention on the side of tradition). All that the Council fathers would accept by way of placating modification was removal of the word "any" from the phrase "without any error." But there can be no doubt of their intent when one reads the transcripts of the discussion, along with footnote 5 of the third chapter of the Council's *Dogmatic Constitution on Divine Revelation (Dei Verbum)*, which cites Augustine, Aquinas, Leo XIII, and Pius XII. "Without any error" is clearly what they meant. For an incisive refutation of each of König's allegations, see Robert A. Sungenis, "The Bible and Historical Criticism," *The Latin Mass* (Spring 2003): 46–48; also Mark J. Zia, "The ABCs of Biblical Inerrancy," *Homiletic and Pastoral Review* (March 2007): 28–31.

4. For John Paul II's words to the PBC, see George Weigel, *Witness to Hope* (New York: Cliff Street Books, 1999), 919. For a critique of Raymond Brown's last book, see Frederick W. Marks, "The Reliability of the Bible," *Homiletic and Pastoral Review* (December 1998); also Frederick W. Marks, "Can We Trust the Bible?" *This Rock* magazine (May/June 2004); and Marks, "Combating Biblical Skepticism," *This Rock* (July/August 2004).

5. Deuteronomy 25:5. See also Genesis 38:8 and Mark 12:19.

6. Romans 3:28. For additional verses used by Protestant exegetes to support Luther's interpretation, see Romans 1:17; 9:32; 11:6; Ephesians 2:8.

7. James 2:24.

8. For James and Paul, see James 2:17–20; Romans 2:6; 1 Corinthians 6:9–10. To be sure, Paul stresses the importance of faith in Romans 1:17 and 3:28: "'He who through faith is righteous shall live' . . . man is justified by faith apart from works of the law." But judging by the context of these passages, he is merely underscoring the early Church's de-emphasis on Jewish dietary and hygienic laws—a de-emphasis confirmed, as mentioned earlier, by the Council of Jerusalem. Immediately before and after the above-mentioned remarks about faith, Paul refers to Greeks and Jews (or Gentiles and Jews), and whenever he does so, his principal concern is how strict to be in requiring Gentile adoption of Jewish customs such as circumcision. Occasionally, Paul tips his hand by mentioning circumcision itself (e.g., Romans 3:30).

    The same may be said of other passages favored by Luther. Take, for example, Romans 9:32, which is governed by 9:30 (the Gentile issue again) and Romans 10:9, 13, which needs to be read in the context of 10:12. In Romans 11:6, still another verse highlighted by Protestant theologians, Paul is not saying that works are superfluous. His point is rather that one cannot earn salvation independently of the grace of God. Luther's favorite "faith" quotation outside

Romans is Ephesians 2:8–9. But here again, the passage only makes sense in the context of Ephesians 2:11, immediately following, which speaks of "circumcision" and "uncircumcision."

9. 1 Peter 1:17; Matthew 16:27. See also John 5:2 and, in the Old Testament, Proverbs 24:12 and Sirach 11:26.

10. For the sower, see Matthew 13. For Paul, see Philippians 2:12. For Peter, see 2 Peter 1:10; 3:17.

11. See Ezekiel 18:24–32; 1 Corinthians 10:12; 2 Corinthians 11:3; Philippians 3:12–14; Matthew 10:22;13:21; 24:13 (for Jesus' warning of the need to persevere). See also 2 John 8 ("look to yourselves, that you may not lose what you have worked for"). In the case of homosexuals, Paul is not referring to people born with certain proclivities, but rather to those who act in certain ways. Peter is equally clear on this point. See 2 Peter 1:10; 2:20–22; 3:17.

12. Matthew 23:2–3 ("Practice and observe whatever they tell you"). As David Currie points out in his marvelous memoir, *Born Fundamentalist, Born Again Catholic,* "the seat of Moses was a product of that historic oral tradition so important to the Israelite faith. Jesus gives the authority of tradition his unqualified approval and commands his contemporaries to obey tradition's precepts. They are not given the option of obeying only those traditions they could justify with a 'chapter and verse'" (p. 53).

13. Acts 4:32.

14. 2 Kings 13:20–21; Matthew 14:36; Acts 19:12.

15. Matthew 23:8–10; Mark 10:18. The meaning is clear: when God tells us one thing and a person whom we respect tells us differently, we must go with God.

16. Mary refers to Joseph as Jesus' "father," and Jesus, who has the Prodigal Son return to his "father," speaks approvingly of Lazarus' appeal to "Father Abraham." See Luke 2:48; 16:24; Romans 4:12 (Father Abraham); 2 Timothy 1:11 (teacher of the Gentiles); 1 Peter 5:13 (re: Mark); Titus 1:4 (re: Titus).

17. 2 Kings 2:12; Isaiah 22:21.

18. Exodus 25:18; 1 Kings 6:23–25; Num. 21:9.

19. Keating, *Catholicism and Fundamentalism, 283.*

20. Galations 1:19. For other examples in the Old Testament of generalized use of the word "brother," see Keating, *Catholicism and Fundamentalism,* 282. Mark may have written in Greek, and Greek has one word for brothers (*adelphos*) and another for cousins (*anepsios*). But there are at least three reasons why the evangelist might have used *adelphos* for *anepsios*: (1) this is what he was accustomed to doing as a Jew, (2) he did not know whether the "brothers" and "sisters" in question were cousins or step brothers and sisters (i.e. offspring of Joseph by a prior marriage), and (3) he wanted to hew, as closely as possible, to Jesus' exact words out of respect for the Master, and, if so, he was simply imitating the seventy-two rabbis who translated the Hebrew Bible into Greek—they used *adelphos* when *anepsios* would have been more accurate (see Keating, *Catholicism and Fundamentalism,* 282–83).

21. Compare Matthew 13:55 with Matthew 27:56 and Mark 15:40. For a powerful refutation of the claim that Jesus had blood brothers, see Keating, *Catholicism and Fundamentalism,* 282–89.

22. Matthew 1:25 (some translations use the expression "firstborn son" instead of simply "son"). For the meaning of "firstborn" see Luke 2:23; also: Exodus 13:2; 34:20; Numbers 3:12–13.
23. 2 Samuel 6:23; Deuteronomy 34:6.
24. Luke 1:34; Matthew 1:25.
25. John 19:27. Roy Abraham Varghese, "Ten Hard Facts About the Doctrine of Perpetual Virginity," *Homiletic and Pastoral Review* (June 2006): 31.
26. See, for example, Alfons Maria Cardinal Stickler, *The Case for Clerical Celibacy* (San Francisco: Ignatius Press, 1993); Christine Cochini, *The Apostolic Origins of Priestly Celibacy* (San Francisco: Ignatius Press, 1990); Lecky, *History of European Morals*, 2:111, 348 (re: a "tradition" that early married priests abstained from sexual intercourse). For the quotation from the Council of Carthage, see the *Homiletic and Pastoral Review* (April 1995): 25.
27. Hebrews 10:34; Acts 5:41; Philippians 4:4.
28. John Farrow, *The Story of Thomas More* (New York: Sheed and Ward, 1954), 206.
29. Anne Barbeau Gardiner, "Supernatural Events Related to the Deaths of Some English Martyrs," *The Latin Mass* magazine (Advent/Christmas 2007): 14.
30. Anne Barbeau Gardiner, "Elizabethan Martyrs," *Latin Mass* (Winter 2008): 18–21.
31. Bernard Bassett, *Born for Friendship: The Spirit of Sir Thomas More* (New York: Sheed and Ward, 1965), 211; Farrow, *Thomas More*, 227.
32. *Catholic World Report* (November 2007): 23. Although Mother Teresa experienced a "dark night" of the soul lasting many years, she remained unflaggingly loyal to her duties and cheerful in the face of suffering. Her "darkness" was simply a lack of any immediate experience of consolation from the Lord.
33. Colossians 1:24.
34. Five times he received thirty-nine lashes. Three times he was scourged. Once he was stoned, almost to death. Three times he suffered shipwreck, and, on one of these occasions, he drifted on the open sea for twenty-four hours. On familiar terms with such calamities as floods and highway robbery, he also grew accustomed to hunger, thirst, and cold (2 Corinthians 11:24–27).
35. 2 Corinthians 12:10.
36. 2 Corinthians 4:10.
37. 1 Corinthians 10:13.
38. Kenneth L. Woodward, *The Book of Miracles* (New York: Simon and Schuster, 2000), 212.
39. John 15:20; Luke 23:31.
40. Gibbon's estimate, as cited by Lecky in his *History of European Morals*, 1: 495.
41. Crocker, *Triumph*, 385.
42. For Lithuania, see Weigel, *Witness*, 670.
43. Best known among the impostors was the Canadian Maria Monk who, in *Awful Disclosures* (New York: Maria Monk, 1836) and *Further Disclosures* (Boston: Crocker and Brewster, 1837), claimed to reveal scandalous practices in Montreal's Hôtel Dieu Convent (from which she said she had escaped). Her books sold in the hundreds of thousands.
44. Quoted in Thomas E. Woods, *How the Catholic Church Built Western Civilization* (Washington, D.C.: Regnery, 2005), 1. Professor John Higham of the University of Michigan

described anti-Americanism as "the most luxuriant, tenacious tradition of paranoiac agitation in American history."

45. *National Catholic Register* (November 26–December 2, 2000): 1. Bill Donohue, *Secular Sabotage* (New York: Faith Words, 2009), 46–47.

46. Luke 23:34; Acts 7:60.

47. Farrow, *More*, 222. One thinks also of Blessed Richard Langhorne, an English lawyer falsely implicated in the fictitious Popish Plot of 1678 and condemned to be hanged for his Catholic associations. He regarded himself as fortunate to die as Jesus did—"O Happy News!" as he put it. On the day of his execution, he kissed the rope as it was being fastened about his neck and when the hangman begged his forgiveness, he freely gave it, asking that God hold no one accountable for his blood (see Anne Barbeau Gardiner, "'I see Myself Honored with the Livery of Jesus,' Blessed Richard Langhorne, Lawyer and Martyr—Part II" *The Latin Mass* magazine (Summer 2009): 26–27.

48. Plunket forgave even those who bore false witness against him. For Guise, see Anne Carroll, *Christ the King, Lord of History* (Manassas, Virginia: Trinity Communications, 1986), 245–46.

49. *The Latin Mass* magazine (Advent/Christmas 2008): 28–35.

50. Beginning with the premiere of Rolf Hochhuth's anti-Catholic play, *The Deputy* (1963).

51. *Il Seitmanale*, (March 1, 1975): 40.

52. Most of the above information, as well as the quotation and most of what follows, comes from Anne Carroll's volume, *Christ the King, Lord of History* (see especially p. 44), along with James Bogle, "The Real Story of Pius XII and the Jews," reprinted from the *Salisbury Review* by *Catalyst* (December 1996): 8–11.

53. Richard Hamilton, *Who Voted for Hitler* (Princeton University Press, 1982); Crocker, *Triumph*, 390; The Ratzinger Report, 167.

54. Quoted by Dalin, *Myth of Hitler's Pope*, 19.

55. Goldstein, *Letters to Mr. Isaacs*, 293.

56. Rabbi David G. Dalin, *The Myth of Hitler's Pope* (Washington, D.C.: Regnery, 2005), 19.

CHAPTER 6

1. Among the heretical patriarchs of Constantinople were Eudoxius, Demophilus, and Nestorius (Carroll, *Building*, 55, 61, 92).

2. Anne Carroll, *Christ the King, Lord of History*, 115.

3. In a letter to the patriarch of Constantinople, the seventh century pope, Honorius, made an ambiguous statement about Christ's will that was seized upon by Monothelites to vindicate the heretical view that Christ had only one will, as opposed to two, in consonance with the doctrine of two natures. Honorius was trying to calm a theologically charged atmosphere by papering over differences, but his eliptical words were fodder for the Monothelite cannon. Technically, he did not err, and he was not addressing the Church as a whole, which is one of the requirements for infallibility. His error lay in *failing* to teach rather than in teaching falsehood. But

that he remained silent, for the most part, aided the cause of Monotholitism. Although the ecumenical Council of Constantinople (AD 680–81) condemned him for heresy, Pope Leo II's endorsement was necessary for the Council's decrees to have any binding effect, and he made the necessary distinctions when he promulgated them (see Carroll, *Building*, 253–54).

4. Henri Daniel-Rops, *The Protestant Reformation* (Garden City, New York: Image, 1963), 1:25.

5. Warren Carroll, *The Revolution Against Christendom* (Front Royal, Virginia: Christendom Press, 2005), 85; Milner, *The End of Religious Controversy*, 273.

6. Laux, *Church History*, 527.

7. E. E. Y. Hales, *The Catholic Church in the Modern World* (Garden City, New York: Hanover House, 1960), 67–69.

8. For all of the above on Ambrose, see *Butler's Lives of the Saints*. 4 vols. (New York: P. J. Kenedy and Sons, 1956), 4: 512–14.

9. Woods, *Catholic Church*, 188-89.

10. For Leo, see Carroll, *Building*, 472–77.

11. For this and all that follows on Gregory VII, see Carroll, *Building*, 500–513; Anne Carroll, *Christ the King*, 161–63.

12. Anne Carroll, *Christ the King*, 167; Eric John, ed., *The Popes* (Harrison, New York: Roman Catholic Books, 1964), 210.

13. On *Unam sanctam*, see Philip Hughes, *A Popular History of the Catholic Church* (Garden City, New York: Image, 1954), 135; Laux, *History*, 393–94. *Unam sanctam* has been interpreted by anti-Catholic critics as denying the possibility of salvation outside the Church and condemning separation of church and state. This, however, is neither what it said nor what it meant. When it spoke of deference to Rome, it meant deference in spiritual matters only (Boniface had already repudiated any claim to be a temporal ruler outside the Papal state), and use of the phrase "every human creature" was probably a throwback to Christ's statement that "No one comes to the Father, but by me" (John 14:6). Christians have always regarded Jesus' death on the Cross as opening the gates of heaven to all who seek the truth with a sincere heart (see Matthew 28:19–20). Papal bulls may or may not be written and/or approved by the pope, and so they are not generally regarded as infallible pronouncements. But one thing is certain: the wording of *Unam Sanctam* was misleading.

Pope Pius IX's *Syllabus of Errors* (1864) invited similar misinterpretation. It denied that "the Roman Pontiff can and should reconcile himself and accommodate himself to progress, liberalism, and modern civilization." Since Turin and other city states had passed anti-clerical laws that not only closed monasteries and convents but attempted to subject education and marriage to government fiat in the name of progress and "modern" civilization, Italians had no difficulty interpreting the pope's message. But observers in England and America were at a loss. How could a pope set himself against all that was modern? Especially troubling was Number 77 of the *Syllabus*, calling it "an error" to say "it is no longer expedient that the Catholic religion should be established to the exclusion of others." Again, while this may have been intelligible to the people of Britain and Scandinavia who had an established church, Americans committed to disestablishment viewed Rome as out of step.

As an aside, papal elasticity on the establishment issue was evident when France's Sun King, Louis XIV, revoked the Edict of Nantes which granted religious freedom to French Huguenots. Pope Innocent XI disapproved openly, and when fifty out of fifty-one French bishops endorsed the Gallican Articles which denied papal authority over the French Church, he persuaded the bishops to reverse themselves.

14. For Boniface, see Carroll, *The Glory of Christendom* (Front Royal, Virginia: Christendom Press, 1993), 339–45.

15. Napoleon forsook his wife, Josephine, to marry a Hapsburg princess, but not with papal approval. For Nicholas I and Gregory V, see Carroll, *Building*, 348–51, 437–38. For Innocent III, see Carroll, *Glory*, 141.

16. Carroll, *Building*, 292.

17. Hughes, *History*, 50. Disagreement on a celibate priesthood reached an impasse in AD 691 by which time the Western custom of fasting on Saturday was not being observed in the East. See Henri Daniel-Rops, *Dark Ages* (Garden City, New York: Image, 1962), 2:23.

18. Luke 6:20; James 2:5 (confirmed by Matthew 19:23). Prostitutes and tax collectors turned out to hear John the Baptist, as opposed to the socially superior Sadducees and Pharisees, just as it was the common people of Corinth, rather than the intellectuals of Athens, who harkened to the message of Paul.

19. See Daniel-Rops, *Dark Ages*, 2:59 for the moral decline of Eastern Christendom in the eighth century.

20. Anne Carroll, *Christ the King*, 153–54 (on Stephen VII's exhumation and trial of Formosus); Warren Carroll, *Building*, 462, 465 (on Benedict IX).

21. Carroll, *Glory*, 641, 671.

22. For Lecky, see his *History*, 2:355.

23. For the wife who clung to virginity, see Lecky, *History*, 2:355–56. For Julius II, see Carroll, *Glory*, 686.

24. Lecky tells of the abbot with seventy concubines (see his *History*, 2:350).

25. Smith, *The Mark of Holiness* (Westminster, Maryland: The Newman Press, 1961), 254. Today's Lutheran bishop of Stockholm, Sweden is a confirmed lesbian living in a registered homosexual partnership with another lesbian priest (*First Things*, August/September 2009, 68). Regarding the preaching of indulgences in Germany, the impression was being given that the moment one dropped a coin into the collection box, the soul of a friend or relative sprang from purgatory to heaven.

An indulgence remits some or all of the temporal punishment due to sin following prayer and/or the performance of good works, and it stems from the power to bind and loose given by Christ to Peter and passed on to Peter's successors. Revenue from the sale of indulgences was usually applied to the building of schools or churches, and those who had been away from the sacraments were sometimes moved to return by the prospect of obtaining a reduction of penance for serious sin. One must bear in mind that penances, in Luther's time, could be extremely arduous. "Two hundred days remission" to a man who had been sentenced to three hundred days of begging in sackcloth and ashes could be quite heartening. But no one could

obtain an indulgence who had not previously confessed his sins to a priest, expressed con-
trition, resolved to change his life, and been forgiven. Plenary indulgences that guaranteed
remission of *all* punishment for sin, both in this world and the next, required total detachment from sin, something few penitents could claim.

There were several problems connected mainly with the administration of indulgences.
They were not always applied to the purpose for which they were earmarked. Secondly, one
might easily gain the impression that "two hundred days" remission was two hundred days less
in purgatory, forgetting that God's time is not man's time. In eternity, there is no such thing as
"two hundred days." Regrettably, some were also led to believe that one could buy the Church's
absolution and hence go on sinning as long as one wanted. This was never the position of the
Church, even in Luther's Germany; but impressions matter.

Due, in part, to Luther's criticism, Pope Pius V forbade the sale of indulgences in 1567,
and they have never been sold since. More recently, in 1967, all reference to a specified number
of days or years was eliminated. In sum, the Church continues to claim the right to grant
indulgences, just as it continues to teach that men can profit spiritually from works, but it has
shut down abuses and eliminated misunderstanding.

26. See Riddle, *Eve's Herbs*, 18–19, 91–92, 126, 136. Riddle's findings on the nature of witchcraft are summarized in chapter 7, note 27.
27. William Thomas Walsh, *Philip II* (Rockford, Illinois: Tan Publishers, 1937), 78.
28. Quoted by Robert D. Smith in *Mark of Holiness*, 254.
29. Woods, *Catholic Church*, 180–81.
30. Lecky, *History*, 1:53.
31. Henry G. Graham, *Where We Got the Bible* (Rockford, Illinois: Tan Publishers, 1987), 136–37.
32. Robert Fox, *A Catechism of the Catholic Church* (Chicago: Franciscan Herald Press, 1979), 129.
33. Paul Johnson, *History of the Jews* (New York: Harper and Row, 1987), 242. See also Daniel Lapin, *The Myth of Hitler's Pope* (Washington, D.C.: Regnery, 2005), 123. Luther instigated the expulsion of the Jews from Saxony in 1537.
34. Riddle, *Eve's Herbs*, 165–68.
35. Riddle, *Eve's Herbs*, 215; Henry Graham, *Where We Got the Bible*, 131.
36. Jones, *Degenerate Moderns*, 250; Warren Carroll, *The Cleaving of Christendom* (Front Royal, Virginia: Christendom Press, 2000), 273; William Cobbett, *The Protestant "Reformation,"* no.238. James I declared, "the more women, the more witches" (Riddle, *Eve's Herbs*, 168).
37. Edward Westermarck, *The History of Human Marriage* (London: Macmillan, 1921), 3:372; I. Ottiger, *Theologia Fundamentalis* (Friburg: Herder, 1911), 2:969 (quoted by Smith, *Mark of Holiness*, 255).
38. Riddle, *Eve's Herbs*, 165–214.
39. Gibbons, *Faith of Our Fathers*, 303–304.
40. Emerson diary quoted by Paul Johnson in *Intellectuals*, 140.
41. Lecky, *History*, 2:301–302.

42. *Human Life Reports* (November 1997):7.

43. James Dobson's volume, *Marriage Under Fire* (Sisters, Oregon: Multnomah Publishers, 2004), not only presents a wide array of statistics on immorality but breaks them down by nationality. Incredibly, the US crime rate trebled between 1965 and 1990 with Canada and Australia not far behind. America also ranks near the bottom of the industrialized world in the caliber of its students. Even its best are verifiably inferior to the best overseas. See Margaret Thatcher, *The Path to Power* (New York: Harper Collins, 1995), 541; "Why America Has the World's Dimmest Bright Kids," *Wall Street Journal* (February 25, 1998).

44. Thatcher, *Path to Power*, 541; Gertrude Himmelfarb, *The De-moralization of Society* (New York: A.A. Knopf, 1996), 224.

45. Woods, *Catholic Church*, 119.

46. Ronald Knox, *Captive Flames* (San Francisco: Ignatius Press, 2001), 22–23.

47. Smith, *Mark*, 255; Woods, *Catholic Church*, 205.

48. Lecky, *History*, 2:392; Woods, *Catholic Church*, 184 (quoting Lecky).

49. Woods, *Catholic Church*, 182.

50. Walsh, *Philip II*, 6733; see also 42, 546, 632.

51. On indulgences, see note 25.

CHAPTER 7

1. St. Vincent, a humble priest of peasant stock, organized the first bureau to help the poor *help themselves*. He aided convicts in God-forsaken French galleys and built hospitals for them in Paris and Marseilles. Among his ancillary projects were: homes for the aged, insane, and lepers; shelters for the destitute (one of which served forty thousand homeless); societies for the reform of sanitation; foundling homes; and soup kitchens (that he personally supervised to ensure the right diet). In addition to relieving destitute members of the nobility, along with the poor, ransoming some twelve hundred slaves of Barbary, and taking charge of eleven seminaries, he provided the impetus for the founding of the Sisters of Charity, an order that is still thriving.

2. For the record, the rector of Notre Dame Cathedral employed a blind organist from 1900 to 1937.

3. Lecky, *History*, 2:85; Woods, *Catholic Church*, 170–80; Goldstein, *Letters to Mr. Isaacs*, 14 (quoting Wilson).

4. This comes out very clearly in the work of Stanley Jaki.

5. For much of the data, both above and below, I am indebted to Vincent Carroll and David Shifflett, *Christianity on Trial* (San Francisco: Encouter Books, 2002), 62–69.

6. Woods, *Catholic Church*, 36.

7. Lecky, *History*, 2:77.

8. Ibid., 5; *Encyclopaedia Britannica,* 14th ed., 7:986b.

9. Lecky, *History*, 2:86–88.

10. Ibid., 4.

11. Ibid., 1:15.

NOTES

12. Carroll, *Building*, 310–11.
13. Lecky, *History*, 2:4; Woods, *Catholic Church*, 14 ff.
14. Carroll, *Building*, 299–302.
15. Daniel-Rops, *Dark Ages*, 2:9–60.
16. Barclay, *Matthew*, 1:156f.; William Barclay, *Letter to the Romans* (Philadelphia: Westminster Press, 1975), 32; William Barclay, *Galatians and Ephesians* (Philadelphia: Westminster Press, 1976), 170f.; William Barclay, *Philippians, Colossians, and Thessalonians* (Philadelphia: Westminster Press, 1975), 199; William Barclay, *Timothy, Titus, and Philemon* (Philadelphia: Westminster Press, 1975), 77f.
17. Carroll, *Building*, 343–45.
18. Lecky, *History,* 2:34–35, 85–86, 90.
19. Carroll, *Founding*, 540; Anne Carroll, *Christ the King*, 99.
20. Carroll, *Building*, 82; Lecky, *History*, 2:25, 34–35, 85–86.
21. Lecky, *History*, 2:39, 85; Carroll, *Building*, 82; Woods, *Catholic Church*, 176.
22. Riddle, *Eve's Herbs*, 87–89, 91–92.
23. Lecky, *History*, 2:378–79.
24. Woods, *Catholic Church*, 212 (quoting Gibbon).
25. Lecky, *History*, 2:335–36.
26. Ibid., 2:363, 373; Riddle, *Eve's Herbs*, 91–92.
27. Riddle, *Eve's Herbs*, 83, 91–92, 126, 136. According to a fourteenth century account of witchcraft, witches had four means of working evil: (1) causing men to be impotent, (2) preventing conception, (3) aborting (causing miscarriage), (4) devouring a child once born (infanticide) or offering it to the devil. Jean Bodin, in *Six Books of a Commonwealth* (Paris, 1576), wrote that midwives employed medical procedures and magical acts to abort fetuses. Henry Boguet, in his *Examen of Witches* (published in the 1580s), says of witches that "they kill them [babies] while they are yet in their mother's wombs. This practice is common to all witches." According to some Dominicans who wrote on the subject, there were seven things witches did: (1) fornication and adultery, (2) obstruction of the generative act by rendering men impotent, (3) castration and sterilization, (4) bestiality and homosexuality (5) destruction of the generative force in women, (6) "procuring abortion" (7) offering children to devils. Observe that all of these practices are related to sexual immorality and all but the first to birth control. Jean Bodin confirmed this in his work, *De la demonomanie des sorciers* (1580). In England, sexual offenses were, by far, the leading offenses of which witches were accused in three Essex villages between 1560 and 1599. In America, Jean Hawkins was accused of practicing "magical medicine," as was Anne Hutchinson, a midwife and medical practitioner banished from Massachusetts Bay Colony. See Riddle, *Eve's Herbs*, 111–15, 132–33. Witches also ran fertility clinics judging from what we know about Catherine d'Medici, who ruled France during the sixteenth century. After trying to relieve her barrenness through prayer and pilgrimages, she turned to witchcraft and devil worship, after which she bore a child every year for the next decade. As for what became of her children, in the words of Anne Carroll: "Francis dead before he was 17, his brain half-rotted away; Isabel, a loving and loyal wife to Philip, but dead in her

early 20s; Claude, crippled from birth and welcoming her death at 27; Louis, Jean, Victor, all dead within a year of their baptisms; Charles, insane and dead at 24; Hercule, stunted and misshapen, dead at 30; Marguerite, so beautiful that men traveled hundreds of miles simply to look at her, yet never able to bear children and pursuing a life of immorality with terrible energy until she grew old and sick and ugly and returned to the God her mother had forsaken; Henri, greedy, perverted, assassinated in his 38th year" (from Anne Carroll, *Christ the King, Lord of History* , 246).

28. Barclay, *Luke*, 17 ("In Palestine the birth of a boy was an occasion of great joy. When the time of the birth was near at hand, friends and local musicians gathered near the house. When the birth was announced and it was a boy, the musicians broke into music and song, and there was universal congratulation and rejoicing. If it was a girl the musicians went silently and regretfully away. There was a saying, 'the birth of a male child causes universal joy, but the birth of a female child causes universal sorrow.'").

29. Lecky, *History*, 2:330, 335–37, 385.

30. Among the women for whom Mozart wrote concertos were Maria Theresia Paradis, Babette Ployer, Mlle. Jeunehomme, and the daughters of the Countess of Lodron. On Lioba and Walburga, see Carroll, *Building*, 293—according to Riddle, female physicians were extinct by the late eighteenth and early nineteenth centuries (*Eve's Herbs*). For Paula, see Erne, *Psalms*, 23–24. Paula was especially helpful to Jerome due to her knowledge of Greek learned from her father (see *Butler's Lives of the Saints*, 1:172, 415). For Melania, see John J. Delaney, *Dictionary of Saints* (Garden City, New York: Doubleday, 1980), 404.

31. On Trotula, see Riddle, *Eve's Herbs*, 31–32. Abbesses such as Bridget of Ireland (c. 450–525), Hilda of Whitby (614–680), and Walburga of Heidenheim (d. 779) had jurisdiction over "double monasteries" composed of male and female communities (see Daniel-Rops, *Dark Ages*, 1:357; *Butler's Lives of the Saints*, 1:415).

32. Carroll, *Building*, 501.

33. Carroll, *Glory*, 14–15.

34. See Warren H. Carroll, *Isabel of Spain: The Catholic Queen* (Front Royal, Virginia: Christendom Press, 1991) for a penetrating analysis.

35. For the charge of the Turkish flagship by a woman disguised as a man, see Carroll, *Cleaving*, 355. For the North African woman, see Daniel-Rops, *Dark Ages*, 2:49.

36. Henry Adams, *Mont-Saint-Michel and Chartres* (New York: Putnam, 1980), 119.

37. Ibid., 119; Lecky, *History*, 2:367.

38. One might also mention artistic depictions of Mary, which portray her as the soul of modesty, and what may be gathered from the reports of apparitions in which her skin color and features vary from place to place, depending on the character of the locals, but not the manner of her dress. At Fatima, for example, she is described as having worn a simple tunic falling to her feet and over it a mantle of the same length which covered her ears and hair. See Walsh, *Our Lady of Fatima*, 51; De Marchi, *Fatima from the Beginning*, 117, 119.

39. Carroll, *Building*, 137.

40. Carroll, *Cleaving*, 354.

41. Woods, *Catholic Church*, 27.

42. Carroll, *Building*, 200; Lecky, *History*, 2:74.

43. Lecky, *History*, 2:76.

44. E.g., in the years 1435, 1537, 1591, 1639, 1781, 1839, 1890, 1912, and 1993. See Appendix 2 for an answer to the frequently asked question, "Has the Church changed?"

45. Carroll and Shiflett, *Christianity on Trial*, 37.

46. For this and other information on the difference between North American and South American slavery, see Stanley Elkins' superb comparative analysis in his volume titled *Slavery*.

47. Anne Carroll, *Christ in the Americas* (Rockford, Illinois: Tan Publishers, 1997), 88, 93; Robert Kagan, *Dangerous Nation* (New York: Knopf, 2006), 240; Carroll, *Glory*, 701.

48. Walsh, *Philip II*, 714.

49. Spanish policy governing the Indians, liberal in many other ways, had no use for eviction or consignment to reservations as compared with the practice in North America where colonists were far more numerous. It should also be pointed out that neither the mother country nor the Church ever resorted to forced conversion. In Mexico, prior to the miracle of Guadalupe in 1531, there were relatively few conversions; similarly in Peru, where few Indians embraced the Faith until Rose of Lima began working her miracles.

50. Carroll, *Glory*, 643.

51. The Portuguese procurator general was given royal orders to "severely prohibit anyone from reducing to slavery, selling, buying . . . [or] separating . . . [the] Indians." See Chris Lowney, *Heroic Leadership* (Chicago: Loyola Press, 2003), 191.

52. For cannibalism, see Warren Carroll, *Our Lady of Guadalupe* (Front Royal, Virginia: Christendom Publications, 1983), 29; Anne Carroll, *Christ in the Americas*, 46, 51; Robert Smith, *Other Side*, 23. For the figure eighty thousand see Carroll, *Cleaving*, 616.

53. *Wall Street Journal* (March 15, 1984):15.

54. Hales, *Catholic Church in the Modern World*, 167.

55. Patrick Allitt, *Catholic Converts* (Ithica, New York: Cornell University Press, 1997), 202.

56. This story and many others like it are engagingly told by George C. Stewart, Jr. in *Marvels of Charity* (Huntington, Indiana: Our Sunday Visitor Press, 1994). For more on the Church and slavery, see Appendix A.

57. John 15:16.

CHAPTER 8

1. In Paul Johnson's words, "there is something repellent, as well as profoundly unhistorical about judging the past by the standards and prejudices of another age" (*Spectator* [November 8, 1997]:8). This is why Vatican II refrained from holding the Church responsible for the errors of individual members—i.e. it never called *the Church* "sinful." And the same holds true for John Paul II. His Apostolic Letter "On the Coming of the Millennium" (November 10, 1994) spoke of the "sinfulness of her [the Church's] children" and the "weaknesses of so many of her sons and daughters" (see Luigi Accattoli, *When a Pope Asks Forgiveness*, 1998, 72).

Likewise, in his address to a consistory of cardinals in 1994 preparing for the upcoming Great Jubilee, he referred to the errors and sins of "her members" or of "Christians." There was no *mea culpa* on behalf of the Church as a Church. In his homily of March 12, 2000, he once again alluded to the sins of "our sons" and "our brothers." In the words of Cardinal Ratzinger, the future Benedict XVI, it was "men of the Church" who were guilty, rather than the Church itself. The Polish bishops put it in a nutshell when they said that "[even] if [there is] only one unworthy person . . . there is need for the Church to ask forgiveness" (Accottoli, 51).

2. Washington, like Jefferson, was a benevolent master who disapproved of slavery in principle and freed his slaves in his will—see Catherine Drinker Bowen, *Miracle at Philadelphia* (Boston: Little, Brown, 1966), 156.

3. Walter Brandmüller, *Light and Shadows* (San Francisco: Ignatius Press, 2009), 127. For Al-Hakim's cruelty, see Carroll, *Building*, 456: he "ordered all business in Cairo to be transacted . . . at night, all women never to leave their houses, and all the dogs in the city to be killed— each decree on pain of death for disobedience." He also "conceived a ferocious hatred for Christianity."

4. Diane Moczar, *Islam at the Gates* (Manchester, New Hampshire: Sophia Institute Press, 2008), 21.

5. Anne Carroll, *Christ the King*, 135.

6. Ibid., 163–64; Warren Carroll, *Building*, 522, 529.

7. When imperial troops sacked Rome in 1527, they engaged in gang rape, torture, and the roasting of children under the eyes of their parents (mentioned by Thomas More in his *Dialogue Concerning Heresies*). One might add that customary reference to a slaughter of one hundred thousand inhabitants of Jerusalem is greatly exaggerated—the number is closer to ten thousand since many fled the city out of fear prior to its capture (Brandmüller, *Light and Shadows, 131*). It should also be said that laying siege to a heavily fortified city entailed such enormous injury and loss of life that armies could not afford a reputation for sparing the lives of those whose stubbornness necessitated the siege.

8. See review of Raymond Secher, "A French Genocide," in *New Oxford Review* (May 2004): 39–42.

9. On Byzantine treachery, see Carroll, *Glory*, 64–66; Moczar, *Islam at the Gates*, 24; Simon Dubnow, *The History of the Jews* (South Brunswick, New Jersey: Yoseloff, 1967–73), 2:, 782–84 (the Greeks, instead of aiding their Latin brethren in the First Crusade, "repulsed them in the Balkans and Asia Minor," and the emperors of the Commenus dynasty "even called upon the Moslems for help against the Latin Christians"). Prince Alexius promised the crusaders two hundred thousand marks in silver, a large sum, plus additional support for their mission and the return of Constantinople to the papal fold (Brandmüller, *Light and Shadows*, 132).

10. Dinesh D'Sousa, *What's So Great About Christianity* (Washington, D.C.: Regnery, 2007), 205–206.

11. Carroll, *Glory*, 8–9.

12. Against enormous odds he reached the Nile with his forces intact only to succumb to illness; ibid., 24.

13. Anne Carroll, *Christ the King*, 175, 225.

14. Tacitus, *History*, 5:5; Johnson, *History of the Jews*, 235; Dubnow, *History of the Jews*, 3:407, 560. On Jewish hopes for Christian failure, enlisting on the side of Islam, and Zionist forces waiting in the wings, see Dubnow, 2:782–84, 799, 803; 3:142–43, 534–35, 540, 575 (Dubnow, for example, mentions that German Jewish refugees, probably passing through Hungary, were told that "the moment the German crusaders arrived in Palestine, 'the threshing floor will become full.' The Jewish army would pounce upon them and begin to 'thresh' them in order to fulfill the prophecy of Micah [4:13]: 'Arise and thresh, O daughter of Zion'"—2:783–84). The great Jewish philosopher Maimonides (1135–1204) was typical in regarding Crusaders with a mixture of amusement and contempt. He welcomed their defeat at the hands of Saladin and thought it would usher in a messianic age in which the Jews would be restored to power. See Joel Kraemer, *Maimonides* (New York: Doubleday, 2008), 133–34, 236; also note 19 of the present chapter.

15. On Talmudic slurs, see David Klinghoffer, *Why the Jews Rejected Jesus* (New York: Doubleday, 2005), 142–44; they were deleted in versions of the Talmud published after 1578. Judaism did not explicitly forbid polygamy until the eleventh century (see Smith, *Mark*, 189). According to Paul Johnson, the great thirteenth-century Jewish sage, Maimonides, sanctioned bigamy (Johnson, *History of the Jews*, 1988 paperback, 200). The Talmudic Aggada, regarded by many Jews as a holy book, said that Christian images could be mocked and Christian prayers cursed (Dubnow, *History of the Jews*, 3:45).

16. Dubnow, *History of the Jews*, 3:239. Centuries later, Maria Theresa placed restrictions on Jewish money lenders in Austria because "their deceit, usury, and avarice" were driving her people "to beggary." Dubnow adds that Jewesses drew jealous looks from Christian women due to their penchant for showy and ostentatious dress, something the rabbis labored in vain to correct (*ibid.*, 3:417).

17. The opening of Spanish archives has changed a lot of minds regarding the severity of the Inquisition. On June 9, 1995, the BBC ran a documentary placing it in a much more favorable light as compared with the Elizabethan persecution of Catholics, and two years later, Yale University Press published a long-overdue revisionist account by Henry Kamen, *The Spanish Inquisition: A Historical Revision* (New Haven: Yale University Press, 1998). See also: Edward Peters, *Inquisition* (New York: Free Press, 1988); Helen Rawlings, *The Spanish Inquisition* (Malden, Massachusetts: Blackwell Publishing, 2006); Peter Kwasniewski, "Rewriting the Inquisition," *Homiletic and Pastoral Review* (March 2005); Patrick Madrid, *Pope Fiction* (San Diego: Basilica Press, 1999), chapter 24; James Cardinal Gibbons, *Faith of Our Fathers*, chapters 17–18; Walsh, *Philip II*, chapter 13, especially 480–81, 493, 503, 513, 632–33.

18. Hughes, *History of the Catholic Church*, 116.

19. Johnson, *History of the Jews*, 177; Goldstein, *Letters to Mr. Isaacs*, 261–62; Carroll, *Building*, 215. The bishop of Segovia was a converso, as was the bishop of Burgos, a former rabbi (Dubnow, *History of the Jews*, 3:291, 310, 597). According to Dubnow, "most" conversos were insincere. They didn't baptize their children or, if they did, they had a purging ceremony. If they went to church, they also went to the synagogue and kept kosher (*ibid.*, 3:306). Dubnov is also clear

that the Christian conquest of Jerusalem not only caused many Jews to grieve, but also led to the mobilization and arming of Zionist forces in places like Arabia, Mesopotamia and Persia. Of the Persian Jews, for example, he writes, "It was not difficult to convince [people] . . . who had quite a few warlike mountaineers among them, that if the alien troops of the remote West could conquer Jerusalem for the sake of triumphant Christianity, then they, the legal heirs of the Holy Land, had the right and the duty to liberate it through force" (*ibid.*, 2:803–806). See note 14 of the present chapter for additional information.

20. Moczar, *Islam at the Gates*, 120. Jews rejoiced in the Muslim conquest of Constantinople in 1453 (Dubnow, *History of the Jews*, 3:200, 394). As Paul Johnson puts it, "Byzantium, the old enemy of the Jews, was no more" and "many Jews believed that the Messiah would now come" (Johnson, *History of the Jews*, 225). Spanish Jews with engineering experience used their technical expertise to help the Turks set up state-of-the-art plants for the manufacture of arms and munitions. In the words of Dubnow, they seemed thus "to war indirectly [against Christendom] . . . by arming the kingdom before which Christian Europe trembled" (Dubnov, *History of the Jews*, 3:394, 472, 474). Whenever and wherever Hussites, Moslems, or Mongols won a victory against Christians generally or Catholics in particular, whether in Russia, Bohemia, the Crimea, or Palestine, Jews were perceived as being treacherously sympathetic with the enemy, and they tended to settle in places vacated by Christian losers. Interesting, too, is that one of the semi-barbaric Mongol-related tribes, the Valaks, who considered themselves descendants of the Jews, plundered Christians while leaving Jewish residents alone (*ibid.*, 2:784; 3:57, 142–43, 192–93, 270). During the bubonic plague of the fourteenth century, Jews were accused of contaminating Christian wells with poisons furnished by the Moslems of Granada, and two centuries later, Luther accused them of plotting to destroy Christian culture (*ibid.*, 3:236–37, 236–37, 311, 680). One cannot say with certainty that such accusations were always accurate, but clearly, that there was a fear of Jewish treason, and it was not easy for state authorities to deal with.

21. Dubnow, *History of the Jews*, 3:331, 597; Goldstein, *Letters to Mr. Isaacs*, 266 (quoting a Jewish historian to the effect that the Inquisition "could not check the Jewish influence on the conversos"). It should be added, in this connection, that fear of sabotage by Jews based on their natural sympathy with Islam was not the main reason for Spanish expulsion. Neither were Jewish plots to murder inquisitors (Dubnow, *History of the Jews*, 3:326, 329). The principal problem for the Spanish crown was twofold: (a) religious subversion—the Jews were perceived as undermining Christianity; and (b) law and order. As regards religious orthodoxy, Judaizing conversos were giving Christians Jewish prayer books, telling them which fast days to observe, bringing matsot for Passover, and urging observance of the Jewish faith (*ibid.*, 3:335). Dubnow points out that *even after 1492*, tens of thousands of conversos "clung loyally to their religion and nation [Judaism]" and not a few had "entered the ranks of the Spanish nobility, clergy, and officialdom." The problem was, in fact, worse than it had been before expulsion on account of the precept passed from father to son: "Be a Christian openly and a Jew secretly" (*ibid.*, 3:597–98).

Regarding law and order, there had been riots in Ciudad Real in 1464, 1467, and 1474, as well as in major cities such as Toledo (1467) and Cordova (1473), and this in spite of concerted peacekeeping efforts on the part of Spanish officials. Fuelling the hostility were reports of converso priests mocking the Mass in the act of celebrating it and Jews under torture pleading guilty to desecrating hosts (Carroll, *Glory of Christendom*, 607; Dubnow, *History of the Jews*, 3:292). On one occasion, a Jew grabbed a cross being carried by a priest in procession and trampled it (*ibid.*, 3:63). Things were such that two months before the fall of Granada, the Jewish community had to ask for royal protection (*ibid.*, 3:334), and the point is that "kings," as Dubnow observes, "could not protect the Jews against the arbitrary attacks of the mob" (*ibid.*, 3:237; Johnson, *History of the Jews*, 225). A pogrom that occurred at Segovia in 1471 came about in spite of an attempt to restrict Jews to the local ghetto (Dubnow, *History of the Jews*, 3:310), and when kings tried to bring pogrom perpetrators to justice, they themselves might be faced with insurrection, as was the case with Alfonso V of Portugal (*ibid.*, 3:313). That it was often difficult for rulers to protect Jews may be inferred from what the Jew says in Abelard's twelfth century *Dialogue* referring to fields, vineyards, and landed estates which Jews were forbidden to own in certain times and places: "There is no one who can protect them for us from open or occult attack." See *Dialogue of a Philosopher With a Jew and a Christian* (Toronto: Pontifical Institute of Mediaeval Studies, 1979), 33. According to Joel Kraemer, Muslim rulers tolerant of Jewish minorities were up against the same problems faced by the Christians. Take, for example, the Jews of Cordoba, which was under Islamic rule during the 1100s, lived in their own quarter "situated near the royal palace . . . for the Jews' protection against possible mob violence. This arrangement created a bond of mutual dependency between the Jews and the ruling establishment that contributed to popular resentment." See Kraemer, *Maimonides*, 26. Paul Johnson, in summing up, writes that "the state was terrified of riots as a symptom of public unrest. It could not prevent the riots or even punish them adequately, so it sought to remove the cause" (Johnson, *History of the Jews*, 225). We also have Isabel's expulsion order which reads in part: "We have tried separation in vain" (quoted by Dubnow, *History of the Jews*, 3:335).

22. Johnson, *History of the Jews*, 230–31 gives a précis of expulsion history. As early as AD 414, Egyptians drove the Jews from Alexandria, and during the seventh century, Mohammed expelled two out of three Jewish tribes from Medina, killing off all the males of a third and selling women and children into slavery.

23. See Michael Wood, *Shakespeare* (New York: Basic Books, 2003), 101 (on Elizabeth). Ancient Judaism imposed such punishments as burning and stoning for over a dozen offenses (Goldstein, *Letters to Mr. Isaacs*, 264). In the Orient, the Persians sawed off the arms and legs of their victims. The Japanese burned men in straw suits. But the English under Elizabeth were particularly cruel. Before executing Archbishop O'Hurley of Cashel in Ireland, they placed his legs in oil-filled boots and roasted them over a fire until the flesh literally melted from his bones.

24. Carroll and Shiflett, *Christianity on Trial*, 105 (comparing the use of torture in various courts). See also Kamen, *The Spanish Inquisition* (for the fifteen minute limit).

25. Goldstein, *Letters to Mr. Isaacs*, 262–63.

26. William Thomas Walsh, *Isabella of Spain* (Rockford, Illinois: Tan, 1987), 275 (re: witches).

27. For Jewish coercion, see Goldstein, *Letters to Mr. Isaacs*, 265.

28. Williamson, trans., *Eusebius*, 111.

29. Carroll, *Building*, 90, 150.

30. Daniel-Rops, *Dark Ages*, 2:38 (on Gaza); Carroll, *Glory*, 606; Moczar, *Islam at the Gates*, 120.

31. Hughes, *History of the Catholic Church*, 116. See also Malcolm Barber, *The Cathars* (New York: Pearson Education, 2000); Belloc, *The Great Heresies* (Rockford, Illinois: Tan, 1991), 85, 90–91; Jack O'Brien, *The Truth About the Inquisition* (New York: Paulist Press, 1950), ch. 3; Brandmüller, *Light and Shadows*, 104. For Dominic, see Butler's *Lives of the Saints*. The Albigensians, who controlled more than a thousand towns in Languedoc, were strong in Provence as well. Influenced by Jewish rationalism, they were in constant touch with the Jews and Moslems of Spain, and so it is not surprising that many Jewish freethinkers became Albigensians and Waldensians. Such sects denied Christian doctrines that were particularly repulsive to them (such as the indissolubility of marriage and the mystery of the Eucharist). That French Jews in Albigensian areas were often appointed to government posts in violation of canon law was another sore point with traditionalists (see John Laux, *Church History*, 351 and Dubnow, *History of the Jews*, 3:21, 24, 40, 269).

32. Anne Carroll, *Christ in the Americas*, 89 (on English penal laws). As William Cobbett observes, in comparing Elizabeth with Mary, her predecessor, "Elizabeth put, in one way or another, more Catholics to death in one year for not becoming apostates than Mary put to death in her whole reign for having apostatized" (Cobbett, *The Protestant "Reformation,"* no. 269). In Elizabethan England, one could not live according to one's conscience, as compared with Isabel's Spain, where the following of one's conscience was mandatory.

33. Ludwig von Pastor, *The History of the Popes* (St. Louis: Herder, 1923–69), 19:511.

34. Anne Carroll, *Christ the King*, 245; Laux, *Church History*, 358.

35. Laux, *Church History*, 358; *The Ratzinger Report*, 146.

36. For Hussite intolerance and atrocities, see Carroll, *Glory*, 506–507.

37. Anne Carroll, *Christ the King*, 248. The Huguenots were not afraid to hire German mercenaries to fight for them, and many of them were in league with England, which was tantamount to treason. In return for cross-channel aid, they gave England the seaports of Havre de Grace and Dieppe while promising to hand over Calais, a strategic plum (Cobbett, *The Protestant "Reformation,"* nos. 273–75, 277).

38. Hughes, *History*, 196. For Gorkum, see Dominican Novices, *Dominican Saints* (Rockford, Illinois: Tan, 1995), 322–27.

39. Hughes, *History*, 196; Anne Carroll, *Christ the King*, 248–49; Walsh, *Philip II*, 289–90, 536; von Pastor, *History of the Popes*, 19:509–511. It should be added that the Huguenots committed terrible atrocities at Nîmes five years before the St. Bartholomew's Massacre and were thought to be on the verge of seizing control of the government of France (which would have put them in a position to conquer the papal states and strike a death blow at Catholicism). According to John Milner, twenty thousand French churches were destroyed by the Huguenots, and in

one province alone (Dauphiny), they burned nine hundred towns and murdered 378 priests or religious (Milner, *The End of Religious Controversy*, 134).

40. Anne Carroll, *Christ the King*, 249.

41. Michael Novak, *On Two Wings* (San Francisco: Encounter Books, 2002), 52.

42. Johnson, *History of the Jews*, 109 (on the Sadducees' cruelty); Goldstein, *Letters to Mr. Isaacs*, 271–72 (on da Costa). See also Exodus 32:27–28; 1 Kings 18:19, 40; 2 Kings 23:5, 20. For Joshua and God's command, see Deuteronomy 7:2, 16, 22–23; 20:16–18; Numbers 31:7, 13–18; Joshua, chapters 6, 9, 10, 11 (especially 10:40).

43. In addition to inventing the hydrostatic balance, Galileo improved the telescope, and some say he was the first to use the latter to study the skies. He also discovered sunspots, the phases of Venus, and the moon's libration. Finally, he demonstrated that the moon is mountainous and shines with reflected light, that the Milky Way is made up of countless stars, and that Jupiter has satellites.

44. See Consultants' Report on Copernicanism (by eleven theologians), Feb. 24, 1616 in Maurice A. Finocchiaro, ed., *The Galileo Affair* (Berkley: University of California Press, 1989), 146. Experimental confirmation of stellar parallax did not occur until the nineteenth century. That Galileo could teach heliocentrism as theory vs. fact was the position of the Congregation of the Index of Forbidden Books, as well as of Pope Paul V, according to what Cardinal Bellarmine declared publicly in a sworn affidavit after meeting with Galileo in 1616 (see Carroll, *Cleaving*, 494). At some point, an unsigned document dated February 26, 1616 (not mentioned in the Bellarmine affidavit) was inserted in the Vatican's file on Galileo. It forbade the mathematician to teach heliocentrism in *any* way, even as theory. But this was presumably a back-up position to be used only if Galileo began teaching his theory as fact, which he, most likely, had not yet done when the document entered the file. Historians are divided on the question of whether the document in question is authentic (ibid., 494). See Carroll, *Cleaving*, 490–95, 537–40 for a concise and balanced discussion of the Galileo affair.

45. For his penance, which included three years of mild house arrest, see Sentence of the Inquisition in Finocchiaro, ed., *Galileo*, 288. The nature of the issue is crystal clear from Galileo's words at his 1633 trial: "I have not held the Copernican system since I was ordered to abandon it" (see Madrid, *Pope Fiction*, 187). This was pure fiction. His book, *Dialogo sopra i due massimi sistemi del mondo* (*Dialogue on the Two Great World Systems*), published just before his trial in 1633, was an obvious attempt to make the case for heliocentrism inasmuch as he presented the strongest possible arguments in its favor while discrediting objections by using a straw man approach. According to a Catholic Answers tract, "The Galileo Controversy," Galileo "claimed that the Copernican theory had the 'sensible demonstrations' needed according to Aristotelian science, but most knew that such demonstrations were not yet forthcoming." Intentional or not, this was another case of dishonesty.

46. Most, *Catholic Apologetics*, 169.

47. Woods, *The Catholic Church*, 69.

48. Stephen Mizwa, *Nicolas Copernicus* (New York: Kosciusko Foundation, 1943), 23–24.

49. On Cambridge, see Williamson, *World of Josephus*, 311. On book burning, see Henry Graham, *Where We Got the Bible*, 128–29, 131.

50. Galileo to Castelli, Dec. 21, 1613 in Finocchiaro, ed., *Galileo*, 28; Carroll, *Cleaving*, 492. For Bellarmine's words, see Richard Blackwell, *Galileo, Bellarmine, and the Bible* (Notre Dame: Notre Dame Press, 1991), 81. For another biblical passage that is relevant, see 1 Chronicles 16:30.

51. Galileo's Considerations on the Copernican Opinion (1615) in Finocchiaro, ed., *Galileo*, 82.

52. See Galileo to Castelli, Dec. 21, 1613 in Finocchiaro, ed., *Galileo*, 51. See also Blackwell, *Galileo*, 197–98. In Galileo's 1615 letter to Christina (quoted in Blackwell, *Galileo*, 78–79), he holds that in matters where science is not certain, one can put one's trust in the Bible (implying lack of trust when science is "certain").

53. For the relevant proceedings of Vatican II, see footnote 3, chapter 5.

54. The Council of Trent (1545–1563) specifically ruled out private interpretation of Scripture, and the emphasis thereafter was on literal interpretation of disputed passages in order to counter the Protestant line on Penance, the papacy, and the Eucharist—see Kenneth Howell, *God's Two Books* (Notre Dame: Notre Dame Press, 2002), 6, 184. George V. Coyne, S.J., director emeritus of the Vatican Observatory, points out in his recently published volume, *The Heavens Proclaim*, that Urban VIII was under intense pressure to silence suspected heretics within the Church on account of his support for the Protestant King of Sweden, who, along with the Duke of Bavaria and King of France, was fighting a Catholic (Hapsburg) coalition of Spain and the German Empire in the Thirty Years War (1618–48). It should also be pointed out that there are still many things about the Galileo affair that remain unclear, including the extent to which Galileo was forbidden to promote heliocentrism when he met with Cardinal Bellarmine in 1616. For some of the latest findings, see John Farrell, "Myths About the Galileo Affair," *Catholic World Report* (April 2009): 30.

55. Galileo to Castelli, Dec. 21, 1613 in Finocchiaro, ed., *Galileo*, 50. In the previous century, Saints Teresa of Avila and John of the Cross stressed the uncertainty of all human knowledge, and even contemporary heliocentrists like Foscarini, in tandem with theologians like Bellarmine, were inclined to agree (with Teresa and John) while taking issue with Galileo (Howell, *God's Two Books*, 196, 198–99). According to biographer David Wooten, who did exhaustive research on the Florentine's religion, Galileo was not even a Christian in any meaningful sense of the word, much less a practicing Catholic (Wooten, *Galileo: Watcher of the Skies* [Yale University Press, 2010], 240–41). Galileo's copyist, Sylvestro Pagnoni, stated that his master never went to church; and in 1627 Galileo wrote a treatise on miracles of the Old Testament in which it would seem that he tried to explain them away naturalistically (*ibid.*, 94, 141–42).

56. Sentence of the Inquisition, June 22, 1633 in Finocchiaro, ed., *Galileo*, 288.

57. Carroll, *Cleaving*, 537.

58. Galileo claimed that his 1632 book, *Dialogue Concerning the Two Chief World Systems*, was not a defense of heliocentrism, but clearly it was. See D'Sousa, *Christianity*, 109. For his perjury, see note 45.

NOTES

59. Sentence of the Inquisition, June 22, 1633 in Finocchiaro, ed., *Galileo*, 288.

60. Madrid, *Pope Fiction*, 188–89. A commission established by John Paul II began investigating the Galileo case in 1991, and in an address to the Pontifical Academy of Science (October 1992), the pope endorsed its finding that the disciplinary measures taken against Galileo were mistaken (Brandmüller, *Light and Shadows*, 251).

61. Most, *Catholic Apologetics*, 168; Carroll, *Cleaving*, 540. For the best summary discussion of Galileo and the Church, see Warren Carroll, *Cleaving*, 490–95, 537–40.

CHAPTER 9

1. The figure for Episcopal priests who have converted to Catholicism over the past generation is estimated to be in the neighborhood of four hundred. See Michael and Jana Novak, *Tell Me Why* (Oxford: Lion, 1999), 154.

2. Raymond Arroyo has written a marvelous biography of the person who is arguably America's most accomplished woman (Mother Angelica).

3. *Catholic World Report* (November 2007): 23.

4. Stevenson's letters edited by Colvin (3:151–53, 214).

5. John J. Delaney, *Dictionary of Saints* (1980), 138.

6. Matthew 7:28–29. See also John 7:46.

7. Matthew 22:34–46 (Sadducees and Pharisees); Mark 12:28–34 (scribes).

8. John 4:18.

9. For the unity prayer, see John 17. For New Testament warnings against sectarianism and separatism, see John 10:16; Romans 15:5–6; 1 Corinthians 1:10–16; 3:4; Ephesians 4:3; Philippians 1:27; 2:2; 2 Peter 2:1. For Jesus' promise of the Advocate, see John 14:16–17, 26; 16:13.

10. According to the *World Christian Encyclopedia* published in the year 2000, there are over thirty-three thousand sects. See also John 17:21 (Jesus prayed for unity "that the world may believe").

11. Many converts from the Protestant ministry have listed this as a reason for crossing the Tiber.

12. Numbers 16.

13. Numbers 12:10.

14. Matthew 16:18–19; John 17:21–22.

15. For Peter, see 2 Peter 1:20; 2:1–3.

16. Romans 16:17; Titus 3:10. See also Galations 1:9; 2 John 1:10–11; 2 Thessalonians 3:6, 14.

17. Ignatius' Letter to the Philadelphians 3.2.

18. Irenaeus, *Against Heresies*, 1. 10, 2.

19. Augustine, *Treatise on Baptism Against the Donatists*, book 5, chapter 1 (AD 400).

20. See Aquilina, *Fathers of the Church*, 38–42.

21. See, for example, no. 2271 (on abortion).

22. See *This Rock* (January 1996): 40 for the results of the Lambeth Conference. The discipline of excommunication is rarely used these days, but it applies automatically to anyone who aids or abets an abortionist.

23. In welcoming Benedict XVI to the White House on April 16, Bush said, "we need your message that all human life is sacred . . . [as well as your message that we must reject the] 'dictatorship of relativism.'" At a follow-up White House dinner, the President said, in like vein, that "the Catholic Church has been a rock in a raging sea," *Wall Street Journal* (April 22, 2008): A23. Catholics are less likely than Protestants to support abortion rights and much less likely than Jews—see *First Things* (December 2005): 21. According to Human Life International, Jews had the largest number of abortions per capita in 1993 and the least children per couple. Israelis, in particular, were slaughtering nearly half of their infants in the womb, according to *Human Life Reports* (May 1993): 2.

24. Forty-two languages in 1998, according to the *National Catholic Register* (April 26–May 2, 1998): 17.

25. Matthew 26:6; Acts 9:43; Romans 12:16; 1 Corinthians 1:26–27; James 2:1–4.

26. John 20:21–23; Genesis 2:7.

27. See Jurgens, ed., *Faith of the Early Fathers*, 1:130–31.

28. For Jesus' fast, see Matthew 4:2. See also 2 Corinthians 11:27; (for Paul); Exodus 34:28 (for Moses); 2 Samuel 1:12 (for David); 1 Kings 19:6–8 (for Elijah); Luke 2:37 (for Anna); Judith 4:11 (for Judith). Catholics of the Western Rite are obliged to abstain from meat or mortify themselves in some other way every Friday. On Ash Wednesday, as well as Good Friday, they must also engage in fasting and abstinence.

29. See Williamson, *The World of Josephus*, 107 (on the singularity of Jesus' attitude toward children).

30. Matthew 18:5, 14.

31. Matthew 10:1; Mark 16:17–18; John 14:12.

32. Acts 5:12; 9:40; 12:7; 16:26.

33. For Augustine's testimony, see his *City of God*, 22:8 and his *Confessions* (London: Burns and Oates, 1954), 242. He found bodies of martyrs miraculously incorrupt long after interment, and his belief in miracles was not limited to signs worked by Christians (see Dulles, *History of Apologetics*, 81).

34. The chapel was modeled on Sainte-Chapelle in Paris, and since the ladder was a normal means of reaching French choir lofts at a time when choirs were all male, this is how the Santa Fe chapel was designed. But needless to say, ladders were inconvenient and even dangerous for nuns in long flowing habits. Consequently, the sisters tried to find someone skilled enough to build a staircase, and it had to be one that would not take up an inordinate amount of space in their tiny chapel. At first they looked in vain. But on the last day of a novena begging the intervention of St. Joseph, a nameless individual appeared who volunteered to do the job. The daily book found in the Mother House of the Sisters of Loretto depicts the person in question as old, gray-bearded, and leading a donkey. His only tools were a saw, a hammer, and a carpenter's square. The tradition that he left without payment is supported by the sisters, who kept a careful record of all expenses and made no entry for the staircase. When Mother Magdalene, the superior, went to the local lumber yard to pay for the wood, no one at the yard knew anything about it. Over the years, various individuals named one or another member of their

family as the builder of the staircase, but none of these claims has ever been substantiated. All of which suggests that the builder may have been St. Joseph himself, as suspected by the nuns. In 1895, the *Santa Fe New Mexican* announced the death of a French carpenter by the name of François-Jean Rochas and stated that he was the builder. Most likely, however, this was simply another unsubstantiated claim. See Mary J. Straw Cook's history of the chapel entitled *Loretto* (Santa Fe, New Mexico: The Loretto Chapel, 1984), chapter 4.

35. See Joan Carroll Cruz, *The Incorruptibles*, 288–89.

36. For Bethesda, see John 5:4.

37. See Genesis 32:23–31 (Jacob); Luke 1:11 (Zachariah); 2:9 (shepherds); Acts 12:9 (Peter). For Paul, see 1 Corinthians 15:8; Acts 9:3–9; 22:11; 26:16.

38. Eusebius, *History of the Church*, 8:7.

39. On the aftermath of these great miracles, the reaction of France and Portugal reminds one of what Jesus had to say about the relatives of Dives. Because they were not attuned to Moses and the prophets, they would not believe even if someone rose from the dead (Luke 16:31).

40. See Carl Anderson and Eduardo Chávez, *Our Lady of Guadalupe* (New York: Doubleday, 2009), 7–31. For an outstanding account, brief but scholarly, see Carroll, *Cleaving*, 616–26. Worthwhile, in addition, is Carroll's full-length treatment, *Our Lady of Guadalupe* (Front Royal, Virginia: Christendom Publications, 1983), and *A Handbook of Guadalupe* (New Bedford, MA: Franciscan Friars of the Immaculate, 1997).

41. For the miracles of Padre Pio, see Woodward, *Miracles*, 367–68.

42. Adams, *Mont-Saint-Michel and Chartres* (1980 ed.), 8, 141. Shaw, speaking of the hereafter, said, "I think perhaps his mother will let me in." On Sargent, see Sally M. Promey, *Painting Religion in Public: John Singer Sargent's Triumph of Religion* (Princeton University Press, 1999). Regarded by contemporaries as the greatest American painter of his day, Sargent spent the better part of three decades at the height of his career executing these murals, and at the end of his life he regarded them, in conjunction with others that accompany them in the Boston Public Library (third floor), as his most important work (Promey, 4). Curious, too, is the fact that one of the symbols Sargent chose for ceiling adornment was the Petrine crown and keys, i.e. the papal insignia.

43. *Time Magazine*,(March 21, 2005).

44. During the 1950s when the Council of Europe wanted a flag, it asked artists around the world to submit designs by the end of the Marian year. Out of forty-seven countries and eight hundred million people, the competition came down to two artists, a German by the name of Arsene Heitz and the Spanish artist/writer, Salvador de Madriaga. The European Parliament tells visitors that the number "12" stands for the twelve tribes of Jacob, along with the twelve apostles and the twelve labors of Hercules; also that the crown symbolizes European unity. But the main inspiration for Heitz was the twelve stars that shone above Mary's head when she appeared to Catherine Labouré, the French nun who had the Miraculous Medal struck in 1832. See *This Rock* (February 2000): 7, 9.

CONCLUSION

1. See Appendix A for an answer to the question of change and continuity in Church teaching. The closest one comes to papal contradiction is the case of Pope Honorius outlined in chapter 6, note 3. False claimants to the papacy ("anti-popes") there have been, and their posturing misled many, including some of the greatest saints; but there has never been more than one legitimate pope.

APPENDICES

APPENDIX A—HAS THE CHURCH CHANGED?

The answer to this question is twofold: yes and no. The "no," however, calls for emphasis at a time when relativism is king. The Church has not budged on the Ten Commandments. It has not sanctioned fornication, abortion, euthanasia, sodomy, or suicide. On biblical inerrancy and the indissolubility of marriage it stands just as it did two thousand years ago.

This said, the definition of dogma takes time. It is unlikely, for example, that anyone in the early Church used the word "sacrament," and it was probably a matter of centuries before theologians would describe a sacrament as "an outward sign instituted to give grace." "Contraception" is another term not likely to have been used. It does not appear in Holy Writ, and it was not until the twentieth century that it was formally condemned—by Pius XI in *Casti Connubii* (1930), then again by Paul VI in *Humanae Vitae*. In the case of Christ's divinity, the apostles believed it and taught it, but it was not formally defined until the Council of Nicaea in AD 325. Papal infallibility became dogma in 1870, and belief in Mary's bodily assumption into heaven entered the books in 1950. There was never a time when these tenets were not generally held; but it is one thing for the faithful to believe, another for the Church to require such belief. As Cardinal Newman observes in his *Essay on the Development of Christian Doctrine*, doctrine is not defined until it is violated.

From time to time, the Holy Father or an ecumenical council will elaborate on Church teaching to clarify a principle or refine the language in which it is couched. This is what Newman means by "development of doctrine." But no pope has ever contradicted another on faith or morals, just as no council has ever clashed with another on dogma, and such consistency stems from the authority Christ gave to Peter and his successors, coupled with the Lord's promise to his apostles that he would send the Paraclete, the Spirit of Truth (i.e. Holy Spirit) to lead them to the fullness of truth and remain with them and their successors forever (Jn. 14:16, 26).

Obviously, there are certain ways in which the Church *has* changed. When a Catholic marries a non-Catholic, the non-Catholic is no longer required to promise *in writing* that the children will be raised Catholic. Catholics may now eat meat on Friday provided they substitute some other form of mortification. There have been many changes over the years in the way the Liturgy is celebrated. The basic elements of the Mass have been in place for well over a thousand years: begging God's mercy, giving praise, reading Scripture, offering gifts, and intoning the Eucharistic Prayer. But who serves, how one serves, what the priest wears, and what he says on the altar—all of this has changed; and such change has been instituted by a Church that (a) formulated the original wording of the Liturgy, and (b) derives its authority from Christ: "I will give you [Peter] the keys of the kingdom of heaven . . . whatever you bind on earth shall be bound in heaven . . . whatever you loose on earth shall be loosed in heaven" (Mt. 16:18–19).

If any of the above-mentioned changes undermined principle there would be a problem. But this is not the case. Imagine, if you will, a young boy who is hit on the head by a baseball pitch, causing him to lose 90 percent of his hearing. As a grown-up, he tells his son he may not play baseball because the game is too dangerous. But no sooner has he said this than batting helmets are introduced, and the same father allows his son to play. Has the old man changed? Not really, because he has maintained the principle of prudence in risk-taking.

Shifting to the world of fashion, is it morally permissible for a woman to wear a knee-length skirt? In the days of Queen Victoria, the answer would have been no, but today, it is common practice. In this instance, the thing that remains changeless is the need for modesty. At all times and in all places, one must take care not to arouse impure thoughts.

The Church no longer forbids the lending of money at exorbitant rates because modern banking has built-in safeguards. Although irresponsible borrowing can lead to trouble in any age, and people still get hurt, the consequences today are less serious than they once were because a person in dire financial straights can simply declare bankruptcy. Debtor's prison is a relic of the past.

Has the Church changed on slavery? We touched briefly on this in chapter 7, but in a nutshell, every well meaning person is entitled to certain essentials, among them food and shelter, rest, recreation, marriage (if they are so disposed), children (if God is so disposed), and spiritual refreshment. In ancient times, when the human rights of bondsmen were recognized, there was no thought of condemning slavery as intrinsically evil. But clearly, things have changed. There are few, if any, places in the world today where the rights of slaves as human beings are respected and protected. So it was that John Paul II, in his encyclical *Veritatis Splendor*, issued a sweeping condemnation of slavery—slavery, that is, *as it exists today*. Even before the papacy of John Paul II, Rome would occasionally come out against isolated cases of abuse. In 1435, for example, the Holy Father insisted on immediate emancipation of all slaves in the Canary Islands where conditions were abominable—under pain of excommunication. A century and a half later, Gregory XIV, for similar reasons, ordered the freeing of all Filipino slaves.

Has there been a shift in Rome's position on capital punishment? Yes and no. In days gone by, the Church's respect for human life caused it to oppose cruel and unusual punishments. But it sanctioned capital punishment because maximum security cells, as we know them today, were non-existent, and prison breaks were common. Nowadays it is financially and technically possible in many parts of the world to incarcerate hardened criminals, and so the Church would limit capital punishment to cases where it is absolutely necessary as a deterrent or measure of economy. In short, Catholicism changes with changing circumstances, but the principles do not change, for, as Paul says, "Jesus Christ is the same yesterday and today and forever" (Heb. 13:8).

The next question is: what does and does not fall under the heading of "change with changing circumstances?" and this is where a qualified arbiter is needed. In the area of sexual morality, proponents of promiscuity will argue that, owing to the availability of condoms, premarital sex is safer than it used to be. Abortion is safer too (for the mother). But safety is not the issue here. The issue is protection of innocent life. Regardless of how safe contraception and abortion may be as procedures—and they still involve risk even on the physical level—they are not *spiritually* safe in the eyes of the Church.

Has Rome altered its position on religious liberty and freedom of conscience? Once again: yes and no, with emphasis on the latter. When Louis XIV forced the Huguenots of France to choose between conversion and deportation, the pope disapproved. When Isabel drove the Jews out of Spain, Rome laid out a red carpet for them. Conversion at the point of a sword has never been the Catholic way. Eighteen hundred years ago, the eminent Church scholar Tertullian wrote Scapula, Roman governor of Africa (c. AD 212): "It is not proper for religion to compel religion" (Most, *Catholic Apologetics Today*, 203), and we have seen how the monk Alcuin protested Charlemagne's forced conversion of the Saxons during the 800s.

Current conditions in many parts of the world, especially the Christian world, favor the separation of church and state. Ethnic mixing is more common than it used to be, and with religious pluralism comes an increased demand for liberty of expression. The Church welcomes separation, especially in the United States, because separation, at its best, leaves religion free. But this does not make theocracy an intrinsic evil. Intolerance of one or another religious group is not wrong *per se*. It depends on the group. Rulers must keep the peace, and the beliefs of certain sects make their job all but impossible. Theocracy was blessed by God in the Old Testament, and since Hebrew Scripture is as much God's word as any other portion of the Bible, it cannot be said that church and state must always be separate or that rulers are never justified in suppressing dissent. Vatican City is itself a theocracy.

Some have held that Vatican Council II's *Declaration on Religious Liberty* (*Dignitatis Humanae*) reversed earlier Church teaching by accepting the idea of a religiously neutral state. This, however, is not so. Long before Vatican II, Leo XIII (1878–1903) wrote that, while error does not have rights equal to those of truth, the Church does not condemn a ruler for allowing various religions a place in the state. Leo's predecessors, Gregory XVI and Pius IX, spoke against religious freedom because, in their time, it meant anti-clerical suppression of parochial schools and religious orders, as well as state control over the appointment of bishops and pastors. They were not thinking of the American system of separation, which is aimed at religious freedom (see Avery Cardinal Dulles, "Development or Reversal?" in the October 2005 issue of *First Things*, 59).

In the second section of its *Declaration on Religious Liberty*, the Second Vatican Council stated that people must not be threatened with prison or death if they err. On the contrary. In section 1, it stated that it would leave "untouched the traditional Catholic doctrine about the moral duty of men and societies toward the true religion and toward the one Church of Christ." As the Catechism of the Catholic Church puts it: "The right to religious liberty is neither a moral license to adhere to error, nor a supposed right to error [CF. Leo XIII, *Libertas praestantissimum* 18; Pius XII, *AAS* 1953, 799], but rather a natural right of the human person to civil liberty, i.e., immunity, within just limits, from external constraint in religious matters by political authorities" (2108). In the words of Cardinal Dulles, "the Church has applied the unchanging principles of the right to religious freedom and the duty to uphold religious truth to the conditions of an individualist age, in which almost all societies are religiously pluralist. Under such circumstances the establishment of religion becomes the exception rather than the rule. But the principle of noncoercion of consciences in matters of faith remains constant" (Dulles, "Development or Reversal?" 60).

Has Rome changed its position on salvation outside the Church? Here, the answer is simply "no." In the Gospels and Acts of the Apostles one can make out three distinct strains of thought on the subject of salvation: (1) those familiar with Christ's words and actions must be baptized into his Church if they expect to be saved; (2) those who through no fault of their own are ignorant of Christian teaching may be saved if they live by the light of their conscience; (3) all who are saved, whether members of the Church or not, owe their salvation to Christ and, by extension, to his Church because he and his Church are one in the same way that man and woman are one in marriage.

Jesus himself warned contemporary leaders that those who refused to believe would die in their sins (i.e. go to hell—see Jn. 8:24; 1 Cor. 15:17–18). He also told Nicodemus that, "unless one is born of water and the Spirit, he cannot enter the kingdom of God" (Jn. 3:5). This, in essence, is also what Peter told his listeners after the Resurrection: "there is salvation in no one else, for there is no other name under heaven given among men by which we must be saved " (Acts 4:12).

For point no. 2, we can go back to Peter: "In every nation any one who fears him [the Lord] and does what is right is acceptable to him " (Acts 10:35). Paul, too, is clear that pagans are bound by the natural law and the light of their conscience (Rom. 2:14).

Point no. 3 is based on what Jesus himself taught: first, that he suffered on Calvary for the salvation of all (Jn. 3:17); secondly, that no one comes to the Father except through him (Jn. 14:6). For bridegroom imagery, see Mt. 9:15; Mk. 2:19; Lk. 5:34; and for oneness in marriage: Mt. 19:5–6; Mk. 10:7. Finally, when Jesus confronted Saul on the road to Damascus, he did not ask Saul why he was persecuting his brethren and plotting against his Church. Our Lord said, "Saul, Saul, why do you persecute *me*?" (Acts 9:4—italics added for emphasis).

Catholicism, in keeping with the Gospel as quoted above, holds first, that there is no salvation outside the Church (see *Dominus Jesus*, a declaration of the Congregation of the Doctrine of the Faith ratified by Pope John Paul II in the year 2000); secondly, that those outside the fold may be saved by the "baptism of desire," meaning that their disposition is such that if they were ever privileged to come to know Christ and his Church, they would convert. As stated in the *Dogmatic Constitution of the Church* issued by the Second Vatican Council, "Those also can attain to salvation who through no fault of their own do not know the Gospel of Christ or His Church, yet sincerely seek God and moved by grace strive by their deeds to do his will as it is known to them through the dictates of conscience" (16).

None of this is new. It may be found in the writings of the popes, as well as in the rulings of ecumenical councils, including the Council of Trent's *Decree of Justification.* Clement I, Justin Martyr, Ambrose, Augustine, Chrysostom, and Gregory the Great are of the same mind, as are Thomas Aquinas, Francis de Sales, and Cardinal Newman.

Augustine is often cited as one who believed there is no salvation outside the Church, and this is true. But it is only one side of the coin. He also taught that "those who seek the truth with careful industry and are ready to be corrected when they have found it, are not to be rated among heretics" (Letter 43:1). In Letter 102:12, he observed that "from the beginning of the human race, whoever believed in Him somewhat, and lived according to His precepts . . . whoever and wherever they might have been, doubtless were saved through Him" (quoted by Most, *Catholic Apologetics Today*, 144–49—see especially 149). Finally, Augustine said the following of those willing to "seek the truth with anxious solicitude, being sincerely disposed to renounce their error as soon as they discover it": they are "not to be deemed heretics" (*Epist ad Episc. Donat* cited by Milner, *The End of Religious Controversy*, 113). For Ambrose specifically, see Ambrose to Studius in "Ambrose Letters 1–91," one volume in the multi-volume *Fathers of the Church*, 1954, 494.

APPENDIX B—THE SEVEN SACRAMENTS IN SCRIPTURE

1. BAPTISM

Jesus, who was himself baptized, instructed his apostles to: "Go therefore and make disciples of all nations, baptizing them in the name of the Father and of the Son and of the Holy Spirit" (Mt. 28:19). He also told Nicodemus: "Truly, truly, I say to you, unless one is born of water and the Spirit, he cannot enter the kingdom of God" (Jn. 3:5).

2. CONFIRMATION

See Acts 8:14–17: "When the apostles at Jerusalem heard that Samaria had received the word of God, they sent to them Peter and John, who came down and prayed for them that they might receive the Holy Spirit; for it had not yet fallen on any of them, but they had only been baptized in the name of the Lord Jesus. Then they laid their hands on them and they received the Holy Spirit." On being a "soldier of Christ," see Eph. 6:13–17.

3. THE SACRAMENT OF RECONCILIATION (FORMERLY KNOWN AS PENANCE)

Christ, who forgave men their sins (Lk. 5:18–24), passed this power on to his apostles: "If you forgive the sins of any, they are forgiven; if you retain the sins of any, they are retained," breathing on them as he did so (Jn. 20:23). The only other place in the Bible where God breathes on man is at the moment of Creation when he literally breathes life into Adam through his nostrils (Gen. 2:7). Message: the Sacrament of Reconciliation is life-giving.

4. THE EUCHARIST

See Mt. 26:26–28; Lk. 22:19–20; and Mk. 14:22–25. Jesus explains the Real Presence in the sixth chapter of John (6:1–13, 48–67), and Saint Paul speaks of the need to receive the "Body of Christ" worthily (1 Cor. 10:16; 11:24–29).

5. HOLY ORDERS (ORDINATION TO THE PRIESTHOOD)

Jesus chose twelve to be apostles, and after doing so, he gave them the power to consecrate bread and wine (Mt. 26:26–28) and the power to forgive sins (Jn. 20:23).

THINK AND BELIEVE

6. MATRIMONY

This was well-established in Jewish tradition. Jesus worked his first miracle at a wedding feast, and it is clear from what he taught that his aim was to restore marriage to the way it was in the beginning. See Gen. 2:18, 24; Mt. 19:5; Mk. 10:7–9.

7. ANOINTING OF THE SICK (FORMERLY KNOWN AS EXTREME UNCTION)

See Jas. 5:14–16: "Is any among you sick? Let him call for the elders of the church, and let them pray over him, anointing him with oil in the name of the Lord; and the prayer of faith will save the sick man, and the Lord will raise him up; and if he has committed sins, he will be forgiven." Also Mk. 6:13: "They cast out many demons, and anointed with oil many that were sick and healed them."

APPENDIX C—WHERE IS PURGATORY IN THE BIBLE?

1. In his Book of Revelation (the Apocalypse), St. John the Evangelist tells us that "nothing unclean shall enter" heaven (21:27). Where do imperfect souls go for purification?

2. David's crimes of adultery and murder were forgiven, but they did not go unpunished (2 Sam. 12:13–14). If David had died the instant he repented, where would he have gone for punishment?

3. Speaking of God's judgment, St. Paul says that if a man loses his reward because he has failed to build on a proper foundation, he may still be saved, "but only as through fire" (1 Cor. 3:15). Where does one experience such "fire"?

4. In the second Book of Maccabees, we read that Judas Maccabeus prayed for the dead that they might be delivered from their sins (2 Mac. 12:42–46). Where were these souls for whom Judas prayed? They could not have been in heaven, for if they were, such intercession would not have been needed (see the concluding section of chapter 2 for the reliability of Maccabees).

5. In both the Old and the New Testament we learn that we will be punished after we die for minor, as well as major, offenses. Where will small infractions be punished? Jesus warned, for example, that if we so much as call a person a fool, we will be held to account (Mt. 5:21–25). He likewise taught that we shall have to answer for "every careless word" we speak (Mt. 12:36). In the Old Testament, God says to Amos: "Surely I will never forget any of their [the evildoers'] deeds" (Amos 8:7), and in the Book of Sirach, we are assured that every kind of sin will be punished (7:8). There must therefore be a place after death where punishment that is not eternal can be meted out for minor offenses that are not expiated this side of death.

6. Two of Jesus' parables *strongly suggest* purgatory even though the word itself is not used. In the first instance, a master has to deal with a servant whose debt he forgives but who refuses to forgive the debts of those under him. The master hands the unforgiving servant over to the torturers *until he pays all that he owes,* and Jesus tells his listeners, "So also my heavenly Father will do to every one of you, if you do not forgive your brother from your heart" (Mt. 18:35). In other words, those of us who are unforgiving will be punished after death until we have atoned for all our sins, and this cannot take place in heaven, which is totally

blissful, or hell, which is everlasting torture. In the second parable, Jesus tells us, "If you are offering your gift at the altar, and there remember that your brother has something against you, leave your gift there before the altar and go; first be reconciled to your brother, and then come and offer your gift. Make friends quickly with your accuser, while you are going with him to court, lest your accuser hand you over to the judge, and the judge to the guard, and you be put in prison; truly, I say to you, you will never get out till you have paid the last penny." (Mt. 5:23–26). Here again, the message is clear. If we sin against our fellow man without making amends in this world, we can expect punishment in the next that will end only with full atonement. What can this mean but purgatory?

7. Among the early Church fathers, Saints Ambrose, Augustine, and Jerome all speak of purgatory while none of the Fathers denies it, and such opinions count because the Fathers were much closer to Christ and his times than we are.

8. Finally, one can argue that purgatory makes eminently good sense since God is fair and impartial (Ps. 98:9; Deut. 10:17; 1 Pet. 1:17; Acts 10:34–35; Rom. 2:11). Will he treat a saintly man who struggles successfully to be virtuous the same way he treats one whose life is flagrantly evil but who dies with repentance on his lips? Suppose, too, that the former has suffered a great deal while the latter's life has been relatively carefree. Both may be saved (Ezek. 18:24). But to assume that both will go straight to heaven makes little sense. Instinctively, we know that there has to be some kind of equalizer short of heaven or hell.

APPENDIX D—MORE ON CELIBACY

Continuing with clerical celibacy where we left off in chapter 5, it is not clear, as many allege, that the Church's position hampers the recruitment of priests. There was no problem in the industrialized West until the 1960s when morality tanked, and at this point many in the American Protestant community experienced the same difficulty. Episcopal's General Theological Seminary in Chelsea (NYC), for example, had 75 percent fewer men in 1992 than it did in 1962 (*New York Times* July 20, 1992: B2 and August 30, 1992: 34). According to David Currie, "a recent survey concluded that about one-half of all Protestant ministers would not enter the ministry if they had it to do all over again. The primary reason was the tremendous stress on the family" (*Born Fundamentalist, Born Again Catholic*, 161).

Another argument for the married priesthood makes the point that one should be married if one wants to counsel married couples. But is this really true? Must one be a woman to succeed as an OBGYN? Are female psychiatrists the only ones qualified to treat women?

Finally, celibacy is said to be repressive, stifling creativity and putting the lid on genius. Anyone who believes this should study history. Celibate genius in the clerical world begins with Jesus, Paul, and John the Baptist. Augustine, Thomas Aquinas, and most of the saints were unmarried. Beyond the clerical world, one can point to Plato, Michelangelo, and Newton. In the realm of music, we have Corelli, Handel, Beethoven, Schubert, and Brahms (Vivaldi was a priest). Painters like Sir Joshua Reynolds, Thomas Cole, and Winslow Homer are on the list as well, along with many writers, as, for example: Jonathan Swift, Alexander Pope, Jane Austen, Emily and Charlotte Brontë (Charlotte was single during the composition of *Jane Eyre*), Washington Irving, Emily Dickinson, and Louisa May Alcott. When one adds the names of such geniuses as Prince Henry the Navigator, Vasco da Gama, Copernicus, Samuel Morse (inventor of the Morse Code), and the economist Adam Smith, it is hard to view celibacy as a handicap. There was certainly nothing stultified about Mother Teresa of Calcutta, or Pope John Paul II who supported her.

APPENDIX E—MORE ON CONTRACEPTION

Those who practice contraception will argue that children from large families see less of their parents on a one-to-one basis and are more likely to be financially strapped, which is true. On the other hand, parents of large families are less likely to spoil their offspring; their youngsters learn at an early age how to take responsibility, and, on the whole, they are better able to fend for themselves. George Washington, who lost his father at the age of eleven, came from a family of seven. Saint Thomas Aquinas was one of seven as well, as was Johann Sebastian Bach (who lost his mother when he was nine, and shortly thereafter his father). Others came from families of:

- **8 children:** Charles Dickens (whose family was poor).
- **9 children:** Rembrandt (eighth of nine), Grover Cleveland (whose father died when he was sixteen), Saint Thérèse of Lisieux, and actor Sidney Poitier (the last of nine).
- **10 children**: Hildegaard von Bingen (the most influential woman of her century), Edith Stein (convert to Catholicism from Judaism, a canonized saint and the youngest of ten), Thomas Jefferson, James Madison, James Polk (all three presidents of the United States), Daniel Webster (ninth of ten), John C. Calhoun, John Philip Sousa, Grandma Moses (most celebrated of American folk painters), Sir Arthur Conan Doyle (author of Sherlock Holmes).
- **11 children:** Saints Catherine Labouré and Rose of Lima (last of eleven), Washington Irving (who worked to put his brothers through school), Stephen Foster (ninth of eleven), Edward Flanagan (founder of Boys Town), and Audie Murphy (the most highly decorated soldier of World War II).
- **12 children:** Joseph Haydn (father of the symphony), Franz Schubert (composer of the Ave Maria), Harriet Beecher Stowe, and Matt Talbot.
- **13 children:** Saint Ignatius (founder of the Jesuit Order and the last of thirteen children), Saint Francis Xavier, Matteo Ricci (first Christian missionary to China), Saint Frances Cabrini (first American to be canonized), and Fr. Michael McGivney (founder of the Knights of Columbus).
- **14 children:** Pope John XXIII.
- **15 children:** John Marshall (greatest chief justice of the U.S. Supreme Court).
- **16 children:** Henry Clay (one of America's best known early statesmen, who lost his father at age four).
- **17 children:** Benjamin Franklin and Fr. Paul Marx, OSB (founder of Human Life International).

- **18 children:** Albrecht Dürer, the greatest woodcutter, portraitist, sketcher, and engraver of all time (his brother Albert worked four years in a coal mine to put him through school).
- **19 children:** John Wesley, the founder of Methodism, and his brother, Charles, the writer of a great many popular hymns (their mother was the last of twenty-five).
- **21 children:** Enrico Caruso, arguably the finest tenor who ever lived and the eighteenth child in a family of twenty-one.
- **25 children:** Saint Catherine of Siena, twenty-fourth of twenty-five, was the most influential person, male or female, of her age (she died at the age of thirty-three and is a Doctor of the Church).

Apart from an historical record that holds out hope for children from large families, one can show that contraception is hazardous to one's health. As I point out in my *Catholic Handbook for Engaged and Newly Married Couples*, barrier methods subject the woman to a "higher risk of preeclampsia during pregnancy, one of the leading causes of morbidity. She also faces intrauterine growth retardation and prenatal mortality. Hormone contraception not only causes blood vessel tumors in the lower coronaries, high blood pressure, and clotting (strokes); it can also lead to bleeding gums, jaundice, baldness, sterility, depression, herpes, loss of libido, visual defects, and problems with breastfeeding.

As for intrauterine devices, they can cause excessive bleeding, perforation of the uterus, and pelvic inflammatory disease. Women have died from use of the Pill. Indeed, they are still dying. It is associated with heart disease and an increase in certain kinds of cancer; and fifty percent abandon it due to such unpleasant side effects as irritability, depression, weight gain, and loss of libido. As in the case of abortion, there are likely to be emotional problems as well (pp. 135–36).

Finally, it should be said that Catholic leaders are not the only ones who have come out against contraception over the years. Martin Luther and John Calvin condemned it out of hand, as did John Wesley. See Charles Provan, *The Bible and Birth Control* (Monongahela, PA: Zimmer, 1989) for more details.

APPENDIX F—MORE ON MARY

The following is a brief summary of Catholic teaching on Mary that includes material covered in the text.

It should be repeated for emphasis that Catholics do not worship Mary. They *venerate* her, and for a variety of reasons. Her "yes" to God, freely willed under extremely difficult circumstances, makes her the new Eve. Her sacrifice resulted in nothing less than the reopening of heaven (through the death of her divine Son), and she is a model for all mankind, having stood by Jesus from his humble birth in Bethlehem to death on the Cross. In Genesis 3 we read of God putting "enmity" between an unnamed woman and the devil; and this "enmity" had to be very special because we all feel a certain repugnance to evil. Genesis tells us further that the offspring of this woman ("seed" in certain translations) was destined to strike at Satan's head (Gen. 3:15). Who, other than Mary, could the "woman" of Genesis be? Whenever Jesus addresses his mother, he calls her "woman" (Jn. 2:4; 19:26) and whenever John refers to Mary in the Book of Revelation, he uses the same title, "woman"—or, more precisely, "the woman" (see chapter 12).

"ALL GENERATIONS WILL CALL ME BLESSED"

The degree of veneration accorded Mary by the early Christian Church is highlighted by something else found in Revelation: "a woman clothed with the sun" brings forth a male child who rules "all nations with a rod of iron" (12:1-5). The only other person described by the Bible as "clothed with the sun" is God himself (Psalm 104:2). Mary's cousin, Elizabeth, who refers to the Blessed Mother as the "most blessed of all women" (see note 26 in chapter 4), could have said, "Why is this granted me that my Lord should come to me?" Instead, she exclaims, "Why is this granted to me, that *the mother* of my Lord should come to me?" (Lk. 1:43). At which point, Mary prophesies that "all generations will call me blessed" (Lk. 1:48). This alone would be reason enough to honor Mary.

STILL OTHER REASONS

Mary is important if for no other reason than the fact that she is the spouse of the Third Person of the Blessed Trinity and the mother of our Lord and God. She gave birth to Jesus, nourished him, and raised him to manhood. At Cana, she inaugurated his public ministry, thereby "giving" him to us a second time (Jn. 2:4-5). When she stood by the Cross at Calvary, Jesus gave her to John—"Behold, your mother" (Jn. 19:27). Since John was the only apostle present at the crucifixion and since his biological mother, Salome, was looking on at the time, one may take this to mean that Jesus gave his mother to *all* of us.

WHY PRAY TO MARY?

Why can't we pray directly to God? This is one of the most frequently asked questions, and the answer, simply stated, is that we *can* pray directly to God. We can and we do. The greatest of all prayers, the Mass, is addressed to God. Catholics are not *obliged* to pray to Mary, but they approach her the way a person in trouble might approach a friend for prayers. She sits beside her Son in heaven; she hears us when we invoke her name; and she has influence. The instant the wedding party at Cana ran out of wine she called upon her Son to work his first miracle, and, though disinclined, he obeyed (Jn. 2:3–5).

MARY AS QUEEN MOTHER

Recall, too, that the apostles were observant Jews, and Jews traditionally honored the mothers of their kings. The queen mother, rather than the wife or father of a king, is normally mentioned when Jewish sovereigns are introduced in Scripture. We know from the Old Testament that the king's mother sat on a throne beside that of her son and had intercessory power (e.g., 1 Kings 2:19). And so it follows that if Jesus is our king, Mary is our queen.

DOESN'T MARIAN DEVOTION UNDERMINE DUTY TO CHRIST?

If so, the fault lies with the individual, not the Church. Marian devotion was never intended to crowd out Bible study or evangelization because Mary's greatest desire is to lead people to her Son. What she said to the waiters at Cana she says to all of us: "Do whatever he tells you" (Jn. 2:5). The Eucharist stands at the center of all pilgrimage activity at Marian shrines, and while Mary's statue graces Catholic churches, it yields center stage to the tabernacle, which contains Christ's Body. Most churches have crosses on their steeples, and there is a crucifix over the altar recalling Moses' elevation of the serpent, along with Jesus' prophecy, "I, when I am lifted up from the earth, will draw all men to myself" (Jn. 12:32).

WHY HAVE STATUES OF MARY?

When one sets eyes on an image of Mary, whether in sculpture, mosaic, or painting, one is inspired to meditate on the virtues of the ideal woman. To be sure, there is a biblical prohibition attached to graven images (Ex. 20:4). But what is forbidden is the act of worshiping and bowing down to them *as if they were God* (Ex. 20:5). Otherwise, it would be sinful to keep a picture of one's wife or husband on one's desk. God, who cannot contradict himself, commanded the Israelites to fashion images of cherubim (Ex. 25:18), and when his people were bitten by poisonous snakes, he instructed them to gaze at a bronze serpent (Num. 21:8).

IS THE ROSARY SCRIPTURAL?

By all means. One meditates on twenty different mysteries, nearly all of which recall a signal event in the life of Christ beginning with the angel Gabriel's announcement of his coming. The Rosary begins with the Creed. Each decade commences with an Our Father, and the Hail Mary repeated ten times in every decade is heavily based on the Bible (see Lk. 1:28). Mary is given the title "Mother of God" for only one reason: she is the mother of Jesus, who is God. Catholics are not *required* to pray the Rosary any more than they are required to believe in Marian apparitions. But, as indicated in the text, there is powerful documentary evidence indicating that Jesus chose Mary as his ambassador to deliver messages at Guadalupe, Lourdes, and Fatima.

THE ASSUMPTION

Catholics believe that Mary was assumed directly into heaven without undergoing bodily corruption, and the dogma is far from unreasonable. If Enoch and Elijah could be assumed directly into heaven (Heb. 11:5; 2 Kings 2:11), why not the mother of our Lord and Savior? There are no historical references to her burial; no municipality claims her remains (as Rome claims the remains of Peter and Paul); and there are no Marian relics. Only relatively recently did the Church officially define the Assumption of Mary as dogma (1950), but it is an ancient belief.

PERPETUAL VIRGINITY

For 1500 years Christians believed that Mary lived her entire life as a virgin. Even Luther and Calvin subscribed to all of the traditional Marian doctrines (including the Immaculate Conception and Assumption). In Mark's Gospel, we read about four so-called "brothers" of the Lord, along with an unspecified number of "sisters" (6:3). But Mark must be read in light of his culture. Since there was no word for "cousin" in Aramaic, the language spoken by Jesus, "brothers" and "sisters" covered a wide range of relations. That Mark's "brothers" and "sisters" are not what they appear to be is clear from Paul's identification of James the Apostle as "the Lord's brother" (Gal. 1:19). Only two apostles had the name James, and neither was the son of Mary and Joseph. Finally, it should be noted that Matthew, who, at one point, refers to James and Joseph as Jesus' "brothers," identifies them elsewhere as sons of another Mary (Mt. 13:55; 27:56).

"UNTIL SHE BROUGHT FORTH HER FIRSTBORN SON"

As mentioned in Chapter 5, the expression "first-born," in popular Semitic idiom, did not imply other children. It was simply the title given to the male that opened the womb. Likewise for Jewish usage of the word "until." It did not necessarily imply future action. The childless Michal, daughter of Saul, was said to have had no children "until the day of her death" (2 Sam. 6:23).

ADDITIONAL PROBLEMS WITH THE SIBLING THESIS
(AS OUTLINED IN CHAPTER 5)

Why, in the absence of a vow of virginity, did Mary respond to Gabriel's prophecy of future conception with the question: "How can this be?" (Lk. 1:34) Most women in her position would have had high hopes for a child. Why, again, did she abstain from marital intercourse during pregnancy? (Mt. 1:25) It is hard to imagine a woman espoused to the Holy Spirit, the third person of the Blessed Trinity, having carnal relations with a man. Lastly, why did Jesus entrust Mary to John at Calvary (Jn. 19:27) if, by the Protestant reading of Mark, she was the mother of at least four sons and two daughters? Under Jewish law, the oldest surviving son was bound to provide for a widowed mother.

THE IMMACULATE CONCEPTION

The dogma that Mary was conceived without stain of original sin (meaning that, like Eve, she had free will but was not subject to sensual temptation, pain, or death) is consistent with the Bible. Not only is it hinted at in Genesis, where we learn of a special "enmity" that would exist between her and the devil (3:15), it is also in keeping with her position as spouse of the Holy Spirit.

PERPETUAL SINLESSNESS

Foreseeing Mary's courageous "yes" at the time of the Annunciation (Lk. 1:38), God not only brought her into the world unstained by original sin but also kept her morally pure. Paul, to be sure, wrote that "all have sinned" (Rom. 3:23;5:12). But this is not meant to be taken literally. Jesus, for example, did not sin. Paul also says that "all die" (1 Cor. 15:22), but there are obvious exceptions (e.g., Enoch and

Elijah). Matthew, reporting on the Last Supper, says that "all the disciples said the same thing" (i.e. "I will not deny thee"); yet we know that Judas was not present at the time (Mt. 26:35).

DOESN'T CATHOLIC TEACHING CLASH WITH THE BIBLE?

Although the Church's teaching is not always explicitly set forth in Sacred Scripture, it is never inconsistent with it. The Holy Father draws on Tradition, as well as Scripture, in defining dogma (see 2 Thess. 2:15), and when he does, he can rely on the special guidance of the Holy Spirit as promised by Our Lord (Jn. 14:16; 16:13), along with Christ's commission to Peter: "Whatever you bind on earth shall be bound in heaven" (Mt. 16:18–19). That Peter alone received the "keys" to the kingdom is one of many indications that Christ entrusted the leadership of his Church to a single individual. Nowhere does the Bible say that Scripture is the sole source of truth. And how could this have been the case during the first three or four centuries of Christianity when there was no agreement on the content of the New Testament? From the very outset, it was the Church, not the Bible, that was "the pillar and bulwark of the truth" (1 Tim. 3:15).

SUMMING UP

In conclusion, some of what we know about Mary comes from Sacred Tradition. But most of it may be found in the Bible, which speaks of a woman beautiful beyond compare—strong in faith, dauntless in suffering, and sublimely humble. Christ is the second Adam, and his mother is the second Eve.

INDEX

INDEX

INDEX

ABOUT THE AUTHOR

Frederick W. Marks, who holds a Ph.D. degree from the University of Michigan, is the author of eight books, including *The Gift of Pain* and *A Catholic Handbook for Engaged and Newly Married Couples.*